Galveston Bay

A⊺M travel guides

NUMBER EIGHT
GULF COAST STUDIES
SPONSORED BY
TEXAS A&M UNIVERSITY—
CORPUS CHRISTI
JOHN W. TUNNELL JR.,
GENERAL EDITOR

TEXAS A&M UNIVERSITY PRESS
COLLEGE STATION

Galveston Bay

SALLY E. ANTROBUS

Manufactured in the United States of America
All rights reserved
First edition

The paper used in this book meets the minimum requirements
of the American National Standard for Permanence
of Paper for Printed Library Materials, z39.48-1984.
Binding materials have been chosen for durability.
∞

Library of Congress Cataloging-in-Publication Data

Antrobus, Sally E.
    Galveston Bay / Sally E. Antrobus.— 1st ed.
        p. cm. — Gulf Coast studies ; no. 8)
    Includes bibliographical references and index.
    ISBN 1-58544-460-x (cloth : alk. paper) , ISBN 1-58544-461-8 (pbk. : alk. paper)
    1. Natural history—Texas—Galveston Bay.   2. Galveston Bay (Tex.)
    I. Title.   II. Series.

    QH105.T4A55 2005
    508.764'139—dc22

                                              2005004842

For Dennis and Audrey Antrobus,
who gave me an abiding love
for the natural world

CONTENTS

PREFACE

Down at the end of my street laps Galveston Bay. At six o'clock on a winter morning in the crisp air of a norther, dawn turns the sky to a pale apricot dome and casts a coppery sheen over the water. Leafless branches frame the gleaming view. Ships glide through the frame. When fog creeps over the coast, I wake listening to a foghorn's boom. When the air is still and shrimp boats are out, urgent if incomprehensible radio exchanges of shrimpers are carried over the water.

Sometimes the bay makes a lot of noise, when the water and the shore are at odds during a big blow. By day it offers the beauty of pelicans, terns, ospreys, and herons of several kinds. At night the bay makes a black reach of quiet in the light bubble of greater Houston; you sense the deepening dark as you get close. I like the ships and shrimp boats, the seafood smells, and the wispy grasses that look so yielding yet support so much small life. But mostly, I just like the bay *because it is there.*

This book is intended as a celebration of Galveston Bay. Along much of its shore just getting to the edge can be difficult because the waterway is boxed in by a large population center with a major port and an enormous concentration of petrochemical plants. Where can we go to enjoy the bay? Is it safe to eat the oysters? How are we to understand the low terrain of a coastal estuary where land and water merge, creating an edge of uncertain identity?

Perhaps it is an advantage to have grown up in mining towns of the high grassland interior of South Africa and to have lived in the Arizona desert, both so different from the marshes and damp woods of the Texas coast: I know that every place has engaging qualities, and my job is to figure out what they are. Upon moving here in 1988, I was excited to learn that alligators occupy the creek at our back boundary, just a few hundred yards from the bay. Watching the bay is a habit I acquired from my neighbor Sonia Doty, who made a point of doing this nightly for years. Armed with a beer, she would perch at the bottom of her bayshore garden and take in whatever was at hand—gulls, ships, windsurfers, small boats, purple martins, clouds.

Knowing little about how estuaries work, I signed up in 1989 for a short course on bay ecology offered at Armand Bayou Nature Center. The course provided some important introductions. One was to the special magic of a bayou at night. Stopping on the nature center's boardwalk to enjoy the Spanish moss draping the trees in the moonlight, I heard a screech-owl call, and then a whippoorwill—hints of how the area felt when it was wild. A second introduction was to the Galveston Bay Foundation (GBF), then the new champion of bay ecology. One of the other students taking the course, Linda Shead, would soon become the foundation's executive director.

My course notes tell me that salinity in the open ocean is thirty-six parts per thousand. In the Gulf of Mexico it is thirty-two, and in Galveston Bay about twenty-five, going down to five or six parts per thousand in Armand Bayou. Over much of its area, the bay's depth is only six to ten feet. At the time, these were just numbers to me, the first building blocks in my grasp of what low salinity and sun-warmed shallow water can do.

Doug Myers, the instructor, emphasized that people living around Galveston Bay should try to learn from the mistakes and triumphs of the Chesapeake Bay community in understanding estuary dynamics and in tackling problems. At two hundred miles long, Chesapeake Bay was the largest estuary in the nation, he said, home to more than twenty-seven hundred species of plants and animals and biologically one of the most productive systems in the world. H. L. Mencken called it "an immense protein factory." Mining, agriculture, industry, and urban development, however, all contributed to its pollution load, nearly resulting in its death. The bay that produced 120 million pounds of shucked oyster meat in 1880 produced only 20 million pounds of oysters in 1980. The Chesapeake Bay Foundation was formed in the 1960s to promote public awareness of the crisis.

The GBF was looking at similar kinds of problems: industrial pollution, runoff bearing pesticides and excessive nutrients, and a serious reduction of submerged aquatic vegetation. A good deal less was then known about Galveston Bay than is now known, and not just because of the normal march of science over the intervening years. There was

Sketches not otherwise credited are from an archive of work by Frederick Weis. He lived near Galveston Bay in El Jardin del Mar and portrayed the area and its occupants in numerous pencil drawings, ink sketches, and paintings. Weis believed in the importance of art to the community, and his bayside drawings span some forty years. Courtesy of El Jardin Community Association.

an extraordinary push going on for better understanding of the bay as a whole, and I began to consider writing a book about it.

Also appearing in my course notes are the names of several other people crucial to the bay conservation effort. At a 1989 GBF meeting to which all the Armand Bayou course registrants were invited—a meeting about Wallisville Dam and proposed deepening of the Houston Ship Channel—I first heard the authoritative voice of the doyen of bay biologists, Bob McFarlane. Photographer Jim Olive gave a slide show about the riches of the estuary, just as he would do at ecotourism symposia in Seabrook in 2001 and 2002, at the Texas Coastal Treasures conference held by the General Land Office in 2002, and at many another gathering in between. I recorded the telephone number of the main speaker for the evening, the indefatigable Jim Blackburn, who remains at the same phone number at the time of writing, ever more sharply active as a protagonist for the bay.

I owe a considerable debt to Mary Beth Maher, Ellyn Roof, and Natalie O'Neill. Having spotted me at environmental events such as local Earth Day celebrations, Natalie nudged me toward closer involvement in bay advocacy. Mary Beth took over where Natalie left off, making sure I was fully engaged, and eventually supplying the wherewithal for me to accelerate work on this book from a slow shuffle to a trot; some of the artwork is also hers. Ellyn passed me choice morsels of information from thirty years of activism and connected me with Richard W. (Dick) Bricker, who generously supplied photographs. Besides recording interesting watercraft, his photo specialty is large archival-quality inkjet prints on canvas, for framing.

My neighbor Dru Dickson was a rewarding friend, keeping an eye peeled for material I might find useful and always generous in giving my family use of her beach for picnicking, swimming, and sailing. Harvey Tidwell, publisher of the monthly *Bay Runner*, provided valuable support by accepting a series of my environmental articles about the bay. Others to whom I am grateful for wisdom and friendship and for guiding my thinking are my husband, Justin Wilkinson; bay activists Nancy Edmonson, Larry Tobin, and Katie Chimenti; and wetlands scientist John Jacob. Any fumbles of fact or judgment are, of course, my own.

My children, Kate and Mark, have found their own ways of enjoying the bay. As babies, they played in its warm shallows. Mark discovered how to have a fine time on a skimboard, tossing the thin oval on inches-deep water at a run, then springing onto the board to plane along. He was having fun even during the high water of storms, while adults stood around in the rain gloomily contemplating the cleanup labors that would be required when the water receded and debris ringed the shore. Kate showed high school friends how to paddle a canoe in bay and bayou. Justin found alligators and spawning garfish in Pine Gully and summoned me to see them; he also tracked down space photos of the bay and joined the Galveston Bay art car support crew.

Most of the sketches are by the late Frederick Weis, whom I consider a kindred spirit for his obvious love of the bay. He and his wife, Adeline, purchased a lot in the bayside community of El Jardin in 1927, at 4914 Geraldine Street. They erected a tiny weekend cabin they called "Studio by the Sea," later adding the home that would become the Frederick S. Weis Community House. An artist and engraver in Houston, Weis retired in 1942 and moved to El Jardin full time, where for thirty years he conducted community art classes. He died in 1976. I am grateful to the El Jardin Community Association for access to his sketches.

Finally, I appreciate the encouragement and comments of Shannon Davies, Jeff Mundy, and John and Gloria Tveten upon their review of the text.

Many people who have lived within minutes of the bay for years seem to ignore it most of the time, scarcely realizing what it has to offer. When I think of how much effort and money we routinely devote to our immediate outdoor setting in lawn maintenance and seasonal yard decoration, I almost want to cry. If each of us gave even a small portion of that time to the wider natural setting of Galveston Bay and gave those dollars to conservation action—that is, if we devoted ourselves a little more to the actual local environment—we could make a world of difference to its future. I urge you to savor the bay.

Galveston Bay

CHAPTER 1

From Bayou to Bayou City

The intention of the following loop is to offer several birding sites to visitors who may have traveled to Houston on business. These locations are within walking distance, or a short drive of downtown Houston or the Texas Medical Center.

Upper coast map, Great Texas Coastal Birding Trail

Steep, heavily wooded banks presented rich texture in a dozen shades of green as we chugged smoothly up the secluded bayou. A great blue heron eyed us suspiciously from a branch. Too close, it eventually decided. The big bird lifted off with a protesting *kraaak* and winged slowly over our heads to alight behind us.

The pilot and all six passengers aboard the *Laughing Gull* were silent, taking in the peace, the darkly shaded curves, the bright lime accent of large leaves on a catalpa tree. A butterfly inspected us briefly. Turtles plopped into the water as we passed. We were taken aback to find such a lovely intimate stretch of bayou right in the middle of downtown Houston. We half expected a buckskinned trapper to swish past in a canoe. Less leery of our presence than the heron, mallards eased under a drooping loop of wild grapevine a few feet from our bow. A red-winged blackbird chirred from a sunny stand of cane, and the ubiquitous mockingbirds went importantly about their mockingbird business.

But the place was not quite as secret as it seemed. Others had found it before us. Our little flotilla passed a couple of small encampments of a makeshift tent or two, places where free spirits apparently lived and the police either did not know or did not care. A lone fisherman looked astonished to see us, and a small cavalcade of dogs watched with curiosity as we passed: boats are rare on the narrow waterway.

No, the water was not perfectly clear. Yes, there were Styrofoam cups and plastic bottles bobbing in the tangles. But even so, the sense of retreat on the last leg of Buffalo Bayou between the Port of Houston Turning Basin and Allen's Landing downtown was a surprise to us all. High and leafy banks screened away the cityscape for most of the distance after the U.S. Coast Guard patrol boat checked us at the turning basin. Except where we passed under bridges, and where a straighter reach of water afforded us a long view of glinting skyscrapers, we might have been miles from anywhere. The bayou could hardly have been more different from the previous leg of our jaunt, the industrial corridor of the Houston Ship Channel with its flanking wharves, refineries, and chemical plants and the larger flow of the San Jacinto River entering the channel from the north.

On a map, the Galveston Bay system can be seen as a kind of giant and slightly skew Mickey Mouse, divided into four segments bearing some resemblance to Mickey's oversized ears and feet (see map). The ship channel comes in at his left ear, carrying the combined flow of Buffalo Bayou and the San Jacinto River. The larger right ear is where the Trinity River enters the bay through a maze of meandering channels and forested islands—also very different from Buffalo Bayou. The Trinity River is the bay's major freshwater artery, its wide delta still largely wild and commanded by the birds, as is much of the low, marshy eastern bayshore. And the enormous feet are the northeast-to-southwest-trending expanses of East Bay and West Bay.

Mosquitoes, Plentiful

The first substantial description we have of life around Galveston Bay comes from a report by Álvar Nuñez Cabeza de Vaca to King Charles V of Spain. Published in 1542 as *La Relación*, the report is available in an excellent annotated translation as *Cabeza de Vaca's Adventures in the Unknown Interior of America*. He was second in command of an ill-fated expedition to conquer what was then known as Florida, a ter-

ritory including the entire coast of the Gulf of Mexico. He and his en-
feebled companions washed ashore in a small boat on Galveston Island
in November 1528.

"It was winter and bitterly cold, and we had suffered hunger and the
heavy beating of the waves for many days," notes Cabeza de Vaca. As
they drifted in, a wave heaved the boat onto the beach. "The jolt when
it hit brought the dead-looking men to" (Cabeza de Vaca 1997, 55).
They crawled ashore, built a fire, found some rainwater, and began to
come back to life. The strongest man, Lope de Oviedo, was sent out to
scout. He determined that they were on an island and found an Indian
settlement.

Once the Indians knew the Spaniards were there, a hundred bow-
men arrived to inspect the newcomers. The Indians initially distinguished themselves by their hospitality. They brought food for the
bedraggled sailors—fish and roots. The Spaniards tried once to leave
but lost their boat and came back ashore worse off than before, now
having lost everything. Freezing and starving, the Spaniards overcame
their misgivings about the likelihood of becoming sacrificial victims
and asked to be taken into Indian homes.

Once again, the Spaniards were surprised at the hospitality they received. But soon the natives began to die from a "disease of the bow-
els," for which they blamed the Spaniards, probably correctly. They
had almost certainly caught dysentery from their visitors. "When they
came to kill us, the Indian who kept me interceded. He said: If we had
so much power of sorcery we would not have let all but a few of our
own perish; the few left did no hurt or wrong; it would be best to leave
us alone. God our Lord be praised, they listened and relented. We
named this place *Malhado*—the 'Island of Doom'" (Cabeza de Vaca
1997, 60).

Cabeza de Vaca reported that the Indians lived on the island from
October to the end of February each year, subsisting mainly on roots,
supplemented with fish caught in cane weirs during November and
December. Food was their major preoccupation. At the end of February when the roots began to grow and became inedible, they moved on.
"Three months out of every year they eat nothing but oysters and
drink very bad water. Wood is scarce; mosquitoes, plentiful" (Cabeza
de Vaca 1997, 62). He reported that only April was a time of festivity
with more than enough to eat, when people ate blackberries all
month.

Pressed to heal the sick because the Indians believed these special visitors must have extraordinary powers, Cabeza de Vaca records that his method was to bless the unfortunate ones, reciting a *Pater noster* and *Ave Maria*, and "pray earnestly to God our Lord for their recovery," concluding with the sign of the cross. Later he came to be treated as a slave; he does not explain how that shift in status came about. In 1530 he contrived to escape from servitude and become a kind of regional trader. "My principal wares were cones and other pieces of seasnail, conchs used for cutting, sea-beads. . . . By barter I got and brought back to the coast skins, red ochre which they rub on their faces, hard canes for arrows, flint for arrowheads, with sinews and cement to attach them, and tassels of deer hair which they dye red" (Cabeza de Vaca 1997, 66–67).

Thus he moved between the bay and the interior until November 1532, when he set out to find his countrymen. Cabeza de Vaca eventually reconnected with three others from the expedition, and most of *Adventures in the Unknown Interior* is about how the four made their way across the continent to meet up with other Spaniards in Sonora in 1536.

Population of a Roving Character

Three hundred years later, the settlements around Galveston Bay still did not amount to much. Writing in the 1830s, Mary Austin Holley gave descriptions of the thirty-three principal towns in Texas. Had she confined herself to populous and flourishing towns, she remarked, her sketch would hardly have been longer than a few lines: "Population is as yet sparse, and widely scattered, and of a very roving character" (Holley 1990, 124–25).

She did mention a recently laid out town named Houston, but it was not the Houston we know; it was on the east side of the Trinity River, forty miles north of the road to San Antonio. Lynchburg, Holley noted, was a new town at the confluence of the San Jacinto River and Buffalo Bayou. Anahuac she described as having about thirty houses and a former military post near the mouth of the Trinity River, in a pleasant situation at an elevation of thirty feet above the bay (Holley 1990, 114–15).

She recorded that New Washington, now known as Morgan's Point, was "as yet a small place, laid out a short time since by Col. Morgan,

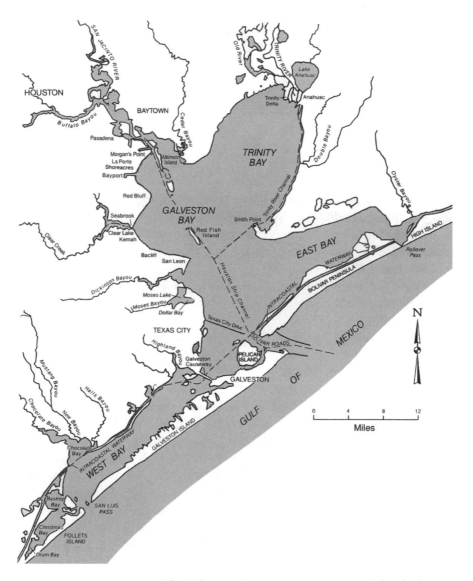

The Galveston Bay system covers some six hundred square miles, including the large Trinity Bay lobe and the long reaches of East Bay and West Bay tucked behind barrier islands. Dredged channels extend for two hundred miles, and industry hugs portions of the shore. Yet no bay in the United States produces more oysters. The shallow estuary sustains major shrimp and crab fisheries, and wildlife refuges flanking it host millions of wintering waterfowl.

a resident and associated with a New York company. It is at the mouth of the San Jacinto River, at the head of Galveston Bay, in Austin's colony. Several well laden vessels have already gone there; and it promises to be a place of great commercial importance. A large warehouse and a hotel for accommodation of visitors are now being built there. It is generally known by the name of Clopper's Point" (Holley 1990, 119).

In what would become the heart of Houston stood Harrisburg, named for the owners of the Harrisburg Steam Saw Mill Company. The mills on Buffalo Bayou were accessible to vessels drawing five or six feet of water, and their loads of lumber were destined for Mexican ports. Harrisburg consisted of about twenty log houses and a handful of frame buildings. "The situation is, probably, rather unhealthy, and the importance of the village can be sustained only by its valuable mills, which furnish more lumber, probably, than all the others in Texas" (Holley 1990, 120).

Galveston looked more promising. As a commercial town, it had one of the best locations on the Gulf because of its superior harbor, wrote Holley. Having the Gulf Stream, "the great river of the ocean, at hand to sweep her vessels, with its mighty and rapid current, to the eastern Atlantic, renders her position for foreign commerce highly felicitous" (Holley 1990, 121).

Mary Austin Holley's *Texas* appeared in 1836, late enough in the year to include the April report of Gen. Sam Houston, commander in chief of the Texas army, on his victory over Mexican president Gen. Antonio Lopez de Santa Anna at the Battle of San Jacinto. Reporting to His Excellency D. G. Burnet, president of the Republic of Texas, Houston said he had received information that Santa Anna was at New Washington and would proceed next to Anahuac, crossing at Lynch's ferry. The Texas army halted close to the ferry. The two sides had minor engagements of artillery, small arms, and cavalry that day, but the Mexican forces were chiefly occupied building a five-foot-high fortification of packs and baggage. They received reinforcements, bringing the respective forces to 1,500 on the Mexican side and 783 Texans, according to Houston's account.

On the afternoon of April 21 the Texans advanced, making the most of the element of surprise. "The rout commenced at half past four, and the pursuit by the main army continued until twilight," said Houston. "Our loss was two killed and twenty-three wounded, six of whom mortally. The enemy's loss was 630 killed . . . wounded 280 . . . pris-

oners 730," among them Santa Anna, who was captured the next day
(Holley 1990, 360).

An Island in Harm's Way

For a time, Galveston would continue to enjoy the ascendancy Holley
had observed. After the Texas Revolution it rapidly became the major
port in Texas. By 1840 immigrants were pouring in and the town's population climbed to four thousand, with about 225 ships visiting each
year and regular steamship service to New Orleans, Mexican ports,
and Havana. A few of the smaller ships navigated to Houston (Cartwright 1991). Galveston's population reached twenty-two thousand by
1880, according to the U.S. census. Today it is home to about sixty
thousand people.

The way the currents flow at the bay mouth indeed produced the
best natural harbor between those of Mexico far to the south and the
flourishing port of New Orleans. Once people recognized that there
was deep water and safe anchorage on the bay side of Galveston Island,
the first phase of Galveston's modern destiny was set. Pirates, then
early entrepreneurs and freight operators, and eventually cruise lines
would occupy the port.

Galveston Island is three miles wide at its widest and about thirty
miles long, part of the extensive barrier island system lining the Gulf
of Mexico shore. The Bolivar Peninsula to the northeast is connected
to the mainland but was also formed as a barrier island. The islands,
however, stand in harm's way, as David McComb describes in *The Historic Seacoast of Texas.* Sand does not stay put. The barrier islands are
endlessly and sometimes catastrophically reworked as severe storms
open and close channels, move the shoreline, and resculpt the dunes.
"Where the sea meets the land there is constant combat. . . . It is a
shifting, dynamic environment" (McComb 1999, 5).

Until the Great Storm of 1900, Galveston's chief concern was not
so much catastrophic effects as the more routine problem of the shifting environment—fending off sand so as to maintain a role as the
prime port in Texas. By the 1880s Houston was beginning to present a
threat to the port of Galveston because the Galveston harbor entrance
was compromised by tidal sandbars. Bars that had been twelve or thirteen feet below the surface in the teens of the century, when pirate

Jean Lafitte held sway, were building up. By 1875 the inner bar at the mouth of the bay allowed only eight feet of clearance—and sailing ships were being replaced by steamers with deeper draft. Cargo had to be lightered from steamships lying at anchor outside the harbor, and it was almost as straightforward to barge cargo to Houston as to Galveston. Galveston needed deeper water (Cartwright 1991).

The first venture in manipulation of the water depth consisted of sinking three rows of submerged pilings to persuade the same current that had created the sandbars to scour them away instead. This produced thirteen feet of clearance over the bar—quite an improvement. But the formulas of the time called for a harbor to be able to accommodate ships drawing twenty-six feet of water at low tide in order to qualify as a first-class harbor. A second-class harbor was twenty to twenty-five feet deep. A port with shallower water was third class—and New Orleans was busy building a harbor that could accommodate any ship afloat (Cartwright 1991, 137).

Not to be outdone, Galveston engineers and entrepreneurs made big plans. They formed the Deep Water Committee and eventually secured a $1.5 million grant from Congress to improve the harbor approach. By 1890 engineers had built two enormous parallel stone jetties out into the Gulf from the tip of the island and the tip of the Bolivar Peninsula to direct the currents and produce more scour at the bay mouth to give larger ships safer passage. Dredges removed sand and wrecks from the channel. "By 1896 there were two miles of stone-capped piers, and the water depth ranged from twenty-seven feet on the outer bar to nearly forty feet along the channel in front of town." That year Galveston welcomed the world's largest cargo ship, the *Algoa*, and within a year the city claimed to be "the second leading cotton port in the world, surpassed only by Liverpool" (Cartwright 1991, 139–40).

Houston Enters the Race

As Galveston flourished, Houston was beginning to entertain grandiose ideas about deep water as well. The Houston Ship Channel is today a defining reality for the bay and a key economic factor for many communities along its shores. When Galvestonians voted in a 2001 referendum to reject a merger arrangement with the Port of Houston Authority, preferring to maintain full control of their port, it was only

Pile driver building a bulkhead for a boat basin, 1955. Armoring the shoreline robs it of productive shallow marshes.

the latest round in a matter that has been contentious for a century and a half.

At the time of Sam Houston's first term as president of the Republic of Texas in 1836–38, Buffalo Bayou was a pretty little river flowing past tiny frontier hamlets served by muddy wagon trails. Just before Texas won its independence, the Allen brothers, real estate speculators, had purchased land along the bayou, and they were depending on waterborne transportation to help them establish a town that would be a center for trade. Chief causes for concern on the bayou were log-jams and sandbars that complicated navigation.

The first steamboat to make it all the way to Allen's Landing, now in downtown Houston, was the *Laura* in 1837. Within two years, five steamboats were regularly calling, and a wharf was built in 1840. A city ordinance created the Port of Houston in 1841, and the following year the Texas Congress gave the little city of Houston the right to improve the bayou for navigation. Most of the abbreviated history of the channel presented here comes from a thirteen-part series published in the Galveston Bay Foundation's newsletter, *Soundings* (see "Port of Houston History" 1990–94, henceforth cited as PHH with part and page numbers).

Activity at the port over the intervening years reflects the dominant economic forces of each era. First, as Mary Austin Holley described, lumber moved through the port from new sawmills. Then there was cotton, as settlement of the surrounding prairie increased. Cotton came to be accompanied by a broader range of agricultural cargoes, and these would later give way to oil as the port's prime stock in trade. For more than fifty years now, oil and other petroleum products have been the single largest category of cargo.

Just as Galveston had sandbar problems, Houston had shallows at Redfish Bar and Clopper's Bar. Vessels small enough to cross these were too small for ocean voyages. When the Allen brothers engaged the larger *Constitution* to make the trip to Houston, there was doubt about whether the ship would be able to turn around. The spot where it did succeed in turning was long known as Constitution Bend and would in due course become the turning basin.

In 1854 a young Yankee of some note visited Texas. Frederick Law Olmsted is remembered today as the landscape architect who designed Central Park in New York City, but he first gained fame as an author of books about the hinterlands. Connecticut-born, he wandered during the 1850s and wrote vivid descriptions of life in the South. Olmsted published *A Journey through Texas* in 1857. On his way to Houston he crossed the Trinity on a ferryboat that gave him some moments of unease on the fast-moving river, even at low water. He wrote of rich bottomlands, canebrakes, and grapevines, of "an almost tropical aspect" to the riverbank vegetation near where the Trinity enters Galveston Bay.

The lower Trinity is still a wooded retreat, but Buffalo Bayou was on a different trajectory, and development accelerated after the Civil War. Shipping mogul Charles Morgan had several ships plying Texas waters, having made a handy fortune during the war by simultaneously building boats for the federal government and running the Union blockade between Havana and Confederate ports. Once the war was over, impatient with fees and restrictions on the lower Mississippi at New Orleans, he moved some operations westward to the Atchafalaya River and dredged a channel from its mouth to the Gulf.

Digging a channel, 1956.

It opened in 1872 at what would come to be called Morgan City in honor of "the commodore."

Morgan was unhappy with the port of Galveston as well because quarantine delays of three weeks or more were imposed on ships coming from Louisiana, in an attempt to protect the people of Galveston from malaria. Hence he was also looking at developing a railroad connection between Houston and New Orleans. When the Buffalo Bayou Ship Channel Company approached Morgan about developing a waterway to Houston, he was receptive.

> In return for agreeing to construct a nine-foot channel at least 120 feet wide from Galveston Bay to the environs of Houston, Morgan received $806,500 in the unissued capital stock of the ship-channel company.
>
> The commodore still owned the dredges that had cleared the channel from Morgan City to the Gulf, and he immediately put them to work cleaning out the channel to Buffalo Bayou. He obtained permission from the U.S. army engineers to make the channel 12 feet deep and succeeded in getting Congress to appropriate money for improvements. (PHH 4:6)

The dredges toiled night and day. By 1876 the channel could accommodate the Morgan ship *Clinton*, drawing nine and a half feet, as far up as Sims Bayou, near where East Loop 610 crosses the ship channel today. By now in his eighties, the commodore built more than a thousand feet of wharves and scooped out a turning basin 250 feet wide. He named that spot Clinton, too, after the Connecticut town of his birth. He began developing a railroad spur serving Houston from there and was also working toward a Houston–New Orleans railroad connection (PHH 4:6).

At its peak, the Morgan Line had a fleet of thirty-two schooners, eighteen barges, ten steamships, seven steam tugs, and two steamboats in service on the channel. Morgan had spent a great deal on dredging at Morgan's Point, and he collected tolls there. A great chain stretched across the channel to ensure that no vessel could pass until the fee was paid. Morgan died in 1878, and his heirs negotiated to turn over the channel improvements to the federal government when the channel from Morgan's Cut to Bolivar Roads at the mouth of the bay was completed.

Morgan's railroad to New Orleans began operations in 1880. Houston was now connected to world trade both by land and by sea, and cotton was booming. Galveston, however, retained the upper hand and was building jetties to deepen its approach channel. Journalists amused themselves satirizing both ports and their fierce contest: "The Houston seaport is of a very inconvenient size—not quite narrow enough to jump over and a little too deep to wade through without taking off your shoes" (PHH 6:12). And the bar at the mouth of the Galveston jetties remained problematic: "When a reporter goes out to inspect the bar, contractors furnish champagne. If he enjoys himself very much, the depth of water on the bar has been known to increase to 16 feet; but this is only on extraordinary occasions" (PHH 6:13).

In 1896, just as Galveston achieved twenty-seven feet of water over the bar thanks to the jetties, Houston was starting to push Congress for a twenty-five-foot-deep channel. The Houston city planners realized that they needed their channel to be even deeper, and they needed financial help to undertake the expensive, ongoing task of channel deepening. Houston congressman Thomas Ball was appointed to the influential Rivers and Harbors Committee of the U.S. House of Representatives, where he pressed hard for federal support for the project.

Horace Rice, a member of the new aristocracy produced by the cotton trade and mayor of Houston from 1905 to 1913, arrived at the inspired idea of sharing the cost of the Houston Ship Channel with the federal government—that is, of selling the plan to Congress on the basis that the city would pay for part of it. In 1910 Congress passed the Rivers and Harbors Act, which authorized spending of $2.5 million on the project, half of it to be furnished by the local navigation district. Navigation bonds were born.

"Before the U.S. Congress could appropriate any money for Houston's proposed deep-water project, a navigation district had to be created and voters had to approve a bond issue of $1.25 million to pay for the district's share of the waterway. Voters were not altogether enthusiastic about the project at first, but the Houston Chamber of Commerce launched a campaign to convince voters that a deeper channel would be well worth the cost"—a gigantic amount for the time (PHH 8:13). From that point forward, the story acquires a familiar modern ring. The hundred-year cycle had begun: publicity, bonds, channel deepening, then another publicity campaign and more bonds and more deepening. The Greater Houston Partnership, successor organization to the old chamber of commerce, now marches beside the Port Commission to promote the channel as the great artery of business.

Arguably, however, the key events moving Houston's port operation forward had less to do with successful lobbying or creative financing than with other forces altogether. The devastation of Galveston by the Great Storm of 1900 improved the case for an inland port protected from the sea, and the first big oil strikes in the area clinched the matter. The Goose Creek oil field near Baytown came in during 1916.

Channel depth reached 18.5 feet in 1908. In 1914, when deepening to twenty-five feet was completed, Houston scheduled a great celebration at the turning basin for the summer of 1915. There were barbecue pits two blocks long, which were to be used to cook food for ten thousand people, and Lt. Gov. William Hobby would address the crowd. But a Gulf storm was destined to spoil the party. The hurricane of August 1915 caused considerable flooding and wind damage. Yet there was reason to be pleased. Naysayers had predicted that the first big storm would compromise the deeper channel, so jubilation reigned when soundings after the hurricane revealed that the channel was still twenty-five feet deep (PHH 9:13).

By the 1930s the channel was being dredged to thirty-two feet. As this round neared completion in 1935, engineers called for further widening, and deepening to thirty-four feet was approved (PHH 10:13). Navigation lights were installed so that the waterway could be used at night. In 1958 the U.S. Army Corps of Engineers recommended deepening to forty feet, and there the depth would remain until century's end. By the late 1980s, as pressure mounted for deepening the channel to fifty feet, citizens began to cry foul. The bay could take no more, they said, without seriously damaging its productivity. This was among the triggers for admission of the bay to the National Estuary Program and for establishment of the Galveston Bay Foundation in 1987 (see chapter 5).

The reason for the outcry involved the "salinity gradient" of the bay, ranging from near thirty-six parts per thousand at the mouths of passes into the Gulf to entirely fresh water in the upper reaches of the Trinity River delta. Fresh water entering the bay from rivers and runoff has a diluting effect, while onshore winds and rising tides push salt water into the bay and increase overall saltiness. Salinity can also vary with depth. The heavier salt water slips underneath the incoming fresh water from rivers so that there is a net upstream flow at the bottom but downstream flow nearer the surface (Warner 1976, 4).

Crabs, shrimp, oysters, and many fish species have special salinity requirements during different life stages. Extremes of low salinity can result from prolonged flooding. Extremes of high salinity can be caused by drought, as impoundments and levees reduce the flow of fresh water into the bay. Either effect can threaten many organisms and compromise some sectors of the bay as nursery habitat. Deepening the ship channel by five feet does not sound like much, but considering that it is hundreds of feet wide and runs for fifty miles, it becomes apparent that the increased volume of the "wedge" of salt water creeping up the bay all the time, 365 days a year, twenty-four hours a day, could have a dramatic effect on overall salinity. Similarly, any given claim on the fresh water that would otherwise flow into the bay may be small, but taken together, excessive upstream commitments of fresh water can mean too little reaching the estuary.

Lighthouses and Ferryboats

Far from the frazzled metropolis, it is easier to feel what the bay was like without the shipping and the freeways and the chemical plants. At the Bolivar lighthouse, for example, things do not look very different from their appearance a hundred years ago. Like Galveston Island, the Bolivar Peninsula is almost thirty miles long and no more than three miles wide. Most of it is only four to eight feet above sea level, but the land at the northern end of the peninsula has the distinction of being the highest point along the coast of the Gulf of Mexico be-

Crabbers at San Jacinto Battleground State Historical
Park on the Houston Ship Channel, long ago. Today the
Texas Department of Health advises that no one should
eat more than a single eight-ounce serving per month of
seafood taken there.

tween the Yucatán and Alabama: the aptly named High Island, at
thirty-eight feet above sea level. The higher elevation is the result of a
salt dome beneath, and the area supports beautiful live oak trees.

James Long established a foothold in 1820 at the southern tip of the
peninsula, called Point Bolivar, at the entrance to Galveston Bay. Here
Fort Travis would later be built, and the site is now a county park.
Long was killed in Mexico and his widow, Jane, eventually departed;
permanent settlement of the area would come only in 1838, after the
Texas Revolution. Point Bolivar proved to have sandbars hazardous to
shipping, and in 1852 the U.S. government built a seventy-six-foot
lighthouse. Rebel soldiers, who did not want the light to aid the Yankee blockade, tore the lighthouse down during the Civil War, but a replacement lighthouse was built in 1872.

"The new lighthouse was 117 feet high, constructed of riveted iron
plates, brick, and concrete, boldly painted with five broad, horizontal
black-and-white bands, and topped with a powerful revolving beacon.
After improvements, its beam could be seen seventeen miles out
at sea" (McComb 1999, 14–15). By the time the Great Storm of 1900
blew in, the Gulf and Interstate Railway connected the Bolivar Peninsula with Beaumont at an excursion fare of one dollar. The first train
came through in 1896, the same year the North Jetty was completed.

High Island had the three-story Sea View Hotel, where guests could dine and dance. A hotel with a dance pavilion and a bathhouse was built at what is now Crystal Beach, then called Patton.

That first tourism boom came undone with the hurricanes of 1900 and 1915. Waves crashed against the cars of the excursion train marooned at Patton station. The storm tide surged over the dance pavilion and washed the town away (McComb 1999, 15–16). The tall, sturdy lighthouse was by far the most secure structure around. Some 120 people saved themselves by huddling inside on the spiral staircase, behind the iron plates. Though the lighthouse reportedly swayed so badly in the hurricane winds that the equipment failed to work properly, keeper H. C. Claiborne rotated the light by hand to keep its beacon burning.

When the 1915 storm blew in with greater advance notice, more people left the peninsula, and only sixty sought refuge in the lighthouse, which once again saved lives. "The light in the tower burned every night during the years of its service except two nights of that storm, Aug. 17 and 18, when the supply of oil used to light the lamps floated away after the surging waters of an 11-foot tide burst open the door at the base of the tower" (Daniels 1985, 38).

The lighthouse served until 1933, when it was decommissioned because other navigational devices ensured the safety of shipping. In 1947 the government sold the Bolivar lighthouse, and it remains in private hands. I was lucky enough to step inside it one day, and it is not easy to believe that 120 people could have sheltered behind those iron plates.

During the 1950s tourism again began to expand. Crystal Beach grew from half a dozen homes to six hundred, mainly for weekenders, and their number has continued to increase. The Texas Game and Fish Commission cut a narrow channel in 1955 at Rollover Pass (see chapter 7), where the distance between the Gulf and the bay was only about a quarter of a mile. The pass now attracts visitors as a prime fishing and birding spot, but storms continue to do their work on the exposed shore. Late in 1996 storm tides washed away many feet of the beach near Rollover Pass. Homes built upon a foundation of sand were lost and damaged, and hay bales were installed along the beach to try to trap sand and restore dunes (McComb 1999, 18).

The birds and the estuary itself are not compromised by the forces moving the sand. Birders are turning up in growing numbers to explore the beaches, islands, and other points around the bay—the Houston

Audubon Society bird sanctuaries at High Island, a bayshore rest stop for migrating songbirds; Smith Point on the eastern shore, almost forgotten terrain until birders began gathering there for the annual Hawkwatch to count migrating birds of prey; and San Luis Pass and the remote reaches of Christmas Bay, far to the south.

The ferry ride across the bay mouth at Bolivar Roads is one of the great unheralded wildlife-viewing opportunities anywhere on Galveston Bay. Dolphins are often to be seen, terns may be fishing, and sea ducks may be there during migration or in winter; sometimes there are frigate birds and always pelicans. The crossing may be smooth and blue; cold and steely gray with slow swells; or blustery with big, wild waves splashing over the bows. This ferry and the port authority's ship channel tour on the MV *Sam Houston* (see chapter 7) are the bargain ways to get out on the water.

A third free boat ride can be taken on the Lynchburg ferry, just a few hundred yards from the San Jacinto Battleground. I first rode it on a warm summer evening of pink sky. As we drove through the petrochemical complex lining Highway 225 and down into the marshes, a great blue heron was fishing in the shallows. Seagulls wheeled. We got in line behind two other cars to board the small, cramped vessel. Passengers do not have much time to absorb the strange mix of quiet marshes and industrial vistas, because the crossing takes just a few minutes.

It evokes another ferry on the lower Rio Grande near Mission, in Los Ebanos, a village named for its lovely old Texas ebony trees. Riding the hand-pulled Los Ebanos ferry in 1999 for fifty cents, I was transported much closer to understanding how things were at Lynchburg in 1836. Cables were rigged on pulleys so that people heaving on a rope on board could pull the craft across the river. Three men did most of the heavy pulling to get three cars and half a dozen pedestrians across the Rio Grande. On the U.S. side a donkey watched the proceedings from a shady spot under an anacahuita tree dotted with big white blossoms. Bright splashes of potted bougainvillea greeted us on the Mexican bank, yielding to a mile or two of cornfields between the river and the little town of Ciudad Díaz Ordaz. Once upon a time things must have looked rather like this where the Lynchburg ferry plies the Houston Ship Channel, with Indian paintbrush and evening primrose in place of more tropical blooms.

The reason for the ferry at Los Ebanos was trade. It served as a crossing for oxcarts loaded with salt from the salt lake known as El Sal del Rey, about forty miles to the north. Cabeza de Vaca had duly reported the salt lakes of South Texas to the king of Spain, and the lake was claimed for the Crown in 1746. Trains of carts and wagons hauled the salt—the first Texas export—south into Mexico and later to Gulf ports.

In the years following Texas independence, when disputes arose over who owned the mineral resources, the arguments went all the way to Congress, where Sam Houston, then a Texas senator, indulged in some oratory on the subject. "It was in one such debate on the floor of the U.S. Senate that Sam Houston referred to 'The Great Salt Lake of Texas' and condemned attempts to wrest its mineral rights from the public as 'one of the most extraordinary and monstrous conspiracies ever formed by the ingenuity of man under the incitements of plunder—conceived in the most grasping and comprehensive spirit of fraud'" (Hastings 1993, 18).

The upshot was rewriting of the Texas Constitution. "Few realize that it was a fight over the snowy salt flats of El Sal del Rey, not a gusher of black gold, that established private ownership of mineral rights in Texas—which set the stage for the state's oil boom" (Hastings 1993, 11).

At Lynchburg, the connections swim into focus and the pictures merge, though the hand-operated ferry has yielded to diesel. Towering nearby is the pale obelisk commemorating the battle that launched the new republic, and lining the channel are the giant chemical plants and refineries, legacy of wealth that followed the mineral rights law provoked by wrangling over El Sal del Rey.

Activists Go Home

Coming back down the bayou after our morning run up to Allen's Landing in the *Laughing Gull*, we assembled once more at the turning basin, the checkpoint where the Coast Guard patrol boat visited us again. Once our companion boats had motored away, we were the sole occupants of the wide basin. It was impressively ugly after the pretty bayou. And it was deathly silent. No vessel was docked there. Not a soul was in evidence on the wharves. Rusting corrugated metal warehouses stood forlorn, some with double doors open on both sides so that we could see right through their emptiness. The only movement

Coastal prairie farmhouse.

was the gentle heaving of rafts of floating plastic and Styrofoam debris lapping at the corners of the crumbling concrete.

The decrepitude was amazing. We were subdued, but not because of the shabbiness alone. Our silence was born of a deeper dismay, for all present that day were involved in fighting expansion of Port of Houston Authority facilities much farther down the bay at Bayport (see chapter 6). On our way back down Buffalo Bayou and the ship channel, we were powerfully aware that the only sites looking well cared for were the public relations dock where the port authority's tour boat MV *Sam Houston* is moored and a few landscaped private docks belonging to chemical plants.

The blatant disregard otherwise evident all along the shore was painful to behold. Only the homeless tent campers and the solitary fisherman—who looked as if he wished we would quickly disappear— seemed to have any kind of territorial view. For the rest, this whole extended waterway in the heart of a major metropolis was being firmly ignored by millions of people. Stunning.

We digested the irony of Houston romantically calling itself the

Bayou City while systematically straitjacketing long sections of its hundreds of miles of beautiful bayous in concrete. Views of dying and dead docks stood in stark contrast to the port authority's chirpy claims of Houston being the nation's leading port in foreign tonnage. It seemed we should hardly bother fearing a terrorist attack on vulnerable port facilities when the installations are falling into disrepair anyway from sheer neglect. Where are the petrochemical giants and their public service budgets when the waterway that has served them so well needs their help? Why can a city with such a can-do reputation not find the resolve to safeguard prime natural assets like the bay and the bayous?

We had to remind ourselves that there are fighters among us. Some are working to preserve or rescue or clean the bayous and bayshore, restoring marshes and sampling to monitor water quality. Others are taking the battle for the bay to the press and to the courts. So many people now live around Galveston Bay and interact with it in so many ways that some are bound to become its fierce advocates and others are willing or eager to help. Whether responding to its beauty through art, enjoying the water for recreation, or making a mint in waterfront real estate, many people today want to support the natural resilience of the great estuary and ensure its long-term viability.

Indeed, late in 2002 the Buffalo Bayou Partnership unveiled a comprehensive twenty-year, $800 million plan for transformation of the ten-mile stretch of the bayou from the turning basin upstream to Shepherd Drive (Thomas 2003). It is envisioned as a showplace of additional park space, wetlands preserves, nature trails, botanic gardens, and performing arts venues. Flood-control components of the plan hold the promise of making it all happen as part of an effort to prevent the kind of calamitous downtown flooding that Houston suffered during Tropical Storm Allison in 2001. There is reason to hope that we will begin to address the visual blight and economic death of Buffalo Bayou, that this portion of it will eventually become the center point of substantial improvements in our urban fabric and green space.

San Antonio has its Riverwalk. In London the historic docks on the Thames are today a waterfront showplace of chic housing and art galleries. Choice hotels have been built alongside warehouses refurbished as a large, upscale shopping complex. Seattle, San Francisco, Baltimore, Bristol, and Cape Town have all done it too. Among the reasons Houston lost a recent bid for the Olympic Games was the bald fact that the city is ugly, which is what happens when the quest for dollars runs roughshod over quality-of-life considerations.

Houston is proving rather slow to wake up to its own possibilities, but early in 2003 a new book celebrating the bayou was published: photographer Geoff Winningham's (2003a) *Along Forgotten River*, profiling Buffalo Bayou all the way from its source on the Katy Prairie west of Houston. Newer yet is *The Book of Texas Bays* by Jim Blackburn (2004), beating the drum for all the bays. Although the Bayou City still has a long way to go in reversing public disregard for the waterway at its heart, at least it appears that we may finally be ready to start out in the right direction.

CHAPTER 2

A Hardworking Bay

Now you know if we wasn't potting and them eggs
mostly hatched, crabs would crawl up out of the water
and conquer the earth. The Bay couldn't hold them all.
And think how mean the bastards are!

Virginia waterman quoted by William Warner,
Beautiful Swimmers

All estuaries are not created equal. Northern fjords may offer easy entry for seawater and be fed fresh water from rivers, but deep water and a rocky bottom are not the ideal formula for biological riches. For high productivity, an estuary also needs shallow water so that the sun can nourish plankton and plants. It needs extensive marshland, shallow coves, and tidal creeks where nutrients abound so that hosts of invertebrates and young fish can find food and shelter (Warner 1976). Galveston Bay has all these things, and lavish productivity to match.

Almost a hundred kinds of crabs of every conceivable and startling design inhabit Texas coastal waters. Only one is of commercial importance: the Atlantic blue crab, *Callinectes sapidus*. The name *Callinectes* derives from Greek, identifying these crabs as "beautiful swimmers," which is also the title of a fine book William Warner wrote about crabs and watermen on the Chesapeake Bay. The name *sapidus* is from the Latin for "tasty" and was bestowed upon this crab by Mary Jane Rathbun, who identified and described around a thousand new species of crabs—surely a record, as Warner observes. "In only one case did she choose to honor culinary qualities. History has borne out the wisdom of her choice. No crab in the world has been as much caught or eagerly consumed as *sapidus*" (Warner 1976, 90).

One mama crab's spongy egg mass yields as many as 2 million eggs, making for enormous numbers of microscopic, newly hatched larvae joining all the other tiny beings collectively known as zooplankton in the warm waters of Galveston Bay. But life for crab larvae is a treacherous affair. Biologists estimate that only about one of every million eggs will survive to crab adulthood. For larvae to flourish, the salinity needs to be just right—about twenty-five parts per thousand, not as salty as the ocean; but they cannot survive if salinity drops below about twenty parts per thousand. There must be enough oxygen in the water, which can be a problem in polluted waterways. Freshwater flooding can wash larvae out to sea, or its flushing effect can lower estuary salinity below the limit they can withstand. And besides all these hazards, many small predators eat crab larvae.

Long before the blue crab looks even a bit like a crab, it struggles through seven larval stages, each time shedding its tiny shell. Then, like other crabs, it metamorphoses into an alarming-looking creature called a megalops, just large enough for the human eye to see. A megalops is a miniature monster somewhat like a crawfish, with two claw arms, three pairs of walking legs, a shrimplike tail, and huge stalked eyes. It can crawl along the bay bottom or achieve some loopy swimming as it travels up estuaries or rivers to the brackish waters that suit it best (Warner 1976, 106).

Although at the mercy of even tiny predators and unable to prevail against strong currents, megalops do have a survival kit. If they are washed out to sea where salinity is too high for them, they go into a kind of suspended animation. They can prolong the megalops stage from a few days to two or three months to wait out the crisis until they reach less-salty water again. Thus, a severe flushing of the bay, as in a year of Trinity River floods, does not necessarily produce a plunge in the blue crab population.

Crabs in Texas reach sexual maturity at the age of about twelve to fourteen months, after eighteen or more molts. The female mates only once and may carry the sperm for several months until she is ready to spawn; spawning peaks in spring and summer. The female fertilizes the eggs and places them on her abdomen, where the spongy mass turns from orange to brown to black before the eggs hatch (McEachron 1987).

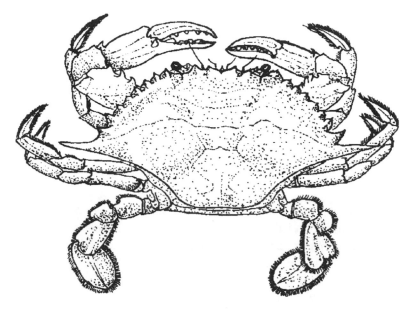

The Atlantic blue crab, Callinectes sapidus, *is the species of commercial importance. All the species illustrated, some of them wonderfully unlikely in design, have been recorded on the Texas coast and probably occur in the Galveston Bay system. Sarah Pounds Leary's drawings are from her bulletin* The Crabs of Texas *(1967). Courtesy Texas Parks and Wildlife Department.*

Crab populations classically experience wide fluctuations, and harvests have tended to do so as well. During the 1930s and 1940s commercial crab landings in Texas were measured in thousands rather than millions of pounds. The range was generally from about ten thousand to sixty thousand pounds of live crabs a year, with Galveston, Aransas, and Matagorda bays taking turns in first place for production (Leary 1967, 16). Galveston Bay took the lead in the 1950s as crab harvests began to escalate. By 1960 blue crab commercial landings from the bay were about two hundred thousand pounds a year, and the statewide tally reached 2 million pounds. The casual and sport harvest was climbing too, reaching twenty-three thousand pounds of crabs taken from Galveston Bay between April and December 1968, according to the Texas Parks and Wildlife Department. By 1989 the commercial crab harvest in Galveston Bay alone had soared to 2.1 million pounds, and it would reach 3 million pounds in 1990.

The increased harvest partly reflected the increased value of blue crabs, and commercial landings have remained high; in 1998 the tally for the bay was 2.6 million pounds. More blue crabs are consistently landed from Galveston Bay than from any other Texas estuary; it produces about a third of the state's crab harvest (McEachron 1987; *State of the Bay* 1994, 2002).

Blue crabs use powerfully muscled swimming legs flattened into paddles to conduct substantial migrations every year. Females migrate down the bay to water of higher salinity to spawn. Because males thus spend more time in the upper bay and are bigger, they are more readily subject to overfishing. To tell a male from a female, check the claw tips: females have bright red fingernails, as it were, which males do not. Another clue is the abdominal apron on the underside. In males this is the shape of an upside-down T, whereas the female's is an upside-down V that bulges out into a bell shape in her final life stage as a breeding adult (Warner 1976).

The Texas Parks and Wildlife Department compiles fisheries data on the basis of "catch per unit effort" (CPUE), meaning the number of individuals caught in a given period of trawling with a shrimp trawl. CPUE data for blue crabs in Galveston Bay from 1982 through 2000 show wide fluctuations (*State of the Bay* 2002, 105). The starting point is a CPUE of around twenty-eight individuals in 1982, and the CPUE zigzags up and down in two- or three-year cycles, peaking above thirty individuals in 1990 but languishing down at only six in 1999. Averaging out the peaks and troughs to a steady line reveals a declining trend over those eighteen years. The average CPUE is down from more than thirty crabs in 1982 to less than fifteen by 2000, suggesting that fishing pressure is substantial.

The Texas Parks and Wildlife Department crabbing regulations are nevertheless quite liberal. Individual commercial crabbers may maintain up to three hundred crab traps. The legal size for crabs is five inches across the carapace; smaller ones must be returned to the water. Egg-bearing females, or "sponge crabs," caught in traps must also be released. Crabs of legal size taken during shrimping operations may be retained.

Remember, though, the 2 million eggs. Crab populations can rebound fast if harvest pressure eases and bay salinity conditions are suitable. In this respect, crabs exemplify the situation for several other species.

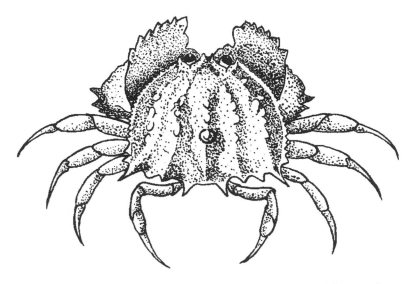

Calappa sulcata

Dance of the Shrimp

Considerably more important commercially than the blue crab are shrimp, the nation's favorite seafood. More than a dozen shrimp species occur in Galveston Bay, of which three of the larger kinds sustain the commercial fishery: brown shrimp (*Penaeus aztecus*), white shrimp (*P. setiferus*), and pink shrimp (*P. duorarum*). The annual shrimp harvest from the bay has been around 7 million pounds since the mid-1990s.

Shrimp lead an accelerated life, growing up in the bays and migrating out to the Gulf as adults. They spawn in the Gulf, each female releasing up to a million eggs. These hatch within twenty-four hours and proceed rapidly through eleven larval stages within a month or less. Winds and currents carry them shoreward, and they enter the bay through the Gulf passes as postlarvae—transparent wigglers about a quarter of an inch long, by now looking like adult shrimp. They drift or migrate into nursery areas in shallow waters, marshes, and tidal creeks, where they find shelter and food. Marshes along the shoreline of East, West, and Christmas bays are prime nursery areas.

Reaching juvenile and subadult stages at about three to five inches long, they move out into deeper waters, clustering for a time in the mid to upper bay. Juvenile shrimp are large enough for the live bait and bay commercial fisheries at an age of about sixty days. The main Gulf fishery begins for shrimp when they are adults, three or four months old; if they evade predators and nets, they may live up to two years. The different species conduct a kind of sequential dance in the bay. Young brown shrimp are in the bays in spring and move out into the Gulf in May and June. White shrimp use the bays during spring, summer, and fall, moving out into the Gulf as the bay cools in the fall. Pink shrimp inhabit the bay from late fall through early spring (Texas Parks and Wildlife Department 1986).

Shrimp landings in Galveston Bay have fluctuated in a dance of their own, keeping shrimpers and regulators in a more or less constant state of uncertainty and argument. Pink shrimp constitute only a tiny percentage of the catch. Brown shrimp account for most of the Texas landings and seem to be holding their own. A long-term declining trend for white shrimp, however, is apparent. The harvest of white shrimp stood at 5 million pounds a year in the mid-1960s, ranged around 2 million to 4 million pounds a year through the 1980s, and then dropped below 1 million pounds by 1990. Shrimping regulations have been amended in various ways to address this population decline, which seems to derive from a combination of fishing pressure, pollution, and reduced freshwater inflow to bays (*State of the Bay* 1994, 170).

Sampling by the Texas Parks and Wildlife Department has shown shifts in numbers from year to year but, like the commercial harvest, also reveals the declining trend for white shrimp. In shoreline bag seine samples of juvenile white shrimp, the peak was more than 3,500 per hectare (2.47 acres) in 1982, dropping to just 250 in a similar-sized area in 2000 (*State of the Bay* 2002, 104). Trawl sampling of larger shrimp in the open bay showed a decline from a CPUE of more than 90 white shrimp per hour in 1982 down to below 20 in 1990; variable years followed, with CPUE values below 20 again in 1996 and at 26 in 2000.

Some kinds of saltwater game fish favor eating shrimp, just as we do. As shrimp boats proliferated along the Texas coast after the 1930s, and especially after World War II, shrimping became a cause of concern. In addition to removing the shrimp, trawling also produced a large incidental catch of fish and sea turtles. By the 1970s shrimp trawls had been identified as a serious problem for turtles, the single greatest cause of human-induced mortality; tens of thousands of sea turtles

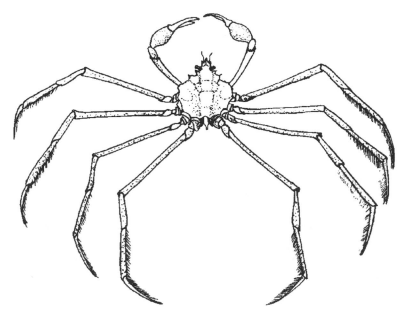

Anasimus latus

were drowning annually in the nets. Today all five species of sea turtles found in the Gulf of Mexico are either endangered or threatened.

Turtles are long-lived animals. In profound contrast to the shrimp life stages measured in days, turtles live their lives in the slow lane. Some species do not reproduce until they are twenty or thirty years old, which means they are slow to recover from losses. Since 1989 shrimpers have been required to use turtle excluder devices (TEDs) in their nets so that most of the turtles trapped in nets can escape. TEDs dramatically reduce needless turtle deaths; estimates of reduced mortality range from 67 to a satisfying 97 percent (National Wildlife Federation 1992).

Increased turtle nesting and recruitment do not show up in a flash after turtle rescue measures come into force. It can take ten years or more to begin seeing the effects of increased survival of adult turtles, but everyone is watching for signs. In 2002 an excited flurry of e-mail resulted when a Kemp's Ridley sea turtle—one of the most endangered species in North American waters—dug a nest on the beach at the southwestern end of Galveston Island. "The Kemp's Ridley laid her ninety-six eggs just two miles east of San Luis Pass," said an alert circulated among interested parties. "The National Marine Fisheries

Service collected the eggs for what's called a headstart program on Padre Island. This Kemp's Ridley herself was a graduate of the 1992 headstart program on Galveston (which ended there that year). One of 2,000 hatchlings that were brought annually from Rancho Nuevo, Mexico, she survived against great odds to return to nest—a victory for conservation" (Seth Davidson, pers. comm., 2002).

As the beneficial effects of TEDs began to register, the idea of reducing the incidental catch of finfish was also advancing. In 1997 the National Marine Fisheries Service announced that Gulf of Mexico shrimpers in some areas would be required to use, in addition to TEDs, bycatch reduction devices (BRDs) in their trawls to allow finfish to escape. The term *bycatch* suggests that the numbers are small, but they are not. In a 1992 study on Galveston Bay, it turned out that *one fish was captured as incidental bycatch for every 1.9 shrimp landed* during the March to November shrimping season. The bycatch is huge. The new BRD regulations for the Gulf were designed primarily to conserve red snapper, because the shrimping bycatch of juvenile snapper had been pinpointed as a major obstacle to recovery of snapper populations. But shrimp trawling is a factor in declines of other fish species as well, and BRDs can obviously benefit numerous kinds of fish.

Although shrimpers have resisted TED and BRD requirements, which have taken effect on a piecemeal basis, there seems little doubt that over time these are likely to become standard in the industry, even if they also cause shrimpers to lose some shrimp ("Gulf Shrimpers" 1997). Throwing away millions of pounds of bycatch when the problem is readily avoidable is rather like cutting down a grapevine to eat a bunch of grapes. Our appetite for shrimp means we are at once removing some of what fish like to eat and killing a lot of young fish as bycatch. Bewailing the low number of game fish, the growing legions of sport fishermen have lobbied successfully for stiffer shrimping regulations. As shrimpers have struggled to make their operations pay, the number of boats out chasing those succulent shrimp has been dropping. Probably no one wants the picturesque shrimp boats or the fiercely independent-minded shrimpers to disappear; let us hope we are approaching a kind of equilibrium.

Oysters, Anyone?

Beyond the appeal of oysters as delicacies on a plate, and perhaps a moment of inquiring whether they come from safe waters, we usually

Glyptoxanthus erosus

have little reason to wonder much about the life of an oyster. But the fact is, the oyster is a wonderful beast. A filter feeder, it can pump up to sixty gallons of water through its body each day, straining the water for plankton and other organic material. Thus, a large, healthy oyster population filters tremendous volumes of water and influences water quality and clarity throughout the bay (Nailon 1990–91).

The commercial oyster in Texas is *Crassostrea virginica*, the eastern oyster, which occurs along the Atlantic and Gulf coasts from Canada to Mexico. This creature can withstand a wide range of salinity conditions, tolerating fresh water for brief periods and being able to survive in waters saltier than those of the Gulf. But it thrives best in the middle salinities of estuaries and tidal zones of rivers. Optimum salinity is fifteen to thirty parts per thousand.

The oyster has a few days of glorious freedom as an embryo and larva, when it swims feebly with fringing, hairlike cilia while its shell begins to form. Then the larva sinks to the bottom to search out a hard, clean surface on which to settle, or "set," and cement itself down. By the time the tiny oyster sets on the bottom, at the age of about ten days, it is just big enough for us to see and is called a spat. The spat lack the adaptability of larval-stage blue crabs. Oyster larvae die if they cannot find a suitably firm surface for setting. Soft muck will not do. Decades of dredging shell from Galveston Bay for road building did not do the oyster population any favors.

Once fixed in place, baby oysters face other dangers. They suffer serious predation by a conch called an oyster drill. The conch drills a hole in the oyster's shell or between the valves and can eat almost a hundred small oysters a day (Hofstetter 1967, 13). Blue crabs, stone crabs, and several other kinds of crabs prey on spat, and some prey on adult oysters as well. Shallow reefs are at risk in winter, when the periodic blue northers bring freezing temperatures and the north wind forces water out of the bays. Low-water conditions may leave oyster reefs exposed to the cold in the shallows.

Although oysters are adapted for the siltation that is a normal part of the turbid daily life in a world of winds and waves stirring up a muddy bottom, sudden surges of clay or mud can smother them. Bottom disturbance during severe storms can bury the oysters. Dumping spoil material from channel dredging can likewise destroy the oyster reefs, as can floodwaters bearing a heavy load of silt (Hofstetter 1967, 12). Floods can be catastrophic: oysters not buried by silt can be killed by prolonged exposure to fresh water.

Assuming none of these disasters, spat reach legal market size of three inches in about eighteen months (by contrast with slower growth in colder northern waters, where they may take three or four years to reach comparable size). Growth of the hard upper and lower shell halves, or valves, is accomplished by the mantle, which is the outermost layer of the soft, squishy part of the animal. "In a growing oyster, the mantle protrudes slightly beyond the open valves, and the oyster grows by depositing layers along the outer edges of the valves" (Hofstetter 1967, 8). Sometimes a speck of grit gets inside and is likewise coated with shell by the mantle, but the true pearl oyster is only distantly related to the commercial oyster and is not found in the United States.

Gradual cupping of the lower valve increases the space within the shell cavity as the oyster grows. Its growth is irregular, depending on water conditions, and the shell surface shows a pattern of "growth rings," each revealing where the edge of the shell once was. A few more things about an oyster's early life are revealed by the shape of the shell. Overcrowding produces clusters of long, thin-shelled oysters. Those growing where the bottom is not quite firm enough for them tend to sink and must elongate to keep the bill above the muck. A broad, well-cupped shell is testimony to a fine life on a firm bottom without too many neighbors.

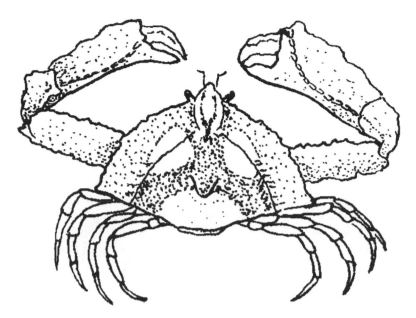

Heterocrypta granulata

The oyster capital of Galveston Bay is Smith Point, population 150 or so, jutting from the bay's eastern shore—a long way by road from Houston, though only a few miles by boat across the narrow waist of the bay from Bacliff or San Leon. Smith Point is not often in the spotlight. Its chance to bask in a glow of publicity came when Richard Bricker published *Pearls on Galveston Bay* in 2003. For a long time I had hankered for a book exploring the vernacular culture of the bay, and suddenly I had one in my hands.

Bricker's portrait of the Smith Point oystermen and their distinctively equipped boats, called luggers, is a celebration of a specialized commercial fishery. He set out to document it, as Warner had examined the crab fishery on Chesapeake Bay. Texas libraries contain "a wealth of fact and fiction" about oil, cattle, and cowboys, Bricker notes, but coastal areas are sadly ignored. "What is going on now will be history in a few years and will be mostly lost if not recorded now" (Bricker 2003, 2; see the books section in the resources listed at the back of this book for ordering information).

Oystering presents no need for the angled booms and wooden "doors" used on shrimp boats to manipulate trawl nets. The business end of a lugger is a small, toothed dredge. Oyster luggers are low and homely but for the tall bamboo canes reaching far above their canopies. The skill of the lugger captain lies in maneuvering the boat to dredge all sections of a reef, using the canes as markers, and then maneuvering the dredge against guiding rollers to spill the oysters onto the lugger.

Bricker details the proceedings in pictures of the crews at work. To get the photos, he had to be out on the water in his own boat before dawn, camera in hand, living the oystermen's life—thinking about sandbars and wakes, watching the bamboo markers, hoping for a good haul. He explains how oyster leases operate and how leaseholders go about transplanting young oysters to their leases. He profiles the boat captains, the crews, and the four seafood companies in town and provides the specifications for all boats based at Smith Point. Bricker may be right that the oyster luggers are unlikely to be with us much longer. The work is taxing and the livelihood is generally modest. Perhaps the time will come when boat owners will also use their luggers at least some of the time for other kinds of trips, such as taking out the birders who have already discovered Smith Point.

Galveston Bay produces about three-quarters of the Texas oyster harvest of some 3 million pounds a year (Blackburn 2004) and has three classifications of oyster beds: approved, conditionally approved, and restricted. About one-third of the reefs in the bay, mainly on the west side, are restricted—closed to shellfish harvest—because chronic exposure to fecal coliform bacteria derived from inadequately treated sewage makes oysters from these beds dangerous to eat.

Leaseholders, however, may transplant oysters from restricted beds to their leases, where the transplants must not be harvested for at least two weeks. Once in cleaner water, the oysters can purge themselves of harmful bacteria. Conditionally approved beds are in areas where known problems arise from flood runoff or similar conditions, and the areas are closed when heavy rains occur. Approved oyster beds meet or exceed minimum health standards on a consistent basis over a long period, under all but extremely unusual conditions.

Most of the oysters harvested in Galveston Bay come from public reefs, which are much more extensive than the private leases. Even the largest leaseholder, Ben Nelson of Smith Point, takes more oysters from public reefs than from his leases. The main advantage of leasing is that the leased reefs can be harvested in summer when the public reefs are closed; the regular season usually runs from November 1 to April 30, and some bay shrimpers switch to oystering for a portion of the year.

Latriella elegans

In the nineteenth century the abundance of fish and shellfish in the Texas bays amazed the arriving settlers. No matter how many delicious fresh fish everyone hauled to market or home to the kitchen, fishing scarcely seemed to make a dent in the plentiful supply. Commercial landings of red drum and trout from Galveston Bay were more than four hundred thousand pounds each in 1890, and the commercial harvest of oysters was 1.6 million pounds, fully ten times larger than either the crab or shrimp fisheries (*State of the Bay* 1994, 49).

The human population of the Texas coast has mushroomed, and technology in commercial fisheries has improved somewhat, but the more important causes of sharp increases in fish and shellfish harvests were two other factors. The arrival of railroads and the mastery of refrigeration meant that the market for seafood was no longer restricted to the immediate vicinity of where it had been landed. Once seafood could be shipped in quantity to distant markets, fishing pressure intensified along the Texas coast, and commercial fisheries boomed.

Overfishing of some species was the inevitable result. The annual commercial harvest of finfish from Galveston Bay climbed above 2 million pounds toward the end of the 1960s. But by 1970 it had halved to 1 million pounds, and it continued to slide. Resource managers and recreational anglers were spurred into action. Commercial taking of redfish (red drum) and speckled trout (spotted seatrout) was banned in 1981. Both species were reclassified as game fish, meaning that they may not be commercially harvested in state waters. Dismayed at what decades of commercial harvest had done to populations of favored game-fish species, anglers threw themselves during the 1970s and 1980s into efforts to beef up the redfish and speckled trout populations. Those efforts are ongoing (see chapter 7 and Coastal Conservation Association in the resources).

Today the commercial harvest of finfish in the bay is only around two hundred thousand pounds a year, mainly mullet, flounder, black drum, and sheepshead. This has become an almost negligible fishery by comparison with the bay's large recreational fishery focused on croaker, sand seatrout, and speckled trout. Sport fishing now contributes millions of dollars to the local economy (see chapter 3).

Population, Industry, and Pollution

Houston in 1890 had a population of just 27,557 souls, still behind San Antonio, Dallas, and Galveston. By 1990 the population of the five counties surrounding the bay had soared to 3.3 million, of whom some 650,000 were living within two miles of Galveston Bay. In the 2000 census the five-county total climbed to 3.9 million, making the Houston metropolitan area number four in the nation, after New York, Los Angeles, and Chicago (*State of the Bay* 1994, 2000).

As we have seen, the first cores of economic activity in the region were lumber and agriculture until petroleum and related products came to dominate exports. Recent decades have seen diversification into other manufacturing, and the population boom has made services and retail the largest providers of employment. Fisheries have made a steady contribution, and tourism is on the increase (*State of the Bay* 2002).

The bay is a key asset to all sectors, not just fisheries and tourism, because marine transportation is the least expensive way to move large quantities of goods over long distances. Impacts of ports on the Texas economy are examined in "Marine Commerce 101," a 1999 special issue of *Texas Shores*, the Texas Sea Grant program journal. As noted there, in the nineteenth century a small sloop of thirty-four tons managed by just three hands could transport the same amount of cargo as about 350 horses could carry overland. In a more contemporary comparison, a single gallon of fuel can move a ton of material sixty miles by truck, two hundred miles by train, more than five hundred miles by barge, and much farther yet by oceangoing cargo vessel ("Marine Commerce" 1999).

About a fifth of the total tonnage of goods moving through all U.S. ports goes through Texas ports, and much of the Texas cargo consists

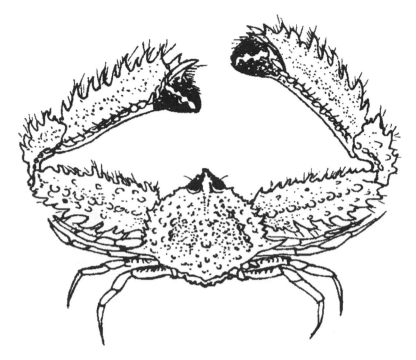

Parthenope serrata

of oil, refined petroleum, and liquid or solid petrochemical products. There is some circularity in the picture. The main impetus for Houston's port expansion was oil. The channel was deepened and improved. Then, because Houston had a well-developed port, industry in turn was able to expand, creating a need for further expansion of port facilities, and so on. Today we are far beyond the initial situation of largely processing locally extracted oil. Instead, much of the raw material used in the local chemical industry comes in on ships and is shipped out again in processed form. More than 60 percent of all cargo tonnage is coming to and from the petrochemical industries (*State of the Bay* 2002).

A jaunt down Highway 225 from Houston through Pasadena to La Porte offers a sense of the scale of it all: a twenty-mile corridor of refineries and petrochemical plants flanks the ship channel. Almost half of all chemical production in the United States takes place in the Galveston Bay area, concentrated along the upper ship channel and at Texas City. The products of these industries are by far our primary exports, and the bay is the conduit for it all.

Local petroleum extraction remains a sizable industry, and it has created other difficulties. In 2000 the five counties surrounding the bay had more than five thousand producing oil wells and some fifteen hundred gas wells on land and in the bay itself. "Produced water"— brine coming to the surface during oil and gas extraction—was still being disposed of in the Galveston Bay system by some sixty dischargers at a rate estimated at up to three hundred thousand barrels a day into the 1990s, raising water-quality concerns. Chronic exposure to concentrated brines, some contaminated with trace metals and petroleum hydrocarbons, "burns" and kills plants and fouls the bay-bottom sediments. The Environmental Protection Agency (EPA) prohibited the discharge of produced water in 1998; it must now be "deep-well injected," or pumped back underground (Roach and Spencer 1992; *State of the Bay* 2002).

Chemical industries inevitably bring air pollution, fires, and accidents. They discharge toxic compounds into the bay. Manufacturing and shipping produce an endless series of small spills (see chapter 5). In combination, the burgeoning local population, the expansion of the chemical industry and its routine discharges of plant wastes, and the inadequate state of pollution regulations brought the Houston Ship Channel to an exceedingly sorry state by the early 1970s, when the EPA listed the channel above Morgan's Point as one of the ten most polluted water bodies in the United States. Parts of it were almost completely sterile, with dissolved oxygen rarely measured above zero—almost nothing could live there. The ship channel showed the worst concentrations anywhere in the bay for nearly all toxic substances measured in sediments or in organisms (*State of the Bay* 1994, 2002).

Most of the effluent from municipal and industrial sources is today subjected to at least some treatment before being discharged. Responsibility for issuing permits to municipal and industrial wastewater sources now rests with the Texas Commission on Environmental Quality. The number of permit holders in the Galveston Bay watershed was estimated at 3,756 in 1987, with about a third of these in the immediate vicinity of the bay. The 1986 Superfund Amendments and Restoration Act required industrial dischargers to report the amounts of certain toxic substances released into the environment. For the upper ship channel, the reported total for 1988 amounted to almost a million pounds of toxic materials of seventy different kinds (Oswalt 1992). Dividing that by 365 days gives close to three thousand pounds per day. But this did not include all facilities; some were not reporting their discharges.

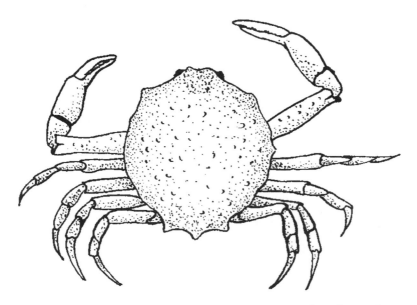

Persephona crinata

Jim Blackburn (2004) suggests that the numbers are much higher. His tally of toxic materials discharged directly from industrial sources in Harris County into the ship channel and Galveston Bay was more than 6.8 million pounds in 2001. He also notes that beyond the direct industrial discharges, more than 50 million pounds of industrial pollutants were sent to publicly owned treatment works for treatment and discharge into coastal waters, mostly into Galveston Bay. Together, says Blackburn, the direct and indirect discharges of toxic materials into the bay could approach 10 million pounds a year, which would mean some *thirty thousand pounds a day.*

The only good thing to be said about this is that at least more data are now being gathered, though the data are difficult to read and understand. Summaries of the extent, distribution, effects, and hazards of contaminants appear in the chapters on water and sediment quality and public health in the 2002 edition of *State of the Bay.* The authors conclude that the worst industrial excesses have been curbed and that the condition of water entering the bay from industrial sources has improved significantly since the 1970s under scrutiny and more systematic regulation.

There remains much room for refinement and public vigilance on discharge permit regulations (and exemptions), monitoring, and enforcement. Monitoring agencies are short of money and staff. Self-reporting is always suspect. The petrochemical industry exerts power-ful political pressure to allow ongoing pollution. Industry wails that cleaning up effluent is expensive, and plants commonly take a bare-minimum approach to compliance with discharge regulations.

How important a source of pollution is sewage, which would not seem to be in the same damaging league as industrial wastewater? Sewage is important because of its quantity. A 1990 estimate indicated that besides receiving large volumes of water used for cooling in power plants, Galveston Bay was annually receiving a total of 224 billion gallons of "process water" discharges. About three-quarters of that flow—174 billion gallons—was from municipal sources, with the re-maining 50 billion gallons coming mainly from industry. In a 1950 study, Galveston officials found that most municipalities were still dumping raw sewage into the bay. A federal study twenty years later found that even then, only 40 percent of the water discharged by the city of Galveston was adequately treated.

Under the circumstances, one might expect water quality in the bay to be a great deal worse than it is. Natural resource scientists de-clare in print, in front of God and everyone, that apart from problems concentrated in and near its western and urban tributaries, for the most part Galveston Bay has maintained good water quality overall. They attribute this to the fact that it is "shallow, well mixed, well aer-ated and undergoes a total water exchange more than four times a year due to freshwater inflow and tidal action" (*State of the Bay* 2002, 69).

For shallow, read extremely shallow. Excluding channels, which range from nine to forty-five feet deep, the greatest depths in the bay are only about twelve to fifteen feet. Much of Galveston Bay is be-tween six and ten feet deep. Trinity Bay is some eight feet deep in the center. Large portions of East Bay and West Bay are no more than four to six feet deep. Basketball players could walk miles through these wa-ters without even wetting their whiskers.

Since more stringent discharge goals were established in 1971 for industrial and municipal sources along the ship channel, upgrading of wastewater treatment has brought a general trend of improvement. Two water-quality parameters that remain of ongoing concern are chlorophyll-a, which is lower than it should be in a healthy water body, and fecal coliform bacteria counts, which are higher than they should be. "Chlorophyll-a needs attention because it has declined steadily for 25 years and the cause of its decline is unknown. Fecal co-liform concentrations in Galveston Bay are of concern because, unlike

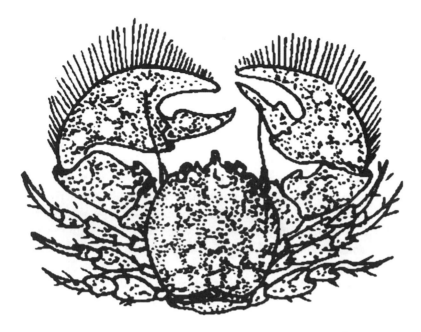

Porcellana sayana

many of the water quality measures, they have not shown improvement" (*State of the Bay* 2002, 81).

The significance of chlorophyll-a is that it reflects the concentration of the principal photosynthetic pigment in green plants, the biological engine of the estuary. It is thus a "surrogate indicator" of the standing crop of phytoplankton or single-celled algae present in the water (*State of the Bay* 2002, 73). I opened this discussion of our hardworking bay with crabs, shrimp, and oysters because they are more pleasant to consider than fouling of the bay with chemicals and sewage. They are also easier to understand than the mysterious workings of phytoplankton. But I can postpone the algae no longer.

The Underwater Prairie

The basis for understanding the functions of an estuary is the concept of primary productivity, the rate at which the sun's energy is captured in usable form when carbon is transferred from atmospheric carbon dioxide into the biomass of plant life. This transfer is high in such ecosystems as tropical rain forests, where the "fixing" of carbon by plants is apparent in the form of magnificent towering trees. We can practically see the trees fixing the carbon. The process is harder to grasp in an estuary because many of the fixing organisms are very small: phytoplankton or algae, microscopic single-celled plants drifting in the water.

Drama they lack, but their productivity is nonetheless impressive. They multiply rapidly and form the base of the estuary's food web. Scientists measure primary productivity in terms of grams of dry biomass generated per square meter per year. On the face of it, a simple sea grass meadow does not seem anywhere near as richly productive as a fecund stretch of rain forest bearing a complex structure of large fruiting trees, undergrowth, and flowering vines, all ringing with the calls of toucans and howler monkeys. Yet by the measure of carbon content in dry biomass, the two are equivalent.

Amazingly enough, when their primary productivity is compared, swamps, marshes, estuaries, algal beds, and coral reefs all score right up there with steamy tropical forests as the ecosystems with the highest primary productivity. All have an average production of more than four pounds of dry biomass per square yard per year, with some areas producing as much as eight pounds (Lieth and Whittaker 1975; Costanza, D'-Arge et al. 1997). Galveston Bay is thus equal to the most exotic of landscapes in its primary productivity, which goes some of the way toward explaining how it has sustained our multifaceted assault for a century.

It takes some mental acrobatics to acknowledge the life-giving power of organisms that we can scarcely see. But power players they are. Four pounds of biomass per square yard per year is more than three times higher than the productivity of the cultivated land that we think of as bounteously productive; crops average only about one and a half pounds of harvested biomass per square yard (Lieth and Whittaker 1975; Costanza, D'-Arge et al. 1997). And the phytoplankton in the bay do it all by themselves, without any gasoline-powered planting, tending, chemical fertilizers, or mechanical harvesting. They are harvested instead by multitudes of other small creatures, the larval life stages of fish and shrimp, which in turn support larger fish.

Across an acre, four pounds per square yard amounts to about eight tons. Where primary productivity is closer to eight pounds per square yard, the yield per acre can climb to much higher. Underwater sea grass meadows are similarly productive, and easier to comprehend.

Stenocionops furcata

Their basic role is providing structure in the water column with their leaves and in the sediment with their roots and rhizomes. The structure they supply baffles waves, counteracts erosion, and removes suspended sediment, thus promoting water clarity.

And there is more. The leaf surfaces of sea grasses increase the "bottom" area on which algae communities can develop—sometimes dramatically. A dense meadow may sport more than four thousand plants per square yard, increasing the bottom area fifteen- to twentyfold. This is the reason why the meadows provide such rich foraging areas for so many young fish and invertebrates, including the commercially and recreationally important species.

The sea grasses themselves are food sources for only a few species, mainly waterfowl and turtles. But sea grasses play a major role in nutrient cycling within the water column and sediments, and their detritus is a key source of organic material. "Entire fisheries may depend directly or indirectly on production by seagrass habitats" (Withers 2002, 85)

The emergent plants of shoreline marshes, consisting mainly of *Spartina*, or cordgrass, have their roots underwater only some of the time. These plants, too, are a veritable pantry. "The agents that mill them and their associated plant and animal life, principally algae and insects, are death and decay," says Warner (1976, 7–8). Again the crop produced consists of minute particles of detritus and nutrients dissolved in the water. His calculation of primary productivity in marshes was up to five tons per acre.

Waiting to receive what Warner calls the "nourishing flow of silage from this decomposing *Spartina* crop" are many forms of life— plankton, larvae, infant populations of fish, clams, oysters, jellyfish, and worms; blue crabs stand by to prey on all these. A cartoon rendering might show big fish eating the smaller fish, and the smaller fish and crabs chasing the wiggling larvae, and these in turn having a riotous feast on dots of decaying vegetation.

All of this is a long, roundabout way of saying what we know but sometimes forget—untold biological riches swirl from warm water and primeval ooze. We need not bother putting numbers and weights and scientific names to the components, provided that we remember the importance of keeping our ooze in good order. When the long-term chlorophyll-a trend in the bay is in steady decline, we would do well to take heed. The indicator of the bay's phytoplankton standing crop is telling us the algae are in trouble.

Priority Problems

The turning of the tide in the ship channel came in the 1970s with strengthening of discharge regulations. Intensifying concern would lead in the 1980s and 1990s to new agency and citizen efforts to ensure the health of the bay as a whole (see chapter 5). Collective judgment about which problems are most acute crystallized in the 1990s into seventeen "priority problems" identified in *State of the Bay* (1994). These are the problems driving current management effort under the Galveston Bay Plan (Galveston Bay National Estuary Program 1995; hereafter cited as GBNEP), and fuller discussion of each can be found in *State of the Bay* (2002, 2–11; downloadable from the Web site of the Galveston Bay Estuary Program, http://gbep.tamug.edu).

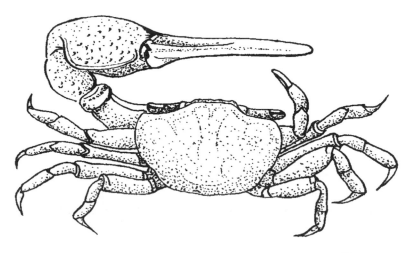

Uca pugnax

The seventeen priority problems intergrade and overlap tightly. Three involve *disappearance*—actual physical losses—of productive shallow wetland habitats to draining, dredge and fill, erosion, subsidence, and shoreline armoring. Eleven involve *degradation* of these same habitats with all manner of pollutants, which of course means further loss of productivity. Two more involve threatened *future losses* of productivity as a result of declining freshwater supply and inroads by exotic species. Is it any wonder that the seventeenth problem involves some species of marine organisms and birds showing declining population trends? The list is a seventeen-point distillation of pure losses. All the priority problems are in fact the same problem: we are straining the bay's resilience in every conceivable way.

Problem number one is wetlands losses. The U.S. Fish and Wildlife Service has estimated that Texas has lost more than half its wetlands since colonial times (Texas Coastal Management Program 1996). Just since 1950 Galveston Bay has lost more than thirty-five thousand acres of emergent wetlands, salt marsh consisting mainly of cordgrass (*Spartina alterniflora*; Werner 1993). Some sources place marsh losses nearer to fifty thousand acres, and nearly all this damage is human induced.

The losses result from conversion of coastal marsh to uplands through drainage projects; from filling of wetlands for development or disposal of dredged material; and from conversion of marsh to open water, especially through subsidence (Werner 1993, 2–3). Open water may look lovely, but marshes are better. Emergent marsh shows shrimp and crab densities five to ten times greater than do other shallows.

The primary wetlands conservation tool at the federal level is the Clean Water Act section 404 permit program, jointly administered by the U.S. Army Corps of Engineers and the EPA. This program regulates filling of "waters of the United States" by requiring permits. Other state and federal agencies have input, depending on the scale of projects. But denial of permits is rare, many small projects are exempt, and many of the larger ones are conducted by the same entity that also carries the regulatory responsibility—the Corps of Engineers itself. *Destruction by Design*, published by the Gulf Restoration Network (1999), gives a depressing account of the Corps' performance. Thus, despite theoretically having in place a sophisticated national regulatory mechanism for wetland protection, and a national policy of no net loss, we in fact steadily continue to lose wetlands.

Recall that eleven of the seventeen priority problems involve degradation. Problem number two mildly notes that contaminated runoff from nonpoint sources—(from the watershed at large rather than from identifiable industrial or municipal wastewater discharges)—degrades the water and sediments of some bay tributaries and near-shore areas. This brings the issue of harm to the bay right to the doorstep of home owners. We are just beginning to face up to the fact that even with stricter regulation of municipal and industrial discharges, a major population center has serious negative impacts on water quality in the bay (see chapter 5 and the resources for more about nonpoint-source pollution).

Galveston Bay is a hardworking bay, a major asset to surrounding communities, with obvious economic value when assessed by standard measures of industry, shipping, and fisheries productivity. Its value as a recreational asset for boaters, anglers, and birders is also high (see chapter 3). And there is one more way of computing the bay's value that is missed by traditional economic yardsticks.

Traditional economics does not recognize that natural systems have economic value beyond the harvestable resources they supply. The discipline of "environmental economics" began to emerge along with the scientific concept of ecology, recognizing that natural systems also supply ecosystem services, which we tend to overlook. The major mechanical and chemical ecosystem services that bays provide are the recycling of nutrients, having effects on the water supply, and treating wastewater. Wetlands filter pollutants from surface waters, maintain groundwater supplies, dissipate floodwaters, and protect shorelines from erosion.

Each of these services has a value that can be calculated on the basis of what it would cost us to supply the service ourselves. And the value of the services estuaries provide is startlingly high—they are the only ecosystems providing more than ten-thousand-dollars' worth of services per acre per year in the 1997 calculations of Robert Costanza and colleagues. Swamps and floodplains come in second, at more than nine thousand dollars per acre per year. After that come sea grass and algal beds, and then tidal marshes. Thus, every component of the Galveston Bay ecosystem scores high as a provider of ecosystem services.

The bay covers six hundred square miles. It has thousands of acres of marshes, forested swamps, and algal flats, providing billions of dollars' worth of free ecosystem services every year. Although the numbers are huge, Blackburn (2004) acknowledges that he is under no illusion about the numbers putting an end to short-sighted decision making; his hope is that they may at least provide a measure of the impact of government-sanctioned destruction of the bays. All the inroads—all the many permits for interference, such as filling of wetlands and discharging of toxic substances—carry costs in lost ecosystem services.

Traditional economics says "access to water transportation and wastewater discharge sites are valuable commercial features" of land around the bay (*State of the Bay* 2002, 49). Biology reminds us that nearly all marine creatures of importance to us depend on healthy estuaries for some portion of their life cycle. Environmental economics says look after the phytoplankton and cordgrass, for they are working hard for us all. And it says we should bear in mind that free ecosystem services supplied by the bay are expenses we do not need to fund as long as we to keep the bay in sound condition. Through marsh restoration projects, we are just beginning to see how expensive it can be to try to compensate for lost services.

When we contemplate the multitude of sins that have been washing into bayous and the bay for decades from neighborhoods and shopping centers from the fifty-mile diameter of greater Houston, and from industrial discharges and spills, sewage plant overflows, garden pesticides, and more, it should not surprise us that we are having a spot of bother with declining chlorophyll-a. We have scarred the bay bottom with dredging for channels and for shell. We have dammed and chan- nelized the rivers that are its sources of fresh water. We have drowned marshes through subsidence caused by pumping groundwater. We continue to pour millions of pounds of toxic materials into the bay and add ever more human inhabitants to its watershed. The astonishing thing is how well the bay has sustained our demands so far.

A space shuttle photograph of Galveston Bay, taken in October 1985, shows the dramatic contrast between the intensively developed western shore and the much more rural eastern side. Pale blazes of industry line the upper Houston Ship Channel, with an outlier near the bay mouth at Texas City. With increasing distance from Houston (upper left), the geometric urban signature yields to agricultural patchwork and then to the swirls and curves of coastal prairie and the Trinity River Delta. Image STS51J-143-126 from http://eol.jsc.nasa.gov, courtesy of Earth Sciences and Image Analysis Laboratory, NASA Johnson Space Center.

The mouth of Galveston Bay is a dynamic junction between the great estuary and the Gulf of Mexico—a focal point for movement of water, sediment, and boat traffic. As photographed from the International Space Station, the lower landmass is Galveston Island, separated from the Bolivar Peninsula (right) by the pass called the Bolivar Roads. Jutting from the mainland at upper center is the Texas City Dike, reaching almost to Pelican Island, Little Pelican Island, and the Houston Ship Channel. Farther west lies the Galveston causeway, crossing the Gulf Intracoastal Waterway, which can be traced from far left to far right. Image ISS004E7306 from http://eol.jsc.nasa.gov, courtesy of Earth Sciences and Image Analysis Laboratory, NASA Johnson Space Center.

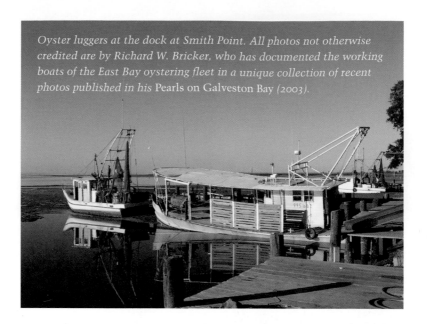

Oyster luggers at the dock at Smith Point. All photos not otherwise credited are by Richard W. Bricker, who has documented the working boats of the East Bay oystering fleet in a unique collection of recent photos published in his Pearls on Galveston Bay *(2003).*

The bald cypress swamp of the Trinity River Delta needs fluctuations in water level to flourish over the long term.

American white pelicans loaf between bouts of fishing. They are mainly winter residents on Galveston Bay, most individuals migrating northward in spring to nest.

Alligators are numerous in Chambers County on the eastern side of the bay and are the theme for Anahuac's Gatorfest in September.

Brown pelicans have been making a gradual comeback. In the 1990s they resumed breeding on Pelican Island after a long hiatus, and more than eight hundred pairs were nesting in the five counties around the bay by 2000.

Some of the boats used for oystering are converted shrimpers, such as the Santana.

The Captain Neal *belonging to Joe Nelson is among the larger luggers at forty-six feet long. Built in 1997, it has a draft of three and a half feet. Luggers carry tall canes used for marking progress on the reefs. The awning is to shade the oysters.*

Tiny oyster spat need to anchor themselves to a firm surface. Old oyster shell is ideal.

Oyster researcher and professor emeritus Sammy Ray shucks oysters for students to sample. He has introduced many to the miracles of shellfish and works closely with commercial oystermen.

Brown pelicans follow the shrimp boat Elizabeth H near Morgan's Point for easy meals. Galveston Bay's annual shrimp harvest has been around 7 million pounds since the mid-1990s. Brown shrimp are the mainstay of this fishery, and more than a dozen shrimp species inhabit the bay.

Booms, nets, and wooden "doors" identify the M-M from Double Bayou as a shrimp boat. Larger vessels trawl in the Gulf, smaller ones in the bays.

Container ship and tug at Morgan's Point, where the narrow upper channel widens out into the bay proper. The Barbour's Cut container terminal built in the 1970s consumed part of the town of Morgan's Point.

The black skimmer feeds by skimming the water surface with its long lower mandible, especially at dusk and at night. Individuals often rest on the sand with neck stretched out, looking for all the world as if dead.

Frigatebirds are recognizable by a deeply forked tail and extremely long wings. They dive for fish and also steal prey from other birds in the air.

The mixed group of white birds foraging in a wet pasture includes great egrets, snowy egrets, and white ibis.

Mergansers are saw-billed ducks that dive to catch fish. They winter along the coast, favoring sheltered salt water.

The roseate spoonbill forages by sweeping its odd bill from side to side in shallow water. These birds breed in several rookeries around Galveston Bay, arriving and departing in splendid cascades of pink.

"Gulf Ghost" earned bay activists the People's Choice Award and third place in the political category in Houston's 2004 Art Car Parade. Coordinated and entered by Charlotte Wells and designed by Dori Nelson, the giant pelican made of recycled sails and palm fronds cut quite a figure downtown. Big-headed fat cats rode on its back, waving outsized cigars and dollar bills, while skull-masked figures walked alongside with signs pleading for bay conservation. Here they also clutch parade trophies. Photo by Justin Wilkinson.

CHAPTER *3*

Recreational Riches

The greatest value of the bay may well reside in its function as an asset in the competition with other regions on quality-of-life issues.

Daniel W. Moulton

What is it worth to have an ordinary, everyday errand run graced by a flock of two dozen pelicans wheeling slowly overhead? What do we gain from knowing that a sea turtle has dug her nest on Galveston Island? How many people know that dolphins can be seen from the shore in La Porte? People who live near the bay know these pleasures, but for many elsewhere in greater Houston, the only obvious way to enjoy the bay is to head for the Kemah Boardwalk and order up some seafood while watching the comings and goings of boats. That kind of limited encounter can also feel like the only prudent way; on television we learn scary things about the bay—high water, oil spills and chemical contamination, fish kills. Rather than being widely acknowledged as an immense natural and recreational asset, the bay is often seen in a much more ambivalent light.

It was not always so. For a long time Galveston Bay was Houston's prime leisure retreat. The first great Camelot on the bay was Sylvan Beach in La Porte. When the town was incorporated in 1892, a large park area was set aside at the beach, including a stretch of fine old

shade trees known as the Grove. La Porte forthwith prepared an exhibit to go to Chicago for the Columbian Exposition, the 1893 World's
Fair, to promote its attractions to the nation.

At that stage, the way to get to Sylvan Beach was to ride a train from
Houston to Deer Park and then rent a buggy for the rest of the run
through thinly populated farmland to the shore. Drivers reportedly
had to stay on the alert for stray horses and cows along the narrow dirt
roads (Foxworth 1986). Visitors had a choice of several hotels at two
dollars a night, and on occasions like the Fourth of July there were foot
and pony races. Huge tarpon and flounder were caught nearby in the
bay. During the 1890s the railroad reached La Porte, roads were sur-
faced with shell for more reliable travel, and dozens of cottages were
built. W. R. Scott, president of the Texas and Louisiana Division of the
Southern Pacific Railroad, had the line extended southward into
Seabrook and built a grand home on Todville Road, where the Girl
Scouts' Camp Casa Mare now stands.

The Great Storm of 1900 damaged the early splendor of the Sylvan
Hotel and destroyed its dance pavilion. The Catholic Diocese of Galveston bought the hotel in 1901 and established St. Mary's Seminary,
which operated there for more than fifty years. But there was bound to
be a resurgence of recreational activity at this beach closest to Houston and accessible by rail. In 1914 during the state Rotary convention,
Sylvan Beach was the setting of an astounding picnic for no less than
fourteen thousand people in an elaborate seating arrangement like the
spokes of a wheel (Foxworth 1986).

Those in Houston who could afford it escaped to the bay during the
heat of summer. They brought pets, servants, and all to Morgan's
Point, La Porte, Seabrook, and North Galveston (now San Leon). "At
the Bay, the constraints of Victorian-era city life were somewhat re-
laxed. Children ran barefoot, evening sails were popular, and friends
and relatives visited for long stays" (Akkerman 1998, 13). Some of the
men commuted by train to work in the city.

The 1920s and 1930s were La Porte's heyday as a holiday destination. In the big-band era it boasted the largest dance pavilion in the
South, often featuring Guy Lombardo as the entertainment. The beach
park and its surrounding attractions were Houston's answer to Coney
Island, enticing some thirty-five thousand people through the gates on
big holidays.

Native Houstonian Walter Cronkite, the grand duke of national
television news anchors, sold hamburgers at Sylvan Beach during va-

cations from San Jacinto High School. Long before entering politics, Lyndon B. Johnson used to visit, when he was still a schoolteacher. Magnate Jesse Jones of Houston sponsored boxing matches there. In the early 1930s actor Clark Gable went to Sylvan Beach during breaks from stage shows at Houston's old Palace Theatre. As a child, the famous heart surgeon Denton Cooley used to dig in the sand there (Foxworth 1986). Sylvan Beach at La Porte was unquestionably the place to go for a good time.

A Boom in Fishing and Boating

Swimming parties and dance floors looking out over moonlight shimmering on the water have yielded to boating and fishing as the main modes of bay recreation. Almost a hundred thousand pleasure boats, from modest fishing dinghies to fancy cruisers, are registered in the five counties surrounding the bay, according to the Texas Parks and Wildlife Department. More than 260,000 recreational fishing licenses a year are sold in those counties. Expenditures on sportfishing in Galveston Bay account for about half of all the money spent on sportfishing in Texas. Surveys indicate that about 20 percent of the people in those five counties go fishing or boating on the bay at least once a year, with an additional 13 percent picnicking, hiking, birding, camping, or swimming (*State of the Bay* 2002, 52–53). The combined total amounts to some 1.3 million people, a third of the population in the region.

To look at the matter in dollars, Dan Moulton of Texas Parks and Wildlife analyzed recreational expenditures to isolate "destination spending" related to Galveston Bay—that is, direct expenditures by visitors after reaching their destination. A 1986 study showed spending of $294 million directly related to Galveston Bay, with $171.5 million of this contribution to the local economy deriving from sportfishing. Bay-related recreational travel expenditures were calculated at more than $400 million in 1995, again with more than half involving sportfishing, and with an overall regional economic impact calculated at some $750 million (Moulton 2003).

For 2001 Moulton found that spending on bay-related recreation had climbed to $708 million, with a total economic impact of $1.27 billion. Outdoor recreation is an industry showing steady and substantial growth, and it produces jobs. Moulton (2003) notes that employment generated by all travel spending in the area was estimated at about 101,000 jobs in 2001, of which recreation supported 20,400 (by contrast with only about 1,400 jobs in commercial fishing). Eco-tourism and marine recreational activities are a rapidly expanding sector under the tourism umbrella.

All this excitement notwithstanding, disregard was also a prominent finding in a Galveston Bay Estuary Program survey of how people use and view the bay. The majority of people in the Houston-Galveston area did not perceive the bay as a site for recreational activities, and most respondents had a negative perception of its quality (GBF, "Galveston Bay," n.d.). We are in the ironic position of simultaneously having excellent recreational opportunities on the bay but also a widespread attitude of dismissiveness toward the same resource. This chapter and the sections on destinations, events, and resources are intended to address that divide.

There are understandable reasons for the disregard. No famous national park hugs the Galveston Bay shore, beckoning us to come and enjoy it. No visitor center is devoted to it. Although the bay lies just a few miles from downtown Houston as the seagull flies, how to get in touch with it is not readily apparent. Most of the bayous that feed the bay are ignored by the great city they drain, or they are feared because they flood. From high bridges where Loop 610 and Beltway 8 cross the ship channel, we can get a look at the water, the ships, and the Port of Houston docks, but the overriding impression is of heavy industry lining the channel. The entertainment complex at Kemah is indeed the first cheerful window on the water.

For someone coming from Houston, the marshes beside the causeway to Galveston Island on Interstate 45 can seem like the place where the bay begins, though by then most of it has already been left behind. And even where the water's edge is accessible, the flat coast offers few vistas where we can understand how land and water relate. Standing at the shore yields only views of merging low elements, a shift from mostly land to mostly water.

A way to get some quick positioning about the physical details of much of the bay system is in *Above and Beyond* by pilot Rob Parrish and photographer Chris Kuhlman (1993), a collection of aerial portraits (see the resources for ordering information). Here one can take in at a glance how the long finger of the Texas City Dike brings a roadway almost to the very mouth of the bay. Within minutes, anglers launching a boat there can be fishing the nearby flats, the deep water

Floundering, 1960.

along the Houston Ship Channel, the long jetties where the bay spills
into the Gulf, or East Bay.

The aerial views are helpful for sorting out the confusing terrain
near Galveston and for a sense of how undeveloped the bay's eastern
shore still is. In an aerial shot of the Trinity River delta, the neat circle
of Lake Anahuac contrasts with a tracery of twisting bayous threading
through *terra* just barely *firma*. Sinuous curves on the river's main
stem look as if they belong in the Amazon. Photos show April Fool
Point and Dollar Bay; a long Gulf shoreline view from Rollover Pass;
the grassy shallows and oyster reefs at Pirates Cove; and the sweep of
Redfish Island, a popular anchorage for boaters staying overnight.

The brief text in *Above and Beyond* is mainly about fishing. Interpretive maps accompany the photos, incidentally conveying that numerous submerged structures dot the bay. Most old pilings are the
remains of oil and gas wells. Although they can be inconvenient for
boaters, such obstacles, along with oil rigs, oyster reefs, wrecks, and
artificially created reefs, also offer shelter to larvae and fish (Dunn
1993; Fulghum 1988). "I look upon these refuges as a fish's idea of a secure retreat or stronghold—a castle," said Barney Farley, a long-time
fishing guide farther down the coast. "Small fish, crabs, shrimp, and
other marine life use these castles to hide from larger fish. To the
larger fish, these places are natural feeding grounds as well as castles
or strongholds against the still larger fish that may prey on them"
(Farley 2002, 24–25).

Drift fishermen must learn about submerged structures, conquer navigational questions, and grasp the bay's moods to avoid getting into trouble on the water. Surf and wade fishermen know the insecure, sludgy feeling of soft bottoms, the easier walking of hard sand or shell, the excitement of seeing fish before catching them. Bay outlets into the Gulf at Rollover Pass on East Bay and San Luis Pass on West Bay are important focal points for anglers, and fishing from piers and jetties can be a good option when the water is too rough for boating or fishing the surf. A pier offers fairly deep water from relative comfort and safety, and some piers are also accessible at night. On the Gulf, small near-shore marine organisms in the surf lure baitfish close to the beach, and these attract the larger predators, such as redfish, trout, croaker, pompano, whiting, sheepshead, and black drum. Occasionally they may also attract sharks and rays, king mackerel, ling, and even tarpon to deeper troughs accessible from the piers.

One means of pinpointing where to go fishing or boating is by looking in the *Texas Beach and Bay Access Guide* published by the Texas General Land Office (2002; see the resources for ordering information). It lists and maps access points by county for the whole Texas coast. The Houston-Galveston section includes two dozen locales in Harris County, eighty-one in Galveston County, and eleven on the east side of the bay in Chambers County. With well over a hundred access points around the bay and its tributaries, boaters can stay busy every Saturday for a year just checking out different places.

The fish most often taken by recreational fishermen in Galveston Bay are the Atlantic croaker, sand seatrout, and speckled trout or spotted seatrout (*State of the Bay* 2002). Flounder, black drum, sheepshead, redfish, and gafftopsail catfish make up of most of the rest of the sportfishing catch. Texas Parks and Wildlife Department pamphlets about game-fish species describe their habits and the best ways to catch them. Fishing is a pastime well served by the Internet, books, and a range of magazines, including *Texas Fish and Game*, *Texas Saltwater Fishing*, *Gulf Coast Fisherman*, *Texas Outdoors Journal*, *Saltwater Sportsman*, and *Texas Saltwater Fishing Magazine* (online). Links to all these can be found at www.texasgulfcoastfishing.com, which also includes fishing regulations; links to sites for angling and paddling associations and equipment suppliers; and listings for about a hundred fishing guides on the Texas coast, of whom a quarter are on Galveston Bay.

Guides, out often and ranging widely, develop an intimate sense of the complexions of different parts of the bay. To produce for their clients, they need to know how to make the most of the clear blue days when a cold front comes through, where the fish will be when the bay is murky brown, and what to do when weather raises white dots and dashes of chop on gray water deepening to charcoal. Sport anglers are proud of their contributions to conservation of game fish through pressing for tighter regulation, supporting research and monitoring activity, and promoting use of retired oil rigs as artificial reef structures (see Coastal Conservation Association in the resources).

Watching the cavalcade of boats emerging from Clear Lake down the Kemah channel to the bay on a spring or summer afternoon makes it clear that this a major boating center. Annual festivities on that channel, like the Blessing of the Fleet in August and the lighted boat parade at Christmas, underscore this (see chapter 8). Newcomers or visitors can tune in through the established monthly boating magazine *Telltales* and the monthly newspaper *Mariner's Log* (see the resources for contact details). Clear Lake has the largest concentration of recreational boats in Texas and the third largest in the nation. There are some thirty marinas in the bay area, with more than eight thousand wet slips and fourteen hundred dry-dock storage lots. Clear Lake alone has nineteen marinas, of which Watergate Yachting Center and South Shore Harbor have more than a thousand slips each.

Watergate claims to be the country's largest private marina, with thirteen hundred slips—slightly more than the number of landside inhabitants in neighboring Clear Lake Shores. That island community was developed in 1927, when the *Houston Post* offered lots for $69.95 to those who purchased a six-month newspaper subscription. The oldest marina is Seabrook Shipyard, which can berth some 850 vessels and offers heavy-duty repair (*Living in the Bay Area* 2001). Add windsurfing, rowing, kayaking, waterskiing, surfing, skimboarding, and the noisy mayhem of Jet Skis, and the community involved in water sports is substantial.

Pledge of the Sailing Community

Houston has a venerable history as a sailing town. The Houston Yacht Club (HYC) was organized in the summer of 1897, following a Fourth of July regatta at La Porte—off Sylvan Beach, of course. The club's first commodore was Dan E. Kennedy, owner of a home at Morgan's Point and manager of the La Porte Improvement Company. Despite the disruptions of the Spanish-American War and the Great Storm of 1900, by 1902 HYC was again holding a seventeen-mile regatta that began just off the Sylvan Beach pier. Large regattas took place at Seabrook and Galveston in the early years as well, and club membership reached two hundred people by 1905.

In her centennial history of HYC, Dora Akkerman notes that the club was organized "not only to promote the sport of boating but also to encourage the science of navigation and provide a cleaner and healthier bayou" (1998, 23). Promoting a healthy bayou involved tasks a little different from today's. One early improvement was to remove a historic hazard to navigation: the wreck of a sunken Confederate ammunition boat near the Milam Street bridge in Houston. "On January 23, 1906, members of the Club detonated a charge beneath the . . . wreck, and hundreds of spectators rushed to the site to gather the relics uncovered by the blast. Cannon balls, bomb shells, cartridges, and coins were gathered as souvenirs" (Akkerman 1998, 22).

Most members initially kept their boats near Allen's Landing downtown. In 1907, when dredging to straighten what was known as Harrisburg Bend on the Houston Ship Channel formed Brady Island, the dredged channel passed north of the new island and HYC settled on the south side, on the original course of Buffalo Bayou. From there, getting to the open bay was much quicker than from Allen's Landing. The club would move again in 1927 to its present facilities in the new development of Shoreacres, just south of La Porte, where it hosted a national regatta for the first time. Membership doubled in the 1960s when the innovation of fiberglass boats brought a boom in sailing activity.

In the centennial year of 1997 the season opening day coincided with the annual benefit regatta for Galveston's historic tall ship, *Elissa*. HYC officers stood on *Elissa*'s deck to salute a flotilla of hundreds of sailboats and powerboats coming from all over the bay to join the celebration. Forty past HYC commodores were present or represented, with first commodore Kennedy's granddaughter among those representatives.

HYC more or less gave birth to several other local sailing clubs. In the early 1900s (when it was called the Houston Launch Club) it held several regattas headquartered at the large, turreted, waterfront lodge called the Seabrook Hunting and Fishing Club. The building suffered heavy damage in the 1915 hurricane and was never rebuilt; in the

Nine-inch turtle on the beach at El Jardin, 1963.

chaos following the storm, a cow was reportedly found on one of its upper floors. HYC maintained a small sailing facility at Seabrook until 1925, when that group became independent, but it too lost its facilities to a storm. Today's Seabrook Sailing Club was organized in 1934.

The Texas Corinthian Yacht Club in Kemah was formed in 1938 by three long-time HYC members who wanted to emphasize amateur sailboat racing. "The founders commissioned Olin Stephens of Sparkman and Stephens in New York to develop a one-design boat for Galveston Bay's strong winds and shallow depths: the Corinthian was the result" (Akkerman 1998, 93). Lakewood Yacht Club was established in 1955 solely for powerboaters, following a rift between sailors and powerboaters; only in 1973 did Lakewood begin to admit sailing members. These clubs and the Galveston Bay Cruising Association have full agendas, from major open regattas to youth sailing and summer camps.

Well before World War I, HYC was already working to stop pollution of Buffalo Bayou. "Any dumping of trash, waste, or oil was perceived as detrimental to the navigability of the Bayou. . . . Club members organized a committee to list all industrial plants along the Bayou and identify the corporate culprits who were allegedly polluting it" (Akkerman 1998, 34). Houston's first antipollution court actions can thus be chalked up to HYC. As a Texas House of Representatives proclamation on the centennial noted, "HYC sailors have traditionally given freely of their time, energy, and resources to numerous worthwhile endeavors; in addition to the club charter's stated goal of 'maintaining a cleaner and healthier bayou,' club members' boats have seen military service in both world wars, and the club's facilities have been used to house both refugees from the 1947 Texas City disaster and military personnel preparing to serve in Operation Desert Storm" (Akkerman 1998, 192). That charter goal has kept HYC at the forefront of conservation efforts on behalf of the bay right up to the present, hosting meetings and helping to fund activism.

Since the advent of the outboard motor, not many people have favored getting around Galveston Bay and its environs strictly under their own muscle power. Kayaking is presently a small sport, but its popularity is growing because of its low impact: no vast expense, no fuel to buy, no permanent slip or boat trailer required—and no damage to submerged sea grasses. Powerboats are not considered a "significant" threat to sea grass in Galveston Bay, but they can leave propeller scars that take years to revegetate, which makes a kayak more suitable for some waters (*State of the Bay* 2002, 90–91).

Buying a sea kayak, or even buying three or four, will not compromise the family budget for a year, and it can be a good way to move around on the water quietly for birding or fishing. A kayaker can nose into secluded places too shallow for most boats to traverse at all. In the wild backwaters of the Trinity delta or upper bayou reaches, birds supply the loudest sounds. Going kayaking with a group provides safety for beginners and shortcuts for learning where to go. For a growing number of people whose inclination is to explore the natural surroundings, kayaking opens new worlds.

Prime Time for Birding

The importance of the upper Texas coast in the world of birding can scarcely be overstated. People are drawn here from across the nation and the globe to share in the riches. We do not draw an international audience for our scenery or architecture, but we do for birding. Galveston Bay is part of the world-class attraction called the Great Texas Coastal Birding Trail. From Boston to San Francisco and from Germany to Japan, birders know about it.

The wonderful thing about an interest in birds is its inclusiveness. It works for the young, the old, and everyone in between, for the physically fit and the not so fit, for the overeducated and undereducated, everyone. It can be satisfying at home or on the road, winter or summer, for an hour or a day—for a lifetime. Once people have caught the urge, it never goes away. Every day contains birds. Many are beautiful; some are comical. They speak to our senses with colors and song, and they serve to connect us with far places in a great web of vibrant life.

We think of migrant birds as living in North America and dashing down to Central and South America for the winter, but we could just as well see them as living to the south and spending some of the spring or summer among us. Indeed, their longer-lasting winter plumage is called their basic plumage, whereas special colors donned for breeding season are called alternative plumage. Obviously it is difficult and dangerous for a bird to undertake a journey of three thousand miles or more. Some of these marathon athletes weigh less than an ounce, and some fly a lot farther—the arctic tern covers up to twelve thousand miles each way, from the far north to Antarctica (Richardson 2000).

The long days of northern summers provide many more hours to gather food for nestlings than are available in the tropics. As spring moves northward, bringing abundance, the birds follow for an energetic summer of breeding and feeding; "northward migration expands the available nesting and food gathering area of the world" (Richardson 2000, 2). When the heat wanes, insectivorous birds must move south again to escape the cold northern winter, which presents few bugs to eat. Birds that fish or feed on aquatic vegetation must move away from lakes and rivers that will freeze. Many of the species that stay in North America all winter eat mainly seeds, which remain available.

During their migration, we have a chance to see a vast array of different kinds of birds around Galveston Bay. With numerous migrants swelling the total, Texas boasts more than six hundred bird species, about forty of which are not found elsewhere in the United States. Most of the Texas species not occurring elsewhere in the nation are found from the lower Rio Grande Valley southward, such as the hook-billed kite, the ringed kingfisher, and the noisy chachalaca. But the bays and woods of the upper coast, within easy striking distance of Houston, also draw plenty of attention.

The easy way into birding is along the Great Texas Coastal Birding Trail, featuring some three hundred sites stretching across five hundred miles from Louisiana to Mexico. The trail is organized into a series of driving loops detailed on three large maps: the upper, central, and lower sections of the coast (see the resources for ordering information). Closest to Houston are the San Jacinto, Katy Prairie, Galveston, Trinity, and Brazoria loops, varying greatly in flavor. Some sites on these loops are small parks in the heart of cities, accessible over a lunch hour and good for repeat visits at different times of year; others are large wildlife refuges that can occupy visitors for a day or a week at a time. Some are woodland or grassland; others are beaches, mud-flats, or marshland; and larger sites include a range of habitats. Brown-and-white signs identify the sites.

One of the specialties on Galveston Bay in winter is the piping plover, a little shorebird with a black breast band and orange legs, named for its shrill, piping call. The North American population is estimated at some four thousand birds, and the species is listed as threatened or endangered throughout its range (Glass-Godwin 1991). Texas hosts the largest wintering population of piping plovers, with a concentration of them around Galveston. After moving into wintering grounds in September and October, they can be found on beaches or on the sand flats on the inland side of barrier islands, feeding on marine worms, mollusks, and crustaceans and often foraging with other shorebirds—the more abundant semipalmated plover, American avocet, and short-billed dowitcher, for example.

Coastal development in the piping plover's favored beach habitats is a difficulty for them. Protecting places where these and other birds concentrate "may be the most significant contribution biologists and conservationists can make to preserve piping plovers," noted Susan Haig of the Piping Plover Recovery Team (in Glass-Godwin 1991). Indeed, Houston-Galveston area bird enthusiasts have proven without peer in working for conservation of natural areas, and we have them to thank for the existence of several sanctuaries on the bay and Gulf where all the rest of us can also enjoy the waterbirds, shorebirds, and birds of the woodlands and coastal prairies (see chapter 7).

Our first migrant songbirds to arrive in spring are those that nest not too far north, such as the prothonotary warbler and Louisiana waterthrush, which we begin to see in the latter half of March. Birds nesting farther north come through later because they must wait for more northerly terrain to thaw. The gray-cheeked thrush, for example, is not seen until late April or early May (Richardson 2000). Migrating birds may not follow the same routes northward and southward, because circumstances differ. A fierce northern blow can be a problem for birds heading northward across the Gulf into the teeth of the wind; they may hug the coast if a storm proves too taxing. On the southbound journey, however, a north wind may speed them on their way directly across the Gulf (Richardson 2000).

Private waterfront access is a jealously guarded privilege. Frederick Weis titled this 1963 sketch "Psychology of the Locked Gate."

A special birding edition of *Texas Parks and Wildlife* magazine in April 1999 included a pull-out birding calendar listing more than four dozen Texas birding places, courses, interpretive tours, and events in March and April, when spring migration is in progress on the upper coast. Events range from weekly warbler walks in the woods at High Island on the Bolivar Peninsula to the week-long statewide competition called the Great Texas Birding Classic. As tourism operators know, birders spend money. As long ago as 1992 six thousand birders visited the live oak woodlands in the tiny Bolivar Peninsula hamlet of High Island during March and April. "They went to witness the spectacular migration of warblers, tanagers, thrushes and other songbirds, and over a six-week period they spent $2.5 million on lodging and other travel-related expenses" (*Texas Parks and Wildlife* 1999, 46).

Scissor-tailed flycatchers reappear on fences and utility wires as spring advances, spotting for where to swoop next in their hawking for insects. Yellow-crowned night-herons are often to be seen patrolling wet roadside ditches, all steely attention, all predator, unfazed by the roar of traffic just a few feet away. The white wisp of the bird's crest dances like a curl of gift-wrap ribbon in gusts from passing vehicles. The end of the ditch vigil is a sharp strike of the heavy bill, and one more crawfish goes down the hatch.

The strident Woody Woodpecker laugh of the large pileated wood-pecker and the muttering and chattering of crows and jays punctuate the season of plenty. Early hours of the morning may bring the deep, mellow hoots of a great horned owl; at dawn and dusk the spooky descending trill of a screech-owl bespeaks young to feed. As summer wanes, the first southbound migrants begin reaching the Texas coast again as early as September. By October, migration is in full swing. November brings again the strange, staccato trumpeting of sandhill cranes from high in the sky as the tall gray birds proceed in elegant Vs so high above as to be scarcely visible despite their large size. Then come the geese, millions and millions of snow geese.

In *Nesting Birds of the Coastal Islands*, John Dyes presents a parallel chronology out on the bay: "Every year for countless centuries, the Galveston Bay area has been host to some fifty thousand pairs of nesting colonial wading birds, gulls, and terns. . . . From the birds' standpoint the islands are ideal, providing the isolation and security they must have for the intense nesting period. The islands offer no direct sustenance, but this is readily found in the shallow bay waters and marshes within easy flying distance" (1993, 1).

The show on the islands runs for much of the year. Early nesters— herons, night-herons, egrets, and cormorants—start gathering in February. In March, the colonial waterbirds begin building nests and laying eggs, all procedures intensifying in April; by May, nesting season is approaching its peak, with the earliest chicks already leaving nests, although most birds are still rearing young. June sees parents working hard to feed growing chicks, and chicks are beginning to disperse. By July, things are winding down. The few birds still nesting have trouble with the summer heat. Most young terns and gulls are already independent in August, scattering out along the coast in September. Roseate spoonbills move into the salt marshes, and egrets and herons head into freshwater habitats.

Nesting on the mile-long shell bank known as Redfish Island, parallel to the ship channel in the center of the bay, are black skimmers, least terns, and Forster's terns. Little Pelican Island near Galveston has a variety of habitats and is among the most important nesting islands anywhere on the Texas coast, with stunning wealth of birdlife. Royal and Sandwich terns, gulls, and skimmers use the sand flats and extensive shell bank, creating a "mixed cacophony of seven to twelve thousand birds" (Dyes 1993, 44); cormorants, spoonbills, herons, and egrets favor the brush.

A hundred years ago egrets and spoonbills were killed by the thousands for plumes to serve the millinery trade. When the killing stopped, there remained plenty of habitat where they could nest undisturbed, and populations recovered. Today threats are more insidious: nesting sites are disappearing. As human pressure nudged them away from traditional nesting sites on the beaches and in the marshes, the birds retreated to old spoil islands created during building of the Gulf Intracoastal Waterway. But the islands have been subsiding and washing away. Now that we have taken up most of the birds' alternatives with our own nesting projects, they cannot easily switch to new places if the landscape lets them down.

Restoration projects are in progress, and several of the islands have become Houston Audubon Society sanctuaries, where wardens keep watch at key seasons to ensure that breeding birds are not disturbed. During the fall and winter months, islands provide safe roosting for pelicans and winter wading birds as well as many songbirds. In the brush and on ponds and bays, winter visitors like horned larks and warblers, pintails, coots, blue-winged and green-winged teal, ruddy ducks, and grebes can be found in the same places as "summer" birds like seaside sparrows and black-necked stilts.

The islands have always been a changing medium—sometimes swiftly changing. The now substantial Pelican Island, for example, earned this name because it was once a major brown pelican nesting colony. But just a few years before that, it barely even qualified as an island. "In 1815, Pelican Island was merely a narrow slip of a marsh, upon which it was impossible to walk dry-footed, except on a spot that was a hundred feet over, which was all that was dry," recorded one early observer (*State of the Bay* 2002, 25).

By 1820 nesting brown pelicans flourished there, and by the 1850s when the first formal surveys were made, Pelican Island was the largest island in the bay, four miles long and about half a mile wide. Pelicans nest on the ground in large colonies where they are safe from marauding raccoons and coyotes. "Biologists counted many hundreds of nests on Pelican Island just offshore of Galveston Island . . . and on Bird Island in San Luis Pass. However, by the early 1900s fishermen became wary of the pelicans' great fish-catching skills and began to crush the eggs of nesting birds" (Sipocz 1993, 30–31). Studies indicated that pelicans eat mainly menhaden (shad), and a few anchovies and mullet—species not targeted by fishermen at the time. But the nest destruction continued, and there was worse to come.

Pesticides, notably DDT, were washing into the bay in the runoff from rivers and bayous. The poisons accumulating in the fish that pelicans ate became concentrated in the birds' tissues, and one effect was that their eggshells grew too thin for incubation. "Between having their nests destroyed by fishermen and the egg shell thinning from DDT, brown pelicans almost became extinct by the early 1960s" (Sipocz 1993, 31). An estimated five thousand brown pelicans nested along the Texas coast in 1918, but numbers were down to fewer than ten pairs between 1967 and 1974 (*State of the Bay* 2002). Like pelicans, the osprey suffered serious declines as a result of this pesticide. Mercifully, DDT was outlawed.

White pelicans are common all along the Texas coast. They nest widely—mainly in southern Canada and the northern tier of U.S. plains and western states but even as far south as Laguna Madre—and winter along the Gulf. Birds not yet of breeding age may stay in Texas all year. They feed by dipping their large pouched bill underwater. In flight they show black wing tips and short tails. They sometimes form a line across the water and "herd" fish into a cove to catch them; I have watched this right in front of Seabrook's strategically located pelican-viewing platform at McHale Park, just north of the Kemah Bridge.

Brown pelicans remain much rarer, but they have shown increases since 1993. At the beginning of the 1990s I used to see a lone individual near the Kemah Bridge in winter. In 1992, according to Andrew Sipocz of the Texas Parks and Wildlife Department, brown pelicans tried to nest on Pelican Island for the first time since the early 1950s. By 2000 more than eight hundred pairs of this endangered species were nesting in the five counties around Galveston Bay (*State of the Bay* 2002). These pelicans can often be seen along the bayfront in Shore-acres, making dramatic dives from twenty feet in the air or more and submerging completely to catch fish.

Every year brings birding surprises. At the end of 2002 a crested caracara—a bird more typical in South Texas—was recorded for the first time in the Armand Bayou Christmas Bird Count. On a Saturday evening in mid-May 2003, bird guide Jim Stevenson of Galveston excitedly informed his e-mail contacts that he and a shorebird seminar

Small boat, 1949.

party had unexpectedly encountered a host of five thousand phalaropes (a kind of sandpiper) at a coastal lagoon on Pelican Island. "This is absolutely unprecedented," he said, noting that anyone nipping out to the island on Sunday might still be able to see them. Birders are not in any doubt about our avian wealth.

Specialty Tours and the Job Market

Television cameras rolled at the Galveston docks in 1992 as three squat little ships called caravels drew in and tied up near where the iron barque *Elissa* is now moored. Replicas of the modest fleet that Christopher Columbus sailed to the New World in 1492, they were part of festivities for the five-hundredth anniversary of his voyage. The *Elissa* looks too small to have crossed the Atlantic numerous times as a workhorse, yet at a length of 162 feet and capacity of 430 tons, it is almost twice the size of the largest of Columbus's caravels. The *Niña* was only 70 feet long, the *Pinta* just a tad longer, and even the flagship *Santa Maria* measured less than 100 feet from bow to stern (*Voyage of Rediscovery* 1992, 7A).

Built of native Spanish oak, the three caravels had been christened by members of the Spanish royal family with much fanfare. Reconstruction was guided by the specifications in Escalante de Mendoza's *Itinerario de Navigacion*, published in 1575. The replica ships took twenty-nine days to make their crossing from Spain, first sighting the New World at St. Barthelemy, southeast of Puerto Rico. They had sailed the whole way, though they did carry small diesel engines for maneuvering in port. Although relying primarily on the ancient astrolabe and quadrant for navigation—the sextant had not been invented by the time of Columbus—they also carried radios and life rafts. Crews consisted of Spanish naval officers and adventurous volunteers willing to face showering on deck in seawater in return for reliving the historic voyage.

The vessels' reception at New World ports scarcely resembled that of the three original caravels. "The mangroves, oyster reefs, and sand dunes of five centuries ago have given way to convention centers and asphalt; the hesitant Native Americans have been replaced by techno-crazed media, by politicians and event promoters" (*Voyage of Rediscovery* 1992, 2A).

The world has grown smaller since Columbus sailed. Now we can reach the playgrounds of Cancun or the Caribbean in almost the time it once took Houstonians to get to Sylvan Beach. In the era of space travel, some of the astronauts at the Johnson Space Center have received their own custom "circumnavigation of Galveston Bay": a field trip to put some flesh on the bones of earth science training they receive before space flights. The excursion was designed to offer them insights about geology and human effects on the landscape around a single large geographic feature visible from space—the bay where they live (Office of Earth Science 1998).

One sample itinerary has a park in Baytown as its first stop. From the marina building, astronauts can see the head of the estuary and receive an orientation about the interplay between marine and alluvial processes. They can also see industrial vistas and learn about oil fields, spill hazards, evidence of subsidence, and recent community attempts to mitigate past damage to the bay. Then they travel north and east over coastal prairie converted to suburban woodland, through 1950s blue-collar housing, and onto terrain known as the Beaumont terrace, where prairie has yielded to rice fields. They cross the Trinity River and hear about the Wallisville Dam before heading south through pine woods into the town of Anahuac (see chapter 7).

A city park in Anahuac is a good place to contemplate the dynamics of delta formation, prehistoric settlement, and human structural changes to the landscape made over the past 150 years by dredging and levees. Leveed fields have been recycled into a wildlife preserve at the next stop, Anahuac National Wildlife Refuge. From there the tour heads south to the Gulf Intracoastal Waterway bridge at High Island, where they learn of the underground salt dome responsible for the elevation of this portion of the coast.

Crossing the bridge onto the Bolivar Peninsula, they see "transgression" of the Gulf of Mexico barrier island before proceeding south to the human-made cut at Rollover Pass. They learn about how businesses and homes are attracted by the cut, and about shoreline erosion, beaches, and dunes. Stops include the former military base at Fort Travis, now a park, and the Bolivar Flats, where a wide beach and extensive tidal flats have accreted against the jetty. Sediment movements around the Galveston jetties, erosion effects at the seawall, the nature of the Bolivar Roads and Houston Ship Channel, effects of oil spills, and changing sediment plumes in the Gulf are among subjects discussed at the mouth of the bay. The next reach is on the Bolivar ferry, with views of the Texas City Dike and Pelican Island.

The wrap-up during the return leg across the Galveston causeway and home up Interstate 45 is all about useful applications of space and satellite photography in earth science, such as for documenting large-scale changes like the effects of hurricanes on shorelines. Astronauts conducted on such a tour wind up with better overall perspectives on the bay than the rest of us can easily achieve. And for them, the world grows smaller yet. They come back from space flights acutely aware of both the fragility and the biological exuberance of Earth. We tend to take our blue planet for granted, but by all astronaut accounts, Earth beckons like a dreamscape to anyone looking at it from an orbit in cold black space.

Few places offer more drastic contrast to the inhospitable void of space than the riot of life in and around Galveston Bay. We can see some of it on boat excursions from Galveston or Kemah. Birders and kayakers have growing schedules of guided trips. Some prototype ecotours have begun out of Smith Point and Anahuac, as Houston begins to recognize the extensive "ecological capital" that its natural surroundings represent (Blackburn 2004). The Columbus commemorative voyage and the landscapes tour for astronauts suggest other possibilities for custom commercial ventures, and no doubt more will spring up as venturesome spirits among us work out how to build careers based on the natural world around the bay (see Ecotours in the resources).

Why do people move to the Houston area? Jobs brought most of us here. Why do people want to move to Austin or Oregon? Clean air, appealing natural surroundings, and varied outdoor recreation are key attractions. Contemplating the long future, we would do well to take note of the recreational riches around us, the boom in bay-related spending, and the groundswell in travel and ecotourism, because these things give us choices. We may also do well to note the fate of La Porte, which largely ignored its natural assets. The once glorious Sylvan Beach park has long since lost its luster and fails even to merit mention on the Great Texas Coastal Birding Trail. People are not lining up to move to La Porte.

"Topping the list of high growth industries is computer and data processing services, followed by health services, health practitioners, research and testing services, communications, electronics components, and management and public relations firms—all industries relying on a well-trained, highly educated workforce," says Dan Moulton (2003, 4). He notes that these sectors have begun to be good job generators for the region, but we are in competition for them with other regions. Outdoor recreation opportunities help these industries to attract and retain a highly skilled and highly paid workforce. "I believe the loss or degradation of the recreational opportunities now afforded by [Galveston Bay] would damage the economy of the region in several ways. . . . In fact, the overall state of the bay may well reflect both the quality of life and the economic competitiveness of the region," Moulton concludes (2003, 4–5).

We can accept that we are stuck on a heavy industrial runaway train and must let all the new high-tech, low-impact businesses of the future go to Austin and Oregon. Or we can insist that the driver switch tracks and set off instead down another line, where we can get Houston a piece of the action and start collecting some of the interest payments on our local ecological capital. It is not too late.

CHAPTER 4

Hurricanes and Floods

*It has become clear that creation of a wide concrete ditch
not only is unsightly and destructive to the ecosystem,
but it also is not effective in preventing flooding.*

Buffalo Bayou Coalition, 1988

In some places, it is possible to forget that despite all our modifications to the landscape, we remain subject to the elements. Galveston Bay is not one of those places. The water and the weather
command respect. Hurricanes, tropical storms, and flooding are inescapable facts of life on the upper Texas coast.

Anyone who has seen the level of the bay come up four or five feet
in just a few hours during apparently calm weather, a day or more before any other effects of an approaching Gulf of Mexico storm are felt,
begins to get the idea. Weather forecasters seem to have trouble pre-
dicting how high and how fast the water will rise. The dynamics of
tidal effects are intricate, and the routes and horizontal speeds of hurricanes are notoriously difficult to anticipate. People living near the
bay have gone to sleep at night after it has been reported on the television news that a storm will make landfall around noon the next day
but have woken to find themselves already cut off by the storm tide,
driveways and streets flooded and cars disabled.

The extreme case I know of in the speed of the rising storm tide was in Galveston during the Great Storm of 1900. Survivors expressed astonishment at how fast the water came up. By six o'clock on the evening the storm arrived, the tide was rising some two and a half feet per hour. As terrified people huddled and hoped inside homes already flooded to a depth of a foot or two, things grew suddenly much worse. "At about seven-thirty, in a single enormous swell, the tide rose four feet in four seconds. The center of the hurricane apparently passed west of the Island between 8 and 9 P.M." (Cartwright 1991, 168).

When the bay is coming up and rain is coming down, high water is likely in the bayous as well as along the bayshore. Flooding hampers traffic. Ferries stop running. And a roiling bout of weather need not be a hurricane to wreak a lot of destruction. In June 2001 Houston got a stern reminder of the damage a lesser storm can do. Tropical Storm Allison produced devastating flooding in many parts of the city and left a $6 billion swath of damage across southeastern Texas counties. Damage estimates first indicated that twenty thousand homes had been flooded, then thirty thousand, settling eventually on forty-four thousand damaged and about thirty-five hundred destroyed (*Storm Signals* 2001). Twenty-four people lost their lives in this storm, twenty-two of them in Harris County.

Several local television networks released videos about how the storm lashed Houston, including *Flood of a Lifetime* (2001) by ABC Eyewitness News. There is room to question that video title, however. Nowhere is it written that the Houston-Galveston area will not face even heavier flooding. The last major hurricane on Galveston Bay was Alicia, which came ashore at San Luis Pass at the western end of the bay in 1983. Alicia was a category 3 storm in the ranking of 1 to 5. Hurricane Carla wrought plenty of havoc in 1961; it was a category 4 storm but made landfall farther south at Port O'Connor.

"We have not had a direct hit from a category 4 hurricane since 1915. A similar storm today with the eye making landfall on the west end of Galveston Island near Jamaica Beach then moving north northwest across Houston would produce damage that would vastly eclipse what happened in Florida from Andrew," said meteorologist Bill Read of the Houston/Galveston National Weather Service office. "Storm surge would start at 15 feet or so on the Island and reach 20 to more than 25 feet on the west side of Galveston Bay. That would flood most of Galveston County east of I-45, all of the Clear Lake area southeast of Ellington Field, much of La Porte to Baytown and much of the area along the Ship Channel. . . . Over 600,000 people live in the category 4 surge zone" (*Storm Signals* 2001). How much damage a category 5 hurricane could do in the Galveston Bay area today is not easy to imagine.

Yet these storms are not the freak occurrences they are often portrayed to be. Although irregular, heavy storms are nevertheless routine events, part of an inexorable cycle. In the hasty modern world, we have trouble seeing things as cyclical when they do not conform to an annual or predictable pattern. But tropical storms are predictable in three respects: we know they will come, we know they will come fairly often, and we know they will bring high water. The only things we do not know are precisely when, where, and how high.

The Great Storm of 1900

Europe received its first description of a New World hurricane in the 1540s from the same Cabeza de Vaca who landed on Galveston Island. The storm struck the expedition while two of its six ships were provisioning at the port of Trinidad in Cuba. It was already raining when Cabeza de Vaca went ashore:

> An hour after I left, the sea began to rise ominously and the north wind blew so violently that the two boats would not have dared come near land even if the head wind had not already made a landing impossible. All hands labored severely under a heavy fall of water that entire day [Saturday] and until dark on Sunday. By then the rain and tempest had stepped up until there was as much agitation in the town as at sea. All the houses and churches went down. We had to walk seven or eight together, locking arms, to keep from being blown away. Walking in the woods gave us as much fear as the tumbling houses, for the trees were falling too, and could have killed us. We wandered all night in this raging tempest. . . . Particularly from midnight on, we heard a great roaring. (1997, 28–29)

On Monday morning when the storm eased, they discovered that both their ships had been lost, with sixty men and twenty horses. Those who had gone ashore were the only members of the expedition who had survived.

The first storm for which local detail is well recorded was in 1818, when the pirate Jean Lafitte lived on Galveston Island in a little fortress town he called Campeachy. His two-story house, known as La Mansion Rouge, was considerably more substantial than the rest of the dwellings, and in 1818 Lafitte more or less presided over a rough-and-ready settlement of some two thousand people.

When a storm threatened, he consigned many of them to the fort and La Mansion Rouge, both on the highest section of the island. He repaired to a schooner to ride out the storm. The fort collapsed, and all the flimsy huts were washed away. Hundreds of bodies lay on the beach. La Mansion Rouge stood firm, though a cannon crashed into it and killed some of the people inside. A dozen ships were smashed in the bay; only three withstood the storm. Perhaps half the colonists were lost (Cartwright 1991, 44–48).

Three big blows came through in 1871, and then on September 16, 1875, a storm tide thirteen feet above normal at Galveston covered the whole island. Farther down the coast the town of Indianola was swept away, and 176 people were killed. Survivors reestablished the little town, only to see it destroyed by the next hurricane, on August 20, 1886. Galveston suffered some damage, and there was talk of building a seawall (Cartwright 1991).

Galveston's name would come to be almost synonymous with the word *hurricane* after the Great Storm of September 8–9, 1900. Isaac Cline, chief of the U.S. Weather Bureau's Galveston Station, hoisted storm warning flags on Friday, September 7. A storm had blown over Cuba on Tuesday and reached Florida on Thursday. As Cline walked along East Beach on Friday, the barometer was falling. Wind was from the north, but the tide was four feet above normal and rising. "The phenomenon of high water with opposing winds was an uncommon occurrence, but Cline knew its name: it was called a storm tide" (Cartwright 1991, 164). He also knew how lethal coastal storms could be. While Cline had been a Galveston weatherman, an 1893 storm had drowned two thousand people on the Mississippi and Louisiana coasts.

The rain began in Galveston just after midnight and fell steadily all night. Before dawn there was water in the streets. By 1:00 P.M. on Saturday, bridges across the bay were submerged—it was too late to get to the mainland. Some twelve thousand people of the city's population of more than thirty-seven thousand had departed, but the rest were stranded. Broadway was the city's highest point, at eight and a half feet above sea level. By midafternoon Cline had recognized the scale of the pending disaster. His final message to the chief of the Weather Bureau in Washington, D.C., just before the lines went dead, advised that "great loss of life was imminent" (Cartwright 1991, 167).

Wind speeds reached one hundred miles per hour before the gauge

Windswept hackberry.

was blown away. The maximum storm surge reached an estimated twenty feet (Bomar 1983). In the southern sectors of the city, two to five blocks inland were swept clean, with not one building left standing. "Where 20,000 people lived on the eighth not a house remained on the ninth, and who occupied the houses may, in many instances, never be known," wrote Cline in his official report to the Weather Bureau (Weems 1999, 153). About thirty-six hundred buildings were demolished (U.S. Army Corps of Engineers, n.d.; hereafter cited as USACE).

Accounts of the death toll vary, but a widely accepted estimate is that some six thousand people died in Galveston and perhaps another two thousand elsewhere along the coast. There is no disagreement about the Great Storm of 1900 having been the single worst natural disaster in U.S. history. Three weeks after the hurricane, people were still removing twenty to thirty bodies a day from the debris.

Chaos reigned higher up the bay as well. At Seabrook the waters rose suddenly over the banks of Clear Creek near the railroad bridge to Kemah. People fled for high ground. Three times the six o'clock train backed up from the Seabrook station to the bridge "and every exertion was used to rescue every soul" ("Loss at Seabrook" 1990, 56). Numerous people were nevertheless drowned, and many buildings were destroyed. Three books offering mountains of grim detail about the 1900 storm are the carefully researched *Isaac's Storm* by Erik Larson (1999), emphasizing Cline's perspectives; *A Weekend in September* by John

Edward Weems (1999), first published in 1957 and much reissued, including extensive interviews with survivors; and *Galveston: A History of the Island* by Gary Cartwright (1991).

In its natural state, much of the Gulf shore of Galveston Island was bordered by sand dunes rising to heights of twelve to fifteen feet above the rest of the island surface. Thus, in its early days, the city was somewhat protected from hurricane tides by the dunes. With rapid development during the nineteenth century, sand dunes along the beach were leveled for beach access or were removed for fill material (USACE, n.d.).

After the Great Storm, the people of Galveston wasted no time developing a means to protect the city from future disasters. A board of engineers was appointed to this end, headed by the former chief of army engineers, Brig. Gen. H. M. Robert—the author of Robert's Rules of Order for parliamentary procedures. The first section of 17,500 feet of seawall was begun 1902, and by 1905 the seawall reached as far as Fifty-third Street.

The next big storm made landfall in 1915 in Freeport, just west of Galveston Bay. According to the Corps of Engineers (n.d.), winds in the 1915 storm exceeded sixty miles per hour for more than nineteen hours and exceeded seventy miles per hour for more than nine hours— much longer than during the 1900 storm. The storm tide in 1915 was also a few inches higher than that of 1900. A three-masted schooner was lifted up and over the new Galveston seawall, and four-ton blocks of granite riprap were hurled across the roadway. On the mainland and the Bolivar Peninsula, more than three hundred people were killed, and there was extensive damage in Chambers County on the eastern side of the bay (Cartwright 1991, 194; Henson and Ladd 1988, 262).

On Galveston Island eight people died—a very different proposition from what had happened in 1900. The seawall got the credit: "The heavy waves caused considerable scour along the foot of the seawall and the riprap apron was undermined in places; however, the concrete section of the wall withstood the storm with no major damage. Without question the seawall paid for itself during this one storm" (USACE, n.d.).

By 1921 the seawall reached more than seven miles, all the way from the South Jetty to Sixty-first Street. It had been built so as to leave three hundred feet of beach in front of the structure, but the 1915 storm washed much of this beach away, and what was left continued to diminish. By the 1930s the shoreline had crept all the way back to the riprap at the foot of the seawall, and the decision was made to pro-

tect the seawall with a system of groins extending five hundred feet
into the Gulf. Congress would authorize another three-mile westward
extension of the seawall in 1950. When this was completed in 1962,
ten miles of the Galveston Island Gulf shore were protected from
storm surges (USACE, n.d.).

A Hurricane Plan

My family was forced to take account of storms soon after moving
here because four billowed up in quick succession during 1988 and
1989, and our home is just a couple of hundred yards from the Galveston Bay shore. The first was Hurricane Gilbert, which caused quite a
stir in September 1988 when it entered the Gulf of Mexico as a category 5 hurricane, a colossal six hundred miles across. The great spiral
of the storm system looked ominous indeed on the television screen.

Gilbert had struck Jamaica as a category 3 storm. It was so large
that when the eye passed over the island, many people thought the
storm was over and went outside, only to be killed when the "other
side" of the hurricane arrived. The next day Gilbert was upgraded to
category 5. Only two category 5 storms have ever struck the United
States: the Labor Day hurricane of 1935 was the most violent in the
turbulent hurricane history of Florida. It killed 408 people, and its
barometric pressure of 26.35 inches of mercury was at the time the
lowest ever recorded in the northern hemisphere, according to John
Williams and Ivor Deudall in *Florida Hurricanes* (2002). The second
category 5 storm was Hurricane Camille, which killed 256 people in
Louisiana and Mississippi in 1969. Since 1988 Hurricane Gilbert has
held the record for the lowest barometric pressure in the hemisphere:
26.22 inches (Williams and Deudall 2002).

Gilbert blasted Cozumel, Mexico, with winds of two hundred miles
per hour, leaving about seven thousand people homeless. Many more
lost their homes as the huge storm crossed the Yucatán and entered
the Gulf. Calculations indicated that Gilbert would next hit Texas
south of Galveston; for us, the time had come to board up the windows
and head for the hills. In the end Gilbert spared Galveston Bay, though
twenty-five Texas counties suffered tornados. The storm went ashore
in northern Mexico, ravaging coastal villages and producing lethal
flash floods well inland at Monterrey, the industrial hub of Nuevo
León (Marshall 1988).

Three more tropical cyclones menaced the upper Texas coast in

1989. The first was Tropical Storm Allison, and it had more in common with the Allison of 2001 than just its name. Both made landfall in June near the western end of Galveston Island, headed into East Texas, and then moved back to the southwest and hung around, producing torrential rains in the Houston area (*Storm Signals* 2001). The other two 1989 tropical cyclones that came this way developed into hurricanes: Chantal in July and Jerry in October. In places Chantal produced eight to ten inches of rain. Tropical Storm Jerry was bearing down on Louisiana when it suddenly intensified into a category 2 hurricane and changed direction to make landfall near Galveston Bay.

Having four storms within a few months showed us that we needed to know which roads went underwater first, so as to avoid those or travel them before the heavy rains came. We saw how much debris rafts up at the water's edge and the damage it can cause. We saw how many trees were lost when heavy winds strained shallow root systems in waterlogged soil. Trees were stripped and snapped, and some simply lay down. We learned that waiting for agency-suggested closures was a mistake. Evacuation is an option the authorities approach with extreme reluctance, delaying it as long as possible and risking the awful prospect of having hundreds or thousands of people stranded in cars on roadways impassable because of flooding.

Carla, Alicia, and Allison

Hurricane Carla on September 11, 1961, is locally regarded as the next most severe storm after the Great Storm of 1900; some consider Carla to have been even stronger. Certainly it was among the most intense in Texas. A category 4 storm, as noted, Carla measured four hundred miles across and made landfall at Port O'Connor. A storm tide of twenty-two feet and winds of 150 miles per hour were recorded. The eye was thirty miles in diameter. A quarter of a million people were evacuated—this came soon after a heavy Louisiana death toll in Hurricane Audrey in 1957, and when Carla threatened, coastal residents heeded the storm warnings and departed (*Storm Signals* 2001).

Returning residents noted "the unmistakable signature of a hurricane: buckled utility poles hanging like corpses from taut power lines, twisted street signs pointing every direction but the correct one, mangled television antennae strewn on roofs and in yards, and boats of all sizes inverted in canals. Dead cattle were scattered about, leaving a

Fallen pine, Hurricane Carla, 1961.

sickening stench . . . even heavy steel boats as much as 70 feet in length [were] displaced up to 500 feet from the shoreline" (Bomar 1983, 71). Port O'Connor was practically destroyed.

The Galveston Bay area saw a good deal of damage, there were forty-six deaths in Texas and beyond, and Carla was still generating rain when it reached North Dakota (*Storm Signals* 2001). As Gary Cartwright points out, the sixty-first anniversary of the Great Storm of 1900 occurred while Carla lay offshore for several days, and Carla's course was similar to those of the hurricanes that devastated Indianola in 1875 and 1886 (Cartwright 1991, 299–302).

Galveston Bay was largely spared from devastating storms during the rest of the 1960s and the 1970s as the Texas coastal population boomed. The storms came in elsewhere. Hurricane Cindy made landfall at High Island in September 1963 but moved up the Gulf shore, bringing floods in several counties to the east of Houston. Hurricane Beulah arrived near Brownsville in September 1967, packing 140-mile-per-hour winds. Several towns in South Texas received more rain in four days than they expect to get in a year, and the storm spawned more than a hundred tornados (Bomar 1991, 76–77). Celia struck at Corpus Christi in 1970, Fern at Rockport in 1971; Edith came the same month but made no Texas landfall. Carmen came ashore in Louisiana in 1977, Amelia in 1978 brought major Hill Country flooding, and Allen came ashore at Port Mansfield in South Texas in 1980. Only Tropical Storm Claudette in 1979 did serious flood damage in Houston.

Hurricane Alicia on August 18, 1983, was sufficiently recent to remain vivid in the minds of many in Harris and Galveston counties. A category 3 storm, Alicia made landfall at San Luis Pass at the southwestern end of Galveston Island and then moved northwest to skirt the western edge of Houston. Top winds of 115 miles per hour were recorded, with a storm tide of thirteen feet (Bomar 1991, 76–77). There were twenty-one deaths (*Storm Signals* 2001). Although this storm was not as severe as Carla, Alicia did substantial property damage because it came ashore in the much more densely populated and industrialized area of Galveston Bay. By the 1980s subsidence had lowered populated areas significantly, placing more homes at risk.

In *Texas Weather*, George Bomar includes a table giving statistics on the winds, tides, and damage in all the hurricanes that struck the Texas coast from 1900 through 1983. A second table lists numbers of tropical storms and hurricanes from 1871 through 1984 and their months of occurrence (Bomar 1991, 226–27). The tally of both kinds of storms is eighty-one in those 113 years—underscoring that although any given spot on the coast will not suffer such severe storms often, this kind of weather does strike our coast as a whole very regularly.

Officially, hurricane season runs from June 1 through November 30, but it is noteworthy that forty-seven of the eighty-one hurricanes and tropical storms Bomar lists arrived in August and September. A chart showing the tracks of the nine Atlantic hurricanes reaching Texas from 1960 through 1983 indicates that all nine hit during high summer, three in August and six in September (Bomar 1983, 79). The 1875 storm at Indianola, the Great Storm of 1900, Carla, Cindy, Beulah, Fern, and Gilbert were all in September. The 1886 and 1915 storms, Alicia, Celia, and Allen were all in August.

The tabulation also shows that storm-surge height has major correlations with damage and loss of life. High winds near the storm center are terrifying, but the greater destroyer and killer by far is the storm surge because of its more widespread effect. The height of the surge depends on the local offshore water depth, bottom topography, and the angle at which the surge strikes the coast. The highest surges come at right angles, and in these cases a storm tide of ten feet is not uncommon up to a hundred miles away from the point of landfall. Where the coastline folds into a bay, the effects in the estuary can be intensified. Hurricane winds can drive bay waters so that water "piles up" in the narrower upper reaches where it cannot spread out (Bomar 1983, 90).

The first weather crisis for Houston in the twenty-first century would be a tropical storm rather than a hurricane. "All flights to Houston are washed out," said a handwritten sign fluttering from the skycap counter at the Baltimore airport passenger drop-off zone when we pulled up there to fly home to Houston on June 10, 2001.

Tropical Storm Allison had raised five-foot tides in Galveston Bay on Tuesday, June 5, and Houston's Hobby Airport was closed because of heavy rainfall. Television viewers saw motorists wading in hip-deep, waist-deep, and then chest-deep water on Highway 225 (*Flood of a Lifetime* 2001). Greens Bayou was up from its usual three to five feet to twenty-nine feet. On Wednesday a Houston Fire Department boat spent all day rescuing people who were stranded, and twelve inches more rain fell in a few hours in Sugar Land.

By late Thursday evening, it became apparent that the storm was looping back. And by Friday, when rain resumed in earnest in Houston, every bayou in the city was already flooded. Radar pictures showed a dramatic concentration of rainfall inside Loop 610. Late that Friday night, with water rising fast, Houston was facing a major disaster. People were stranded all over town. Bands of heavy rain continued to fall through Saturday. Sections of Interstate 45 near downtown looked like a lake, with a dozen semitrailers scattered in the water at zigzag angles like bathtub toys.

Houses were in the middle of rivers, and rivers were in the middle of houses. Hospitals at the Texas Medical Center were incapacitated with water filling their lower levels, so that power had to be cut off and patients had to be carried down stairwells on stretchers. Nurses worked twenty-four-hour shifts. The downtown tunnel system sported four feet of water. Parts of the city had received from 13 to 27 inches of rain in twenty-four hours, 36 inches of rain in five days. On Sunday morning, hundreds of people were still being rescued each hour.

Allison's impressive deluge was not unprecedented. Looking at the rainfall for three- to five-day storm periods, meteorologist Daniel Huckaby noted that Tropical Storm Claudette in 1979 produced some incredible rainfall totals. An Alvin observer recorded 43 inches of rain in twenty-four hours, which remains a U.S. record. League City got almost 25 inches, Pearland more than 22 inches. The floods of October 1994 brought 26 inches of rain to Liberty, 25.5 at Baytown, and seventeen deaths in southeastern Texas (*Storm Signals* 2001). We can be quite sure more storms like these will visit us.

Flood Buyouts and Cop-Outs

Large cities and high water can be poor companions, depending on what is promoted by private developers and permitted by government. Houston and New Orleans are at the top of the list of communities nationwide in terms of flood insurance payments to "repetitive loss structures." Residents of Texas, Louisiana, and Florida buy more federal flood insurance policies and make more claims than people do in all the other states combined.

In the 1978 through 1995 period covered in the National Wildlife Federation (NWF) flooding report *Higher Ground*, all fifty states were represented. Louisiana had almost 18,000 repetitive loss properties, on which payments of $585 million were made. Texas was close behind with $525 million paid out on 11,410 properties. No other state had more than 10,000 properties affected. Houston and New Orleans accounted for almost a third of the $1.8 billion in National Flood Insurance Program payments between 1978 and 1995 (NWF 1998, 95, 145).

The NWF report argued that the buyout solution held considerable promise for Houston. Nearly half the claims paid out in Texas under the program were in Harris County. The problem, of course, is that during periods of heavy rainfall, the bayous quickly fill and overrun their banks. The disregard with which the powers that be in Houston often view the bay applies also to the bayous flowing into it. Lack of zoning has allowed development in floodplains and floodways. And by way of flood-control measures, Houston has largely relied to date on speeding up runoff by straightening, widening, and concrete lining of streams.

Detention ponds have not found much favor, and subsidence because of groundwater pumping has lowered the already low terrain. "As a result, physical geography, combined with rapid development, has expanded flooding problems well beyond the boundaries represented on floodplain maps" (NWF 1998, 158). Responsibility for controlling runoff has rested with public agencies; private developers have only recently been pressed to reduce or capture runoff by including detention areas and highly permeable cover in their designs.

During the period surveyed by NWF, 986 single-family homes in

Driftwood, 1959.

the Houston area had flood damage twice; 826 had flood losses three times or more. Buyouts in floodplain areas seemed a practical way to reduce flood losses (NWF 1998, 158). Texas established a Division of Emergency Management within the Department of Public Safety and targeted 560 properties for buyouts, using 75 percent federal and 25 percent local funding. By March 1998, 452 of these had been purchased. Land purchased in voluntary buyouts reverts permanently and by law to open space, recreational uses, or natural floodplains.

As the NWF report pointed out, besides being an investment in averting disaster for people in high-risk areas, voluntary buyouts enhance the urban environment and make a start at reclaiming the natural and beneficial functions of floodplains. Various government agencies and citizen groups have also been working on mitigation projects in which tracts of land are devoted to creation of forested wetlands and detention basins.

But flood troubles are multiplying. Fred Garcia of the Harris County Flood Control District noted that 31 percent of the 1978–95 repetitive losses in the city of Houston were outside mapped floodplains (NWF 1998, 162). A significant problem is the creation of new areas of flooding.

Consider the example of White Oak Bayou in northwestern Harris County, where neighborhoods that had never flooded were suddenly underwater in 1998 and again in 2001 as increased runoff from new upstream development caught up with them. In 1992 some four hundred homes there had flooded. Despite a series of channel improvements and creation of some detention sites, in 1998 about a thousand homes flooded during September rains from Tropical Storm Frances. "Flood victims wanted to know . . . why were they receiving such very conflicting information from insurance brokers and mortgage companies about their location on the 100-year floodplain? Why are new neighborhoods being constructed on 'higher ground' and why is nothing being done to protect the older lower neighborhoods that did not flood during 1989 and 1992 but did flood in 1998?" asked Kevin Shanley, the president of the Bayou Preservation Association (1998, 1).

Who was checking that detention ponds installed by developers of new subdivisions really served their intended purpose? Strangely, continued Shanley, neither the Harris County Flood Control District (HCFCD) nor the City of Houston had advised the flood victims or home buyers that HCFCD had developed a new floodplain model showing an enormous increase in the hundred-year floodplain along many parts of the bayou. The City of Houston was still issuing permits using old floodplain data (Shanley 1998, 5). Residents challenged the Flood Control District and developers in a lawsuit.

The 1998 flooding deriving from Tropical Storm Frances began in Jersey Village. Within hours, 1,167 homes were damaged; most had never flooded before. According to flood insurance rate maps available at the time, most were outside the hundred-year floodplain, and residents had seen no need for flood insurance. But upstream development had paved thousands of acres of previously undeveloped land without constructing detention ponds for the increased runoff. According to an investigation by the *Houston Press*, HCFCD documents showed that the district knew residents of Jersey Village were at risk but was suppressing the information until new flood insurance rate maps took effect in April 2000. The county was simply *hoping* that there would not be a big flood in the meantime (Wallstin 2001).

As the *Houston Press* also reported, flood-control policy in the county had made some strides since 1979, when Tropical Storm Claudette and two other heavy storms ravaged the city; flood insurance claims filed in Harris County that year exceeded the combined total for the rest of the country. Jim Green, then director of the Flood Control District, decided things had to change. He worked to provoke the county's first official drainage policy, basically requiring "that new real estate development could not aggravate known flooding problems or create new ones. Developers would have to submit engineering plans to show how they planned to maintain stormwater runoff from their new projects at predevelopment rates" (Wallstin 2001, 26).

Developers, however, proved creative at finding ways to undermine and delay compliance, and the *Press* reported another observer noting that Harris County commissioners had received "more than $600,000 in recent political contributions . . . from engineers, developers, architects, and contractors who make their living off new development" (Wallstin 2001, 28).

Even the legal system seemed to be looking the other way: on June 11, 2001, Judge Eric Andell dismissed the White Oak Bayou homeowners' lawsuit. "Under normal circumstances, Andell's ruling might have generated some attention. But June 11 was not a normal day in Houston. It was the Monday following Tropical Storm Allison, which flooded some 30,000 homes—5,000 of them in the White Oak watershed—and inflicted hundreds of millions of dollars in damages to downtown Houston and the Texas Medical Center" (Wallstin 2001, 31). Andell signed his order at a hotel because the courthouse was flooded.

Farsighted spirits have argued for years that Houston can achieve better flood control by *not* straitjacketing waterways in concrete. Swamps, marshes, and curvy creek channels are natural flood-control mechanisms, excellent at slowing and accommodating floodwaters. An obvious illustration is Clear Creek, much of it still a natural waterway but lately threatened with Corps of Engineers plans for "control." Substituting armored channels for natural watercourses continues to be advanced as the way to speed floodwaters past trouble spots.

A bayou that has been converted into a concrete ditch cannot inspire us, raise our spirits, or contribute to an appealing cityscape. It does not serve as nesting habitat for birds, nor can it serve as a sponge to hold or slow floodwaters. It is merely a sluice. All a sluice can achieve is to move water faster, which is guaranteed to intensify downstream flooding, just as tinkering with the timing of one red light moves a traffic bottleneck down to the next intersection. It does not solve the problem. Casting an eye over a sluice is like watching a child wobble off down a bumpy road on a new bicycle: you know the child is going to fall, and the best you can do is hope the fall is not too serious.

This is not a new song. Two decades ago, Frank Smith (1984, 1), chair of the Bayou Preservation Association, invoked philosopher Lewis Thomas's remarks to a gathering on NASA's Global Habitability project: "The long record of evolution instructs us that the way other creatures get along in nature is to accommodate, to fit in, to give a little whenever they take a little. The rest of life does this all the time, setting up symbiotic arrangements whenever the possibility comes into view."

Smith suggested that when it came to flooding, Houston had compelling reasons to give a little. The flat coastal plain and heavy rains meant that with groundwater withdrawal and systematic acceleration of runoff, we had cooked our own goose: "We have created a flood-prone city where we might have created a flood-proof city, had we set up a few more symbiotic arrangements whenever the possibility came into view" (Smith 1984, 1). In coping with storm water, just as with industrial discharges and other issues affecting the bay and surrounding communities, corporate leaders in Harris County have proven less than equal to the challenge. I repeat: much depends upon what private enterprise promotes and what government permits.

Ecological Force of Storms

A hurricane or tropical storm may destroy highways and buildings, but it cannot destroy an estuary. For all the hundreds of thousands of years before we got here, storms have lashed the coast. Hurricanes are natural phenomena, intensifying physical processes and exerting a considerable influence on natural systems along the Texas coast.

When hurricanes and tropical storms visit, the bays and bayous are flushed with fresh water, salinity swings wildly, and sand moves more than ever. Depths and boundaries change. Passes may open between the Gulf and the bays, or they may suddenly close. A few hours can see coastal erosion and deposition that would normally take months or years. The overall effect is comparable to that of pressing the fast-forward button to speed up a movie.

How everything shakes out depends on whether storms are distinguished by extreme rainfall, extreme high water, or extreme wind velocity. The flush is the greatest effect on the bays. In combination, the enormous inflow of fresh water from heavy rains, the inrush of seawater with high tides, and the opening of passes through barrier islands can change life in an estuary dramatically. Three months after Hurricane Beulah brought heavy rains to South Texas in 1967, scientists recorded much lower salinities than usual in Laguna Madre,

Damaged pier.

which is normally highly saline. They also recorded much higher numbers of fish species.

Within two years, commercial landings of spotted seatrout went from zero to more than a million pounds. The shrimp fishery experienced a similar boom in the Tamaulipas portion of Laguna Madre during the 1970s, after Hurricane Beulah opened passes through the barrier island that had been closed since 1960. The shrimp catch climbed from some five hundred short tons a year in 1971 to a peak of almost five thousand tons in 1977 (Withers and Dilworth 2002, 250–52). The connections between these events are somewhat speculative, and the interplay of ecological factors is intricate, but it is clear that the passage of large storms has bearing on the boom-and-bust cycles of some marine species.

The big storms affect waterfowl too. As we have seen, the Texas coast is crucial migration and wintering habitat for millions of waterfowl of more than two dozen species. They converge on the wetlands of our coastal prairies, bays, and lagoons. Some drought years in the 1950s meant low winter waterfowl numbers. After Hurricane Carla's heavy rains filled many South Texas coastal ponds in 1961, there were dramatic increases in wintering duck and goose populations (Smith 2002, 169–72). Then in 1967 after Hurricane Beulah reduced the salinity of Laguna Madre, the shoalgrass meadows in that estuary built up, and so did the waterfowl population feeding on the shoalgrass, most notably the redhead ducks. Today 75 percent of the world's redhead ducks winter on Laguna Madre. These ducks feed almost exclusively on shoalgrass and have abandoned other traditional wintering areas such as Chesapeake and Galveston bays because of sea grass declines (Withers 2002, 98).

A hundred years ago, people were more respectful of oceans and rivers, knowing the power that water could unleash. Now that we have armored long stretches of shoreline and we can buy flood insurance, 80 percent of Americans live within an hour of the beach. Some of us have so much invested in coastal or bayou real estate that we simply do not care to face the knowledge of how fragile and hazardous this can be. But viewing hurricanes and storms as alarming and dangerous masks their inevitability as a feature of our natural conditions. They are among the forces driving local ecology, and they will not stop because we moved here. We know they are certain to strike any given stretch of the coast eventually.

In these circumstances, a hurricane- or flood-protection strategy composed of 70 percent hope and 30 percent built structures is not a sound long-term proposition. Trying to hold such dynamic forces in check with seawalls and channelization of drainages is little more than tinkering. And to the extent that structures supply the illusion of control, they are a recipe for more trouble ahead because people are less inclined to evacuate when storms roll in. Surely we can be smarter than this.

A better prescription might be 70 percent reinstatement of natural protection plus 30 percent evacuation. "The best kind of hurricane protection is to ensure maximum stabilization and integrity of natural environments," note Wes Tunnell and Frank Judd (2002, 288). Stabilization does not mean pouring more concrete. It means restoring dune barriers and sea grass flats and bayou floodways wherever possible. It means reducing the punishment we mete out to the estuary in the form of toxins and destruction of vegetation in shoreline shallows; it means trying to keep the bay in sound condition.

The bay and the creeks and the hurricanes and tropical storms are not the enemy. The enemy is unintelligent development. Agencies charged with trying to protect us cannot do so in the face of political pressure from property developers who ignore long-term feasibility in favor of short-term profit and let the nation's taxpayers pick up the tab through federal flood insurance.

Possibly the greatest hazard during storms is failure of imagination. We think of our homes as safe havens and of our roadways as secure routes, even though we get abundant indications to the contrary some-where along the Texas coast every few years. Aside from the surfers heading for Galveston when the water rises to enjoy the excitement of a big storm, it is not easy for the rest of us to see something as de-structive as a hurricane or tropical storm as a rejuvenating blessing. But for a proper grasp of the long sweep of Texas coastal ecology, this is exactly how to view these fearsome forces.

I heartily endorse the idea of throwing a hurricane party to cele-brate the wildness of the elements and the energizing effects of flush-ing out the estuary. For those who live close to Galveston Bay, though, I recommend taking the cat and the important documents and head-ing well inland before starting the party.

CHAPTER *5*

Bay Politics

With Galveston Bay, the economy and the environment are inseparably linked. If the siege of Texas' greatest estuary continues unabated, not one or the other will lose, but both.

B. C. Robison

"Captain, I can't stop. I can't stop this thing. I can't stop now. Lord a' mercy, Skipper. There ain't nothing I can do, Captain."

Thus spoke one man in a tape recording of a conversation between officials on two vessels just before the vessels collided in the Houston Ship Channel near Atkinson Island at 6:20 P.M. on Friday, June 23, 1989. One was the 407-foot Panamanian-flag tanker *Rachel-B*, carrying various chemicals and headed for Belgium when the incident occurred. The impact tore a hole in the ship's bow, but there was no leakage because the punctured compartment was empty.

The other vessel was a 275-foot northbound barge, the second of three pushed by the tug *Gayolyn Ann Griffin*. The barge contained refined industrial oil. Some 250,000 gallons of it spilled into the waters of the upper bay. Mercifully, high winds blew the oil westward, sweeping most of it into the Bayport channel three miles away. The quarter-mile-long channel could hardly have been a better place for retrieval and cleanup.

The tape recording was played at an investigatory hearing the U.S.

Coast Guard held within a few days of the collision. The Coast Guard called it "dumb luck" that most of spill had been contained. A tropical storm was buffeting the bay, and high water would have hampered or prevented shoreline or open-water containment efforts just about anywhere else. Garner Environmental Services of Pasadena brought in a huge vacuum device called a supersucker to collect much of the oil.

By six on Monday evening, 150,000 gallons of oil had been removed from the channel. Petty Officer Third Class Bob Morehead, a spokesman for the Coast Guard, said about 40,000 gallons of oil remained in the channel. Some of that later moved back out into the bay, and the remaining 60,000 gallons were unaccounted for—perhaps below the surface or along beaches and channel banks. The *Houston Chronicle* said this was the worst spill in Galveston Bay since 1981, when the *Olympic Glory* had dumped more than 800,000 gallons of crude oil into the bay after collision with a Liberian chemical carrier a little farther north, near Morgan's Point (Urban 1989).

While spill control crews were still salvaging oil at Bayport, oysterman Joe Nelson of Smith Point on the eastern shore of the bay reported patches of oil about a quarter-inch thick passing over oyster reefs five or six miles away and headed toward East Bay, where there are more reefs. Viewing the area from a helicopter on the Wednesday after Friday's accident, the Coast Guard reported seeing a light sheen of escaping oil in a half-mile-wide swath extending about two miles from Bayport. What Nelson had seen, the Coast Guard suggested, probably derived from a different source. A tugboat had gone down on the intervening Monday in the Houston Ship Channel about two miles from San Leon, much closer to Smith Point.

Meanwhile, the parties involved in the spill were hashing out the question of who was at fault. The local port pilot assigned to guide the *Rachel-B* out of Bayport told investigators that the ship had had trouble making the turn into the main Houston Ship Channel because of sedimentation where the Bayport side channel joined the main channel. Attorneys implied that the *Gayolyn Ann Griffin* had not been in its proper shipping lane, but another tugboat captain testified that the barges had been where they should have been (Urban 1989).

On the Thursday after the spill, the U.S. Army Corps of Engineers confirmed that the Bayport channel had not been maintained and had seen a buildup of sediment. It had originally been dredged by the Port of Houston Authority to a depth of forty feet and a bottom width of three hundred feet. But it had not been dredged since 1984. Indeed, sediment problems at Bayport were common knowledge among local mariners. A Houston Pilots Association notice to vessel operators in late 1987 had noted the risk of navigational problems and an urgent need for maintenance dredging. It appeared that the reason the Corps had not been dredging the channel was that it was waiting on an economic feasibility study of maintenance requirements for the channel.

"While the Bayport Channel piles higher with silt, neither the federal government nor the Houston Port Authority will claim responsibility for dredging clear the shipping way," led a *Chronicle* story on July 1, 1989, a week after the *Rachel-B* collision. "Each agency says the other is responsible."

Since the 1984 dredging, six feet of sediment had built up in places. Both the Corps and the port authority had received complaints from shipping lines and pilots about the diminished channel, and conservation groups were singing the same tune. John Grimes, chair of the Galveston Bay Conservation and Preservation Association, was quoted as saying the dredging was long overdue. The *Chronicle* examined the muddle:

> In the past, the port authority had the task of keeping the privately owned waterway at its designated 40-foot depth. According to a congressional source who requested anonymity, the port authority went to Congress in the early 1980s to persuade legislators to give the Bayport Channel's maintenance duties to the Army Corps of Engineers, which maintains the Houston Ship Channel.
>
> The result was a provision in the Water Resources Development Act of 1986 authorizing the Corps to assume responsibility for the Bayport Channel. . . . [Port spokesman F. William] Colburn said, "If it's the Corps of Engineers' responsibility, why should we dredge it?" (Urban 1989).

Corps spokesman Ken Bonham, however, said his agency would not technically assume responsibility until economic and environmental studies had been reviewed and that the channel must be at its proper depth before the Corps took over. Port officials agreed to dredge the channel one last time, even while insisting that maintenance responsibility lay with the Corps. Industrial property owners along the Bayport channel were pressed to help pay. The problem, inevitably, was the cost, which the Corps estimated at about $3.5 million and the port authority estimated at $7.4 million.

There have been other sizable spills, for other reasons. In 1996 more

than 200,000 gallons of heavy fuel oil leaked from a 275-foot barge belonging to Buffalo Marine Service when the barge ran aground between
Pelican Island and the Bolivar Peninsula, rupturing some of its twelve
oil storage compartments. The oil spread out in a slick five miles long,
stretching from the mouth of the bay into the Gulf of Mexico. Initial
cleanup efforts were impeded by high winds gusting up to fifty miles
per hour, which probably also had a bearing on why the barge ran
aground in the first place. Workers largely succeeded in protecting the
shoreline through use of booms (CNN 1996).

One of the worst spills of recent years was nearby in the Gulf in
June 1990. The 885-foot Norwegian supertanker *Mega Borg* leaked
some 5 million gallons of oil about sixty miles off the coast of Galveston, toward High Island (CNN 1996). On June 8 while the *Mega Borg*
was lightering—transferring a portion of its petroleum cargo to a shallower draft ship for transport into port—there were explosions in the
pump room and fire broke out. The ship contained 44 million gallons
of light Angolan crude, presenting the possibility of a gigantic environmental disaster in Texas coastal waters if all the oil spilled.

At times the intense flames reached a hundred feet in height. Much
of the spilled oil burned or evaporated, and 75,000 gallons were recovered. The fire burned for a week and was not officially declared extinguished until June 15, but it "aided clean-up efforts by rapidly con-
suming the oil as it continuously leaked from the vessel. Once the fire
was extinguished the areal extent of the slick dramatically increased,
raising concerns about the potential landfall of the oil slick" ("*Mega
Borg* Oil Spill" 1990). The coast was largely spared, but an oil slick
eighteen by ten miles in size was observed almost forty miles away
from the ship.

Just a month later, the alarm went up again for a serious spill right
on Galveston Bay. The tanker *Shinoussa* collided with two barges in
the Houston Ship Channel in July 1990. Final estimates suggested that
up to 700,000 gallons of oil were spilled into the bay. This accident occurred near Redfish Island. The ship channel had to be closed, and
commercial fishing and sportfishing were temporarily banned in some
areas. Many feared the effects on shrimp and oysters. Oil-eating bacteria that can break down oil and convert it into fatty acids without
producing toxic by-products were among the measures employed to
address sections of both the large 1990 spills.

The *Rachel-B, Mega Borg,* and *Shinoussa* accidents all took place
within a period of thirteen months in 1989 and 1990. Like hurricanes,

Ship collision between the Norwegian freighter Milross *and Sinclair tanker* Albert E. Watt *in the Houston Ship Channel at Five Mile Pass, March 24, 1958. The pass is north of Seabrook, near Red Bluff. In 1963 a Chinese freighter and a banana boat ran into each other at Five Mile Pass. Survivors in lifeboats came ashore at El Jardin, attracted by the recently installed gas lights at the waterfront (Klopp 2002).*

oil spills do not exactly qualify as freak occurrences, although not all spills are large. Texas General Land Office (GLO) figures indicate that crude oil and diesel fuel spills in Galveston Bay in 1998 numbered 94, with totals of 125 in 1999, 126 in 2000, and 130 in 2001. These are routine events, averaging two or three per week. The largest in these 1998–2001 GLO records were a crude oil spill of 14,364 gallons in 2001 and a diesel spill of 14,406 gallons in 2000. Crude and diesel are just two of the twelve categories of spills on which GLO maintains records; and GLO notes that the records are incomplete because observers "must report a spill for it to be recorded" (GLO 2003).

The *Rachel-B* collision illustrates the complexity of bay and spill management—the multiplicity of agencies and other entities involved and the kind of bureaucratic argument that can induce problems. It indicates the cosmopolitan nature of shipping: the ship flew a Panamanian flag, but its owners were Japanese, and its skipper was Korean. The episode also introduces many of the key players in the politics of decisions and actions affecting the bay: the Corps of Engineers, Port of Houston Authority, U.S Coast Guard, chemical and shipping industries, port pilots, and other mariners. Add to these a series of natural resource agencies such as the U.S. Fish and Wildlife Service, Environmental Protection Agency, Texas Council on Environmental Quality, and Texas Parks and Wildlife Department. Then add other interested parties, such as local governments, sport anglers, commercial fishermen, and organizations representing various kinds of recreational users and conservation interests, and you can have a mighty full house when bay-related controversy arises.

During the Cold War years, Houston and the surrounding cities felt an ongoing sense of threat over the multiple targets that a major port with immense petrochemical installations presents. The Texas City fire in April 1947 (see chapter 7) was a kind of wake-up call; when a ship explosion set a series of other fires, some people initially thought there had been an act of aggression. Yet that, like the collision between the *Rachel-B* and the *Gayolyn Ann Griffin*, was merely an accident. It takes only moments of uneasy contemplation to conjure up what kind of mayhem an intentional attack could produce. By the time of the September 11 terrorist attacks in 2001, the mouth of the Houston Ship Channel also had a container port at Barbour's Cut, and as the press frequently noted, inspectors check only a tiny percentage of all the millions of shipping containers entering U.S. ports each year. Grim cargo could be entering without inspection and getting trucked right through the neighboring cities on the highways.

It is misleading, however, to focus on the special sense of hazard that events such as major oil spills, the Texas City fire, or the September 11 attacks provoke. The fact is that there are plenty of hazards all around us all the time, simply in the course of business as usual. Oil spills are only the most dramatic and visible of the routine issues in bay politics, because fish kills and oiled birds have great resonance on television. But considering the number of legally permitted toxic discharges into the bay and the quantities of chemicals involved, there is little question that normal life with its staggering complexity of wastes—all flowing into Galveston Bay every day—is as harmful to bay resources as oil spills and other isolated crises.

Emerging Bay Advocacy

For a long time after taking the lead in the wrestling match with Galveston for predominance in port operations, energetic Houston boosters, including the port authority and the industrial facilities growing up along the ship channel, had a relatively free hand. They grew accustomed to winning whatever they wanted. The decades of rapid population growth following the close of World War II were an era of unparalleled grimness in toxic pollution entering the bay. By the time the federal government stiffened environmental laws during the 1960s and 1970s to address degradation problems all over the nation, the upper Houston Ship Channel was essentially a dead zone (see chapter 2).

What finally galvanized citizens into bay activism, however, was not the poisoned ship channel but an astonishing Corps of Engineers proposal to build a twenty-five-foot-high levee all along the bayshore from Morgan's Point to Kemah, to armor the coast against storms. As proposed, it would have been a hundred feet wide with a roadway on top. Whatever would this brutal scheme do to waterfront property and shoreline nursery marshes? The organization that sprang up to defeat the levee project in 1974 was the Galveston Bay Conservation and Preservation Association (GBCPA).

Several GBCPA stalwarts lived in the long-established bayshore communities of the Seabrook–Shoreacres–La Porte–Morgan's Point section of the shore that would have its waterfront destroyed by the levee. The Bayport channel had been cut to the south of them in the 1960s, and the Barbour's Cut terminal was built to the north at the beginning of the 1970s. Now they were to be sacrificed to coastal armoring as well as to the industrialization surrounding expanding port facilities. Citizens mounted such an outcry that the levee proposal was abandoned.

Hindsight suggests that killing the levee project might be viewed as the beginning of a turnaround in bay politics. For the first time, residents were insisting that "the public sector must be made accountable to the independent sector. Accountability . . . involves responsiveness on the part of government and business to citizen input" (*Progress* 1981). GBCPA was successfully making the case that the Corps, port, and industrial complex could no longer expect to prevail unchallenged.

In 1975 GBCPA began negotiations with major oil-drilling companies to regulate drilling in the bay; agreements were signed limiting wells to one or two instead of six or eight per square mile of oil and gas leases (*Progress* 1981). In 1976 the organization helped defeat an Atlantic Richfield Company proposal to build a supertanker terminal at Bayport within three hundred feet of homes in Shoreacres. Beginning in 1978 GBCPA led opposition to recertification by the Texas Water Commission of the McGinnis Pits near West Galveston. These pits were major receivers of toxic sludge from maintenance dredging of the ship channel, and there was mounting evidence that toxic materials were leaching from the pits into the bay.

Next, in 1979 the organization joined others in an eventually successful effort to defeat a proposed supertanker port at Pelican Island. GBCPA was among those filing a lawsuit against the Corps of Engineers in May 1981 on the granting of dredging permits for this port. The proposed "Super Port" would have required hundreds of millions of taxpayer dollars for dredging a ship channel fifty-six feet deep. Rick Middleton, a lawyer in the suit, said it was "absolute folly to think that you can move supertankers a fifth of a mile into one of this country's busiest ports without risking a catastrophic oil spill" (GBCPA 1981b, 3).

By 1980 bay advocates had effectively dissuaded B. F. Goodrich from building a Bayport plant that would have exposed schools and neighborhoods to the hazards of chlorine spills and by-products. Air pollution was prominent on the agenda during the early 1980s, as was challenging various hazardous waste landfills and landfill proposals of the Gulf Coast Waste Disposal Authority (GCWDA). Song lyrics in the GBCPA meeting minutes for April 1981 bear a note indicating that they are sung to the tune of "Home on the Range":

> O give me a home
> In the chemical foam
> Where the benzene and PCBs play
> Where ev'ry encore
> Is a gas-pipe's loud roar,
> And the sky is not bluish all day.
>
> *Chorus:*
> *Home, home on the Bay!*
> *Where the flares and the smokestacks all play*
> *Where the air is all brown*
> *Through the north side of town*
> *And the skies are obscured night and day!*
>
> We've heard the "ho-hums"
> O'er the rusting brown drums
> That are flavoring Galveston Bay.
> All the hard-hats have jobs
> Making poisonous blobs,
> But all they can see is their pay.

We shed quite a tear
And we waited to hear
What the Austin authorities say;
"Don't worry a bit;
Here's another permit
For the GCW-DA!"

O the businessman's oath
Is encouraging growth
Ev'rywhere and any old way.
Viet-Namese, fish the Bay
All you want to, but HEY!
Be sure you don't get in our way!

GBCPA was threatening the waste disposal authority with lawsuits over pollution violations at its forty-acre Texas City facility treating industrial waste from the Union Carbide and Monsanto plants and over improper disposal of pesticide wastes at its Bayport industrial treatment plant (*Houston Post* 1981).

The Corps of Engineers had meanwhile requested permission from the EPA to dump dredge spoil into Galveston Bay just north of the Texas City Dike, although EPA had directed that this practice be stopped after 1977 because of harm to the bay due to toxic materials in the dredge spoil—lead, mercury, and arsenic. Supporting objections by EPA and the U.S. Fish and Wildlife Service, GBCPA chair Paul Vavra noted that *maintenance* dredging appeared to be immune to restrictions (GBCPA 1981a).

A striking aspect of documents dating back twenty and thirty years is how many of them bear the names of people who were still active in bay conservation circles in 2003, among them Scott Eidt, Mary Beth Maher, Ellyn Roof, Dick Rogan, Ed Sartain, Sammy Ray, Eddie Seidensticker, and Stennie Meadours. They evidently took to heart the advice received from Grace Singer of the Center for Environmental Studies at Princeton when she addressed the 1979 GBCPA annual meeting at the Houston Yacht Club. She talked about techniques employed in New Jersey to fend off projects proposed for unsuitable coastal locations.

"Seasoned veterans from several urban battles . . . had rejected the paternalistic 'father knows best' attitude of previous political bosses, existing in several large cities even today. They had developed a strong distrust in their government officials," said Singer (1979, 6). Several citizen groups banded together into a coalition and engaged in a heavy public relations effort using the slogan "Thanks but no tanks" (in New Jersey, pronounced "Tanks but no tanks"). They ensured large numbers of people at public meetings and produced thousands of signatures on petitions, and they involved the minority populations, who had typically not been included in environmental fights.

"Most important perhaps," said Singer, "these groups were persistent over a long period of time, convincing the power structure of their ability to sustain a strong position. This is always a problem for citizens who have full-time jobs and must devote extraordinary amounts of time, effort, and sometimes out-of-pocket costs to maintain a viable stance" (1979, 7).

By the late 1980s, in line with national developments, environmental concerns were starting to find a respectable place at the negotiating table. Victories were slow, but they were beginning to stack up. When a mainstream glossy like the *Houston Metropolitan* magazine ran a piece titled "Galveston Bay under Siege" (Robison 1989), it was apparent that at least some people were starting to think differently than before. The bay was in grave danger, the article said, citing proposed deepening of the ship channel to fifty feet and construction of the Wallisville Dam as two of the most damaging in an "arsenal" of numerous proposed projects "aimed at the bay by the U.S. Army Corps of Engineers" with potentially harmful impacts (Robison 1989). GBCPA had trained its spotlight on both the Wallisville project and the proposal to deepen the ship channel.

The economic downside of damaging the bay was also getting some column inches. The same article cites a 1986 Texas A&M University report showing that Galveston Bay accounted for almost a third of the state's commercial seafood harvest, two-thirds of the oysters, and about half the money spent in Texas on sportfishing.

Activists were still up against a high wall of tradition, but comprehensive thinking about the bay was at last beginning to gain some traction. In passing the Water Quality Act of 1987, Congress designated Galveston Bay and several other major bays as "estuaries of national significance." Through that legislation, these bays entered the National Estuary Program (NEP), which was designed to tackle the growing problems arising from industrial and residential development, pollution, and overuse of bay resources. NEP is a program of the EPA, and its mission is a multiple-use mandate: to protect and restore the health of estuaries while also supporting economic and recreational activities (EPA 2002).

Oil rig off Seabrook, 1945.

The first step was to create local estuary programs consisting of partnerships between resource agencies and the people who depend on those waters for their livelihoods and quality of life. Local groups were to determine how best to revitalize and protect the bays. Thus, a major benefit of NEP lay in bringing communities together to decide the future of their estuaries—to identify problems and recommend solutions, with EPA assisting in implementation through grants and technical help.

One conclusion from the ecological crisis that confronted the Chesapeake Bay in the mid-1980s was that reliable science was crucial as a basis for comprehensive bay management. A Scientific/Technical Advisory Committee (STAC) for Galveston Bay was appointed to identify problems and pinpoint trends needing intervention. Work undertaken by the STAC was the first systematic effort by representatives of a wide range of interests to assess the bay on an ecosystem scale. Existing data from many sources were analyzed, and new research was launched to fill the most glaring gaps. The result of five years of work was a volume titled *The State of the Bay: A Characterization of the Galveston Bay Ecosystem* (1994), published with the explicit objective of improving resource management.

There were unexpected findings, some in the category of good news. For example, nutrient overenrichment of the bay system had been a concern. For "nutrients" read chiefly nitrates and phosphates; too much of these causes plankton to flourish far beyond normal levels, and the explosion of tiny organisms depletes the oxygen supply for other inhabitants of the bay. Ward and Armstrong (1992) found this syndrome only in localized areas; it was not a baywide phenomenon.

Other researchers documented loss of wetland habitat (White et al. 1993). The leading single factor in the bayside loss of more than twenty-six thousand acres of emergent wetlands (marshes) was conversion to open water, mainly because of subsidence resulting from groundwater withdrawal. The effort to reverse this trend had already ended pumping of groundwater and provoked a baywide series of projects to reestablish areas of smooth cordgrass, often with volunteer groups conducting the planting.

Although some problems were being addressed and some were less pronounced than resource managers had feared, others came into sharper focus. The issue of nonpoint-source pollution galloped to the fore, as it has in other estuaries. It has become the greatest factor preventing attainment of water-quality standards nationwide, and it is an extremely tough problem to address. Point-source pollution means pollution derived from readily identifiable sources, such as industry and municipal wastewater facilities. Nonpoint-source pollution means all the rest—runoff from extensive areas of land, urban and rural.

Point-source pollution of Galveston Bay is immense, as described in chapter 2, but it has declined somewhat as a result of federal water-quality legislation and permit requirements that came into force some thirty years ago. "In contrast, all indications are that nonpoint sources of pollution have steadily increased to the present day, and significantly influence the water and sediment quality in various portions of Galveston Bay"—notably in the ship channel, which is a funnel for Houston's runoff (*State of the Bay* 1994, 121).

Low levels of dissolved oxygen in urban bayous and other poorly flushed tributaries are one result. Toxic contamination and elevated bacteria levels are others. Because nonpoint sources of pollutants are so diffuse and cover wide areas, they are nearly impossible to police. Because the pollutants travel, usually in rainwater runoff, it can be nearly impossible even to identify sources, much less address them. The sources cannot be measured in terms of standards for effluent, as industrial pollutants can. And their arrival in a water body like Galveston Bay is often related to uncontrollable events such as heavy storms, so that the effects differ greatly from place to place and from year to year. Understanding and tackling nonpoint-source pollution thus presents multiple difficulties for scientists and resource managers.

Worse, the more we educate ourselves about it, the uglier the picture looks because of the inescapable conclusion that all of us and the way we live are to blame (*State of the Bay* 1994, 122–35). Home owners tend to accuse industry, while industry points a finger at agriculture, and farmers blame home owners. Farmers say they have to use pesticides and fertilizers to grow food for us all. Industry says it cannot manage expensive pollution controls and still stay in business, providing jobs. Residents of cities and suburbs overuse pesticides and flush hazardous wastes or pour them into storm drains because it is hard to find proper ways to dispose of them. People wonder what difference one pan of oil in a storm drain can possibly make when chemical plants legally discharge thousands of pounds of dangerous substances into waterways.

It is easy to feel that individually we can achieve almost nothing to clean up our act—that we are at the mercy of a great, churning leviathan of a system, powerless to check its momentum. Yet it also true that the actions of individuals can make a difference. According to a 1992 study commissioned as part of work on the Galveston Bay Plan, the land use generating the greatest load of almost every category of pollutants is "high-density urban" (*State of the Bay* 1994, table 6.3). This means dense residential development, shopping centers, industry, and construction sites. That study found high-density urban areas contributing 87 percent of all the oil and grease; 59 percent of fecal coliform bacteria; 50 percent of pesticides; 33 percent of "total suspended solids" or sediment (construction is a large contributor); and 31 percent of nitrogen and phosphorus (fertilizers).

Cities, in short, are the problem. Although agriculture covers far larger areas, the only pollutant category in which it produces more than 30 percent of the loading is its 31 percent in suspended solids—topsoil. Even for suspended solids, urban areas contribute more (33 percent). Despite large-scale fertilizer and pesticide applications on farmland, the study found that agriculture contributes only 18 percent of the nitrogen and 24 percent of the phosphorus pollutant load in the runoff, whereas high-density urban development is responsible for 31 percent of both. The discrepancy in pesticide loads is much more pronounced: 10 percent is coming from agricultural land but 50 percent from high-density urban areas, with another 24 percent from lower-density residential land—the suburbs.

Adding 50 percent to 24 percent gives 74 percent: *three-quarters of all the pesticide in the runoff entering Galveston Bay is coming not from farms but from towns and suburbs.* This is a cultural issue, not a question of feeding the nation. The main reason for the primacy of urban areas as a source of pesticides is that home-owner applications occur essentially year-round and are often highly intensive, whereas agricultural applications are seasonal and usually more limited and dilute. It behooves the millions of us who live in cities and suburbs to face the fact that we cannot blame the farmers, who number only thousands. We could do the health of the bay quite a favor if we found alternative ways to tackle garden pests and traded lawn for other ground covers that need less weed killer and fertilizer.

With publication of the Galveston Bay Plan in 1995, the Galveston Bay Estuary Program shifted from research to implementation. There were eighty-two action items in the plan, in eleven categories: protecting habitat, species, public health, and freshwater inflow and bay circulation; working to control spills and dumping, waste and sediment quality, and point and nonpoint sources of pollution; shoreline management; research; and public participation and education, including the State of the Bay symposium held every other year.

A plan, of course, is only as good as its implementation. Progress requires that losses and damage already sustained or under way be halted or reversed and that new projects not do further damage. Unfortunately, we cannot bank on these things. At the same time that the Galveston Bay Estuary Program was forming in the late 1980s, the Port of Houston Authority and the Corps of Engineers were proposing to deepen the Houston Ship Channel to fifty feet and widen it to six hundred feet to accommodate larger ships. By then, however, the gathering momentum of comprehensive thinking about the bay had placed the community in a stronger position than ever before to undertake defending the bay.

The Ship Channel Standoff

Environmental attorney Jim Blackburn was born in Alexandria, Louisiana, and grew up in South Texas, where wildness was close at hand. All his uncles hunted and fished. While clerking to work his way through the University of Texas, he felt uncertain about law as a career until he realized there was a place for him in environmental law. A paper he wrote about the legal status of oceans earned a feeble grade from a professor who had once been an attorney for Humble Oil—but it won first place in a national environmental law essay competition.

Ship proceeds down the Houston Ship Channel, 1945.

Rice University offered Blackburn a scholarship for a master's degree in environmental science; he would become a lawyer, a planner, and a faculty member at Rice.

In 1984 GBCPA hired him to help oppose a permit application by the Houston Lighting and Power Company (HL&P). Cooling towers at HL&P's power plant between Kemah and Texas City had been damaged in a storm, and HL&P wanted to abandon them. This would have meant releasing heated water into Galveston Bay, and GBCPA demonstrated that the releases would be unacceptably detrimental to marine life. HL&P wound up having to rebuild the cooling towers.

By then Blackburn was also involved with the Bayou Preservation Association, fighting to preserve the few remaining natural sections of bayou in the Bayou City. When the Port of Houston Authority's proposal to deepen the Houston Ship Channel to fifty feet came along, and the issue was to come up on the ballot for a bond vote, a membership organization was needed to coordinate public resistance. Blackburn and attorney Dick Morrison, then on the Texas Parks and Wildlife Commission, set about forming the Galveston Bay Foundation (GBF), which Blackburn chaired for its first two years, 1987–89.

The foundation sought to "unite disparate groups and individuals behind a common goal of preserving a resource" (GBF 1990, 4). In 1988, using a one-hundred-thousand-dollar grant from the Moody Foundation, GBF launched its first conservation programs. Linda Shead was appointed executive director in 1989 and would retain that role for more than ten years. Most important, GBF was a voice for the bay, opposing the Wallisville Dam and channel deepening projects. "It seemed as though we were marching to the precipice as far as protection of the bay was concerned. It was obvious that instead of each user looking out only for its own special interests, we needed someone watching 'the whole pie.' We decided that the only way we could make real progress was to bring all the players to the table at the same time, people who generally are at loggerheads over bay usage and issues," said Shead (in Barrington 1999, 8).

The fight against the Wallisville Dam was so extended that it spanned a series of changes in the law and the circumstances. What was eventually built was a low saltwater barrier across the Trinity River south of Interstate 10, gated so that it can be closed to keep salt water from moving upriver. This was but a distant relative to the original concept, which involved a dam that would have drowned close to twenty thousand acres of forested swamps and marshes.

The Trinity supplies more than half the fresh water entering Galveston Bay. Its delta is still building, a plume of fertile muck laced with nutrients. The dam would have disrupted the Trinity's flooding pattern and prevented larval organisms from migrating to freshwater nursery wetlands above the barrier. The Corps of Engineers, the federal court system, the City of Houston, and an endangered species were all players in a saga that was in and out of court from the 1960s through the 1980s. A fascinating account of it appears in the *Book of Texas Bays* (Blackburn 2004).

GBF (1990) got busy on environmental inventories of Armand Bayou and Christmas Bay and on trying to curb industrial point-source discharges in the ship channel. Committees on oil spills and permit review came into being. Soon GBF had a thousand individual members and a staff of five. Its first Bay Day celebration took place in 1990 (see chapter 8), the same year the Texas Waterway Operators Association donated an aluminum workboat that was christened *Bay Ranger*, which got heavy use supporting the foundation's education and conservation activities.

GBF's board had more than a hundred members, including county, state, and federal elected officials and representatives of numerous nongovernment organizations, such as conservation groups, yacht clubs, the Houston Pilots Association, and groups of anglers and shrimpers. Advisory trustees on the board represent agencies from the Harris County Flood Control District and Sea Grant College Program to the Port of Houston Authority and U.S. Army Corps of Engineers. In short, inclusiveness was the key concept.

GBF evolved ever-broadening reach, helping create an oil spill response program, acquire critical habitat, and monitor wetland permit applications. It involved hundreds of volunteers in activities supporting the bay ecosystem, such as planting cordgrass, monitoring water quality, and undertaking a program to boost the oyster fishery. Participants hung bags of shell from their docks so that tiny oyster spat could establish themselves in water of suitable salinity and later be placed in the bay to seed new oyster reefs. GBF's many ongoing programs carried costs that could not be met by membership dues, and over time the foundation came to receive much of its funding from corporate sponsorship by local industry.

The proposed deepening of the Houston Ship Channel, Blackburn said, would more than double the cross-sectional area of existing channel cut, due to slope at the sides. The large volume of salt water intruding into the shallow bay would compromise salinity in a water body already faced with multiple challenges to its ecological integrity. The project would pull $250 million out of the local economy just to expedite movement of channel traffic. Money could be invested more wisely in real economic growth without tearing up Galveston Bay, he said.

The ship channel fight was another extended public controversy, beginning in 1986 and not concluding until well into the 1990s. The Port of Houston Authority, the Corps of Engineers, and much of the business community pressed hard for the channel deepening. When voters rejected the port bond issue on the ballot, negotiations began. In the end a compromise was reached: the channel would be expanded to 45 feet deep and 530 feet wide, producing a much smaller wedge of salt water. In addition, the Beneficial Uses Group (BUG) was born, whereby the project came to include conservation-oriented disposal of dredge spoil for marsh planting and bird island restoration.

In the course of the controversy, some people began to sense trouble at GBF. Some of its conservation activities were cooperative ventures with none other than the Port of Houston Authority and the Corps of Engineers, both of which wield a great deal of power in bay-related decisions—and both promoters of the channel deepening. Although the channel issue was a hot one in the conservation community by 1990, the GBF annual report for that year mentioned it only politely and in passing. There were those who foresaw that precisely because of its inclusiveness, GBF could turn out to have limitations as an advocate for the bay. A two-thirds majority of its board to oppose harmful projects might become difficult to achieve.

This became sadly clear in the late 1990s when the port authority released a master plan for development of a giant container port at Bayport, on a thousand-acre green site. Members who had watched GBF win good compromises for the bay on Wallisville and on channel deepening kept wondering when the organization would whirl into action on Bayport. It did not. Those opposed to the Bayport terminal waited many months before finally grasping that GBF was hamstrung by its dependence on corporate support, including from the Port of Houston Authority. Fighting Bayport would divide its board and risk gutting its programs. Its activist days were over. Others would have to step in if citizens were to fight the plan (see chapter 6).

Defining the Galveston Waterfront

Besides the drawing power of its beaches, Galveston has gained prominence in the nostalgia market of late, with a proud restoration movement and a series of annual events making the most of its waterfront and fine old buildings. But things could easily have been otherwise. The force of public opinion was as crucial to the preservation of Galveston's historic district and waterfront as it was in the battle to avoid deepening the ship channel.

The elegant architecture of Galveston's heyday nearly vanished during the first decades after World War II. In the 1960s the Strand was the crumbling preserve of vagrants and derelicts. "Once proud Hendley Row, the oldest stretch of commercial buildings on the Island, was known informally as the Wino Hilton" (Cartwright 1991, 301–302). The effects of Hurricane Carla in 1961 did not help. Some people mourned the replacement of gracious and distinguished old buildings with dull new ones or with parking lots, but no one could see how to revive the tired downtown.

As the nineteenth-century buildings came down, the Galveston Historical Foundation (GHF) was in a rut. In this case, the community needed a nudge from newcomers who shared an interest in history and culture and who brought in the fresh perspective of outsiders. "They saw the Strand, for example, not as a row of decaying buildings but as one of the great collections of Victorian architecture anywhere in the country. It was obvious to these people that the Island was throwing away an incomparable treasure" (Cartwright 1991, 303).

The turnaround came when Ed Protz of Atlanta became grants

Still in sight but no longer in service, 1959.

coordinator for the Moody Foundation. He persuaded Mary Moody Northen and the foundation to provide $250,000 in seed money for a revolving fund that would allow GHF to intervene by buying old buildings and holding them until renovation financing could be found. A wealthy North Texas ranching family named Wallace saved the Hendley Row buildings from the wrecking ball. A key development was GHF's hiring of Peter Brink, who arrived in 1973 from Washington, D.C. He knew all about fund-raising and rustling up grants, and he had a sharp sense of the potential in Galveston's architectural heritage. Brink pulled several smaller groups together to beef up the GHF initiative.

Emily Whiteside came to town to lead the Galveston Cultural Arts Council. She visited the old State Theater, closed by then and most recently in service as an X-rated movie house. Peeling back rotting boards on its marquee, she saw granite underneath—a Romanesque arch bearing the word *OPERA*. "A ghost reached down the back of her neck as she realized that what she had discovered was the 1894 Grand Opera House, one of the few of its kind still in existence. This was one of the great finds of the restoration movement, and foundations got in line to back it" (Cartwright 1991, 305–306). As the preservation movement gathered steam, forty buildings on the Strand were eventually purchased and restored through the efforts of the GHF.

More recently, Galvestonians united to preserve their options on the waterfront. The docks were tired, sagging, and underused, but ways to finance modernizing them were proving elusive. The Port of Houston Authority was angling for a merger, aiming to take over Galveston's port facilities to meet its own expansion needs. Under the proposed deal, Galveston would have deeded its public docks to the Port of Houston Authority, which would then rebuild them. The Galveston Wharf Board voted 7–0 in favor of the merger, and the city council backed it as well. Citizens feared, however, that the takeover would be the leading edge of an ugly industrial trajectory. Unwilling to allow their city government to deed away control to Houston, they pressed for the matter to be subject to a referendum.

Resisting the port authority's ad campaign for its takeover, Galveston voters said no. When the merger came up on the ballot on December 18, 2001, it was rejected by a vote of 4,060 to 3,041, as reported in the *Houston Chronicle* on January 13, 2002. Voters thought their city council and wharf board were barking up the wrong tree. The people of Galveston wanted to retain control of their historic waterfront and explore other possibilities for making it an economic proposition.

This was not the first time a public vote had rescued the waterfront. Almost thirty years before, the city had seen a bitterly divisive fight over the future of its shrimpers, known as the Mosquito Fleet. The picturesque little shrimp boats had tied up at Pier 19, at the foot of Twentieth Street and just off the Strand, for a century. They were becoming a kind of living history exhibit against a backdrop of oceangoing vessels. Yet the wharf board decided in 1974 to evict the shrimpers. "The prestige of the port was at an all-time low, and the board was grasping for a plan to improve its financial situation. The Mosquito Fleet wasn't paying its fair share of rent, and port authorities wanted Pier 19 as a roll-on, roll-off loading dock for imported cars" (Cartwright 1991, 307).

The wharf board had a suggestion. Would the shrimpers like to move to new docks across the channel on Pelican Island? Shrimpers rejected the offer. Coinciding with the growing restoration movement in the city, the wrangle drew in Mary Moody Northen and the GHF on the side of the shrimpers. After a three-year fight, voters settled the issue in a 1977 referendum, insisting by a margin of two to one that the Mosquito Fleet should stay at Pier 19. "This was more than just a symbolic victory for the Galveston Historical Foundation. The referendum established that the electorate overwhelmingly supported a historic waterfront" (Cartwright 1991, 307).

Galveston almost became a city with no grand old Victorian shop fronts or eighteen-foot ceilings, no shrimp boats trailing their entourage of bobbing pelicans, no chance to hold a nostalgia festival such as Dickens on the Strand (see chapter 8). It could have had a supertanker port at nearby Pelican Island and a downtown waterfront of asphalt acres with snappy little imported automobiles glinting in the sun. Instead, it has joined the narrow ranks of working ports that also manage to preserve a sense of history and a setting where visitors can enjoy the bay.

My files about bay politics bulge and overflow with items about bulkheading of the shoreline, fecal coliform bacteria counts, destruction of bayou vegetation, and the gloomy track record of chemical plants caught making illegal toxic releases. Newer items describe Galveston voters rescuing what their city council and wharf board were ready to give away, and the Houston Audubon Society saddling up to resist a proposal for a giant bridge across the Bolivar Roads. For a time I received several pieces of mail each day from the Texas Commission on Environmental Quality pertaining to permits for legal discharge of toxic wastes.

The industries located around the bay want to be able to discharge wastes into it, and the rest of us want industry to flourish because it creates jobs. Transportation and commercial interests want to be able use the waterway for shipping goods, and the rest of us want those goods at low prices. At the same time, we want a bay as clean and healthy as possible—safe for boaters and swimmers, doing its quiet work as a nursery, producing seafood that can be eaten without fear.

We cannot feel confident that the Corps of Engineers is exercising its environmental mandates properly when intense public pressure is often needed to prevent projects damaging to the bay. We cannot feel confident that industry is giving its best effort at reducing toxic discharges, and as the Galveston case illustrates, even city governments may need prodding to avoid taking easy ways out.

The conclusion must be this: All who care about Galveston Bay should be wide awake, watching closely, and ready to take action. We and the elected representatives who genuinely respond to our wishes may be able to ensure a sound future for the bay and the communities around it, but we are the only ones who can. We can often prevent damaging plans from coming to be. Finding ways to tackle nonpoint-source pollution, to which we all contribute, remains a major task still lying ahead.

When all our finesses go right, we can get support for restoration of marshland and bird islands from the economic power brokers of the region, but their main interest is bound to be profits, and they will lean on elected representatives accordingly. Corporate thinking works on short-term or, at best, on medium-term horizons. As far as industry is concerned, conserving the long-term soundness of the bay is incidental, a nuisance required by law, like taxes. We are a long way from corporate recognition that a healthy bay will be a far more profitable entity than an estuary in need of expensive remediation.

Resource agencies recognize this, but they are often hard pressed to follow through with what they know is best. In pursuit of profit, the powerful in our communities have done well at skirting the public interest and risking the resilience of the bay. Unless they are reined in by tireless public pressure, as at Wallisville and in Galveston and on deepening of the Houston Ship Channel, the giants of industry and property development will often prevail over conservation voices. We can rely on some help from resource agencies, but they cannot ensure the bay's future without us. Only we can do it.

CHAPTER 6

The Container Port Juggernaut

*Real-life issues are messy and ambiguous and
contradictory and tough. But their complexity should be
a reason to engage them, not a reason to turn away.*

Kathleen Dean Moore

Down at the elbow of land where the upper reach of the Houston Ship
Channel widens out into Galveston Bay lies a traditional Texas-style
ice house known as the Point. In summer its sides are open to bay
breezes, and in winter a wood fire beats the chill. At any season, this
establishment is a fine spot for watching the stately progress of ships
and barges along the channel. The ships loom just a few feet away from
patrons at the Point, and for the modest price of a beer and a burger,
anyone can witness the important business of transworld shipping
from up close.

Next door on one side is the Port of Houston container terminal at
Barbour's Cut. On the other side is the residential community of Morgan's Point. One route to the ice house is to drive north from La Porte
along Bay Ridge Drive, passing an assortment of bayfront homes, some
historic and imposing, some merely old and quaint. The other approach is from Highway 146 along Barbour's Cut Boulevard past the
container port. Using one route to reach to the Point and the other to
depart offers a sense of what a container port means to a community:

the quiet of a leafy established neighborhood yields to ugly industrial sprawl and baking acres of asphalt. Thousands of heavy trucks have destroyed the road surface. For two or three miles, hundreds upon hundreds of metal boxes are stacked five high in a spreading blight of container yards.

Port of Houston Authority publicity presents a different view of what a container port means. The lead article on the front page of a *Houston Chronicle* special advertising supplement in June 2000 was all about a new container facility planned a few miles south of Barbour's Cut, at Bayport. Construction was "scheduled to begin early next year," the supplement said. The article was designed to make readers think development of the new terminal was sure to happen and about to begin—thoroughly misleading when the project was still years from receiving a construction permit and faced stiff citizen opposition.

Later the port authority began placing full-page color advertisements headlined "The Portfolio" in local magazines. In the March 2003 issue of monthly *Baycomber*, for example, a large picture showed a woman in a pleasant kitchen preparing stir-fry. Lemons and olives and a vase of flowers stood artfully on the countertop. Smaller inset photos showed elegant living room furnishings, a bottle of mineral water, some yellow and white daisies. Captions expanded upon the wholesome mood: "Tons of sizzle and seasoning—more than 5,500 tons of extra virgin olive oil passed through the Port of Houston last year . . . more than 9,000 tons of fresh fruits and vegetables . . . nearly 50 tons of cut flowers . . . fine upholstered couches." In case anyone failed to grasp the idea, the bottom line was spelled out: "The Port delivers the goods."

The same message was being broadcast on television spots, and the port authority was identified as a sponsor of the news time slot on Houston's National Public Radio station, KUHF—more subtle placement of publicity dollars. By August the campaign had grown explicit. The ad in that month's *Baycomber* still carried the bottom line about the Port delivering the goods, but the main head read: "Building Bayport—environmentally safe, economically vital." Under a picture of swimming pelicans was a glowing description of the port's "environmental modifications."

The reason for these ads is that the Port of Houston Authority is heavily supported by Harris County taxpayers through property taxes. Many cities have ports that pay for themselves with operating revenue, but not Houston. Despite its claims about record cargo volumes, the port authority is not a profitable enterprise. More than half its cumulative reported income from 1995 through 2002 came from property tax, according to a financial analysis released by GBCPA. Only 28 percent of its reported net income for that period was operating revenue, with the balance coming from interest income and a state subsidy.

In a comparison of ports the Port of Houston Authority ranked head and shoulders above all of the nation's ports in its level of general obligation (bond) debt, an amount of $331.6 million. The taxpayer cost to retire these general obligation port bonds is $529.5 million, including $178.9 million in interest, as reported in the Port's Comprehensive Annual Financial Report for 2002 (GBCPA 2003d).

The financial situation reveals the reason the port authority pays hundreds of thousands of dollars each year to manipulate public opinion through local advertising: it needs voter support when port bond issues come up on the ballot. Ads can also sell an unpopular project and dupe people into thinking that critical decisions have already been made.

Citizens Besieged, 1998-99

The Port of Houston Authority made public its master plan for the proposed Bayport container port in June 1998. As outlined, it would occupy twice the acreage of Barbour's Cut; it would be a thousand-acre juggernaut on the coastal prairie of upper Galveston Bay. The site has residential development just a few hundred yards away, with some five thousand people in adjacent neighborhoods, ten thousand within two miles. Some of the neighborhoods have been there since the 1920s. The plans showed the port facilities reaching well into Seabrook and raised the specter of seven thousand trucks a day grinding into town, all belching diesel exhaust. Taxpayers would pay for this megaport to be built. People were stunned.

The gigantic project would prove to be a case study in bad faith on the part of the port authority and the U.S. Army Corps of Engineers. It would also prove a focal point for citizen activism as people realized that these government entities were directly threatening local quality of life. The proposed new port was advertised as a major regional economic engine, but it would seriously damage bay resources and flourishing residential communities. The obvious thing to do was to get this engine hauled to a less sensitive spot on the line, where it could do its work without doing so much damage. Citizens began to organize.

The Seabrook City Council wasted no time adopting a resolution opposing the Bayport location for the facility. Within three months the cities of Shoreacres, Taylor Lake Village, and El Lago and the El Jardin Community Association had passed similar resolutions opposing the Bayport site as inappropriate land use alongside residential communities.

The next step was to press the Corps of Engineers—the agency that would have to issue a permit for the project—to require an environmental impact statement (EIS). The port authority had hoped to get away with a much less intensive environmental assessment, but on a project so large and directly on the bayshore, it was not difficult to make the case for the fuller procedure of an EIS.

While the port kept singing its dirge about Barbour's Cut being stretched to capacity, citizens argued that Barbour's Cut could be made more efficient, that other potential sites for a new container port would be less damaging to natural wetlands and the coastal prairie. Environmentalists asked why the project drawings showed wharves engineered to a depth of fifty-six feet even as the port kept saying it had no intention of deepening the ship channel beyond the forty-five feet already authorized. In December 1998 the Corps of Engineers determined that an EIS would be required for Bayport.

Meanwhile, things were warming up at another potential site. Texas City unveiled a container port plan, announcing it as an alternative to the Bayport expansion. Although under consideration in the Bayport plan as a possible alternative site, Texas City was now applying for its own permit to build a container port. The site was at Shoal Point, an island made of dredge spoil material and flanked solely by heavy industry. This proposal entailed no tax support; the new port would be built by private investors. "We have a very viable alternative for the Port of Houston to consider," said Texas City mayor Chuck Doyle. "Our port is already the eighth largest in the U.S. and the third largest in Texas. We are also the only port on the Gulf Coast that has been approved to dredge to 50 feet" (Fuller 1998).

A year after the Bayport plan had been announced, Port of Houston Authority chairman Ned Holmes (1999) summed up the agency's view about Seabrook as the pivot of Bayport opposition. Speaking at a Houston Property Rights Association luncheon, he declared: "You have a metropolitan area with 4.4 million people that is being compromised

Water returning after a norther to the pier at the Harris Ranch, 1955. This historic property was deeded in the nineteenth century to one of Houston's founders and was still in the hands of his heirs when a portion of it was threatened with expropriation as the twenty-first century opened. Adjoining land where the Port of Houston Authority wants a container port, the old Harris Ranch is in danger of disappearing under asphalt and container yards.

by a city of seventy-five hundred people. . . . Now, is that hardhearted? Yeah, yeah it is. But is it realistic? Yeah, it is." The airy dismissal of residents' concerns was typical of port pronouncements—the views of the people most closely involved with the bay were simply seen as a nuisance.

In August 1999 as part of the EIS process, the Corps of Engineers held a "scoping meeting" for the Bayport project, to identify people's concerns. Between twenty-five hundred and three thousand people squeezed into the Pasadena Convention Center, an unprecedented turnout for such a meeting. Traffic backed up on the approach road as cars filled the parking lot and spilled over onto the grass. Large signs proclaimed opposition to the project, and antiport stickers and flyers were everywhere. More than a hundred people signed up to go to the microphone and speak for their allotted three minutes, raising issues that needed to be addressed in the EIS. Nearly all expressed opposition to the plan.

Holmes was the opening speaker. He said the port authority was considering how to protect a grove of old oaks along the southern side of its Bayport land. People chuckled at his reverently declaring protection for the oaks, though he did not mean to be funny. State legislators acquitted themselves better. Senator Mike Jackson of District 11, the western side of Galveston Bay, listed a series of problems with the project, saving until last the one he considered most critical: air pollution.

Even without the new port, the Houston area was and is violating national standards for ozone in the air—standards intended to ensure that the air we breathe is not poisoning us. Our region needs to reduce nitrogen oxides substantially to come into compliance. The exhaust of thousands more trucks a day and assorted other diesel-powered equipment at a new port, not to mention the ships themselves, would obviously only worsen the air problems. Fine particle matter is an especially dangerous air pollutant, and diesel combustion is a major source of particulate matter. Moreover, air pollution is no respecter of jurisdictional boundaries—this a regional problem, not a local one.

State Representative John Davis of District 129 in southeastern Harris County said he was suddenly hearing from people he had never heard from before. He said he had received no calls or letters supporting the port but numerous calls and letters opposing it, particularly from small-business owners. Most disturbing was that many of his constituents felt the port authority was determined to make this project happen, regardless of its impacts or of how anyone felt about it (Antrobus 1999).

Congestion on highways near the bay was a pressing issue. Many speakers groaned about how large increases in truck and rail traffic would extend commute times and worsen the hazard of grade-level railroad crossings. The pressure of additional trucks and trains would also increase traffic density on other major routes—again a regional issue. One speaker wondered ominously whether congestion would compromise Highway 146 as a hurricane evacuation route; another pressed home questions about trucking accidents and preparedness for coping with resulting spills of hazardous substances.

Land and home values in the bay area would scarcely profit from the air, light, and noise pollution or the traffic arising from the proposed container port. Many other matters were raised, from conflicts between recreational boaters and large-scale shipping to erosion by ship wakes and contamination by bilgewater. Songwriter Bill Oliver stepped to the mike with his guitar and delivered a sharply satirical ballad about the proposed new port, breaking through the tense atmosphere in the hall to draw hearty laughter and applause.

Several speakers emphasized the importance of a regional approach, citing alternative potential sites for a new Galveston Bay container port, such as in Texas City; or on Spillman's Island beside Barbour's Cut, where a new port could take advantage of existing road and rail infrastructure; or on Pelican Island at Galveston, where impacts of increased shipping on the bay would be lower because the new port would be close to the bay mouth. Texas City, Galveston, and Freeport were all mentioned as examples of places that already had deeper water and fewer ground transportation and air pollution conflicts. City Manager Bob Herrera of La Porte—speaker number seventy-nine at 11:21 P.M.—gave a forceful presentation identifying citizen concerns. The scoping meeting ran until 1:20 A.M. No one who attended that hearing will soon forget it.

Now in the interesting position of having two permit applications on the table for a Galveston Bay container port, the Corps of Engineers held its Texas City scoping meeting in October 2000. It could not have been more different from the Bayport session. Attendance was around two hundred people. No one had any trouble parking. Thirteen members of the public signed up to speak, but one failed to turn up, so there were just a dozen speakers. Even though they raised environmental concerns, every single one of them also endorsed the Shoal Point plan.

These speakers had another theme in common. Several noted how open the Texas City preliminary discussions about the project had been, and how willing officials had been to alter the plans in response to environmental concerns. An emblem of this openness lay in—of all things—shirts. Texas City officials were much in evidence at the scoping meeting, as were representatives of the major Shoal Point investor, Stevedoring Services of America (now called SSA Marine), and of the environmental consulting company Shiner Moseley, which would develop the EIS. All were identifiable by identical blue polo shirts, illustrating their pride in the partnership. Far from spending an estimated $1.5 million on a publicity campaign of television ads to persuade voters to endorse port bonds, as the Port of Houston Authority had done,

Texas City needed no bond money and had merely dropped a few dollars on matching shirts so that citizens could easily pinpoint everyone involved with the project.

At the Bayport hearing, the opening address had been by the chairman of the mighty port authority. On Shoal Point, the opening address came from a project engineer, and the hearing was over by 8:07 P.M. As the Corps of Engineers worked through the two competing permit applications, it was blindingly clear that the people of Texas City wanted a new container port, but people living higher up the bay did not.

Turmoil in Seabrook, 2000–2002

As the largest of the small cities that would be impacted by the Bayport plan, Seabrook was a fulcrum for tensions. It began to suffer stress fractures. Some members of the city council were not listening to the rising crescendo of citizen opposition to Bayport. Instead, apparently persuaded that there was no way to prevail over the muscular Port of Houston Authority and get the container port moved elsewhere, some on the council were quietly negotiating with the port authority for capital improvements in the city, such as new sewage treatment and fire department facilities. Citizens were furious; a new sewage treatment plant was a poor trade for the long downward slide in residential property values that would accompany a giant container port. Voters petitioned successfully for a recall election in early 2000 and replaced four council members, including the mayor.

Three of the replacement council members, however, also turned out to be unwilling to oppose the Bayport plan, although they were silent about this until after being elected. There would be more excitement in Seabrook at the end of 2002, when one of these three council members resigned in public disgrace. Stopped for a late-night traffic violation during the Christmas party season, the council member claimed to have been pulled over not for running a stop sign but for supporting the Port of Houston Authority! Police tape recordings captured an undignified outburst that was aired on television, where it certainly qualified as tons of sizzle and seasoning (Seabrook Police Department 2002).

Officials of bay area cities, GBCPA, and citizen activists of every stripe raised hurdle after objection after barricade against the port through 2000, 2001, and 2002. A key theme was that decaying com-

Frederick Ulrein
1938

Woodland occupies higher ground along the shore near
Bayport, supporting large birds such as the pileated
woodpecker and great horned owl.

munities and plunging property values surrounded new ports in other
cities, showing that vast container terminals near residential and commercial areas had negative impacts far outweighing the benefits of any
jobs they brought.

"Until you visit the Port of Los Angeles/Long Beach, it is impossible to imagine the enormity and impact of a facility like Bayport,"
said Houston environmental planning consultant Peter Brown after a
research visit to California ports (GBCPA 2000a, 1). He called Los Angeles a "convincing example that no amount of buffering or remedial
measures can alleviate the effects of such large facilities." Community leaders and residents of the neighboring cities of Wilmington and
San Pedro described how for thirty years the port had been insensitive
to community needs and had broken numerous promises made to residents (GBCPA 2000a, 2).

For a time in 2001 the action shifted to the Texas legislature. Representative Rick Noriega introduced Texas House Bill 564, calling for
sunset review of the Port of Houston Authority. He wanted evaluation
of port management and accountability because of the $387 million

port bond election in 1999—in which the ballot wording was all about "environmental enhancements" and said nothing about Bayport. Representative John Davis quickly signed on as coauthor of the bill, as did three more members of the Harris County delegation. Port commissioners are appointed, not elected. The idea was that sunset review would provide a means for citizens to insist on accountability regarding how the port authority was using public funds; but the bill was dropped.

The Bayport opposition was also exploring problems in the assessment of wetlands that would be affected by the project. During the run-up to publication of the draft EIS, the stated acreage of wetlands over which the Corps of Engineers claimed regulatory jurisdiction veered wildly, from well over a hundred acres to less than three acres, even though much of the Bayport site was dotted with prairie potholes. Under Corps rules, if wetlands are to be filled for a project, the Corps must choose the site least damaging to the environment. Policy guidelines require no net loss of wetlands. Opponents saw the juggling of the wetlands numbers as illustrating bias on the part of the Corps.

A large crowd was expected for the public hearing on the draft environmental impact statement in December 2001. Indeed, close to five thousand people trekked downtown to Houston's George R. Brown Convention Center for the hearing, once more far outstripping previous attendance at any such meeting. Elected officials spoke first. State legislators and mayors and council members from Pasadena, Seabrook, Shoreacres, Taylor Lake Village, El Lago, and other communities spoke out once more against the Bayport site. Most were frustrated with the draft EIS and its biases and incompleteness. In view of its failings, many speakers requested that a supplemental draft EIS be prepared.

Early 2002 saw a stream of further calls for a supplemental draft EIS—from the Houston-Galveston Area Council, five city councils, and the City of La Porte, which noted in written comments that concerns the city spokesman had expressed at the scoping meeting three years before had still not been addressed. The La Porte and Clear Creek school districts both adopted resolutions opposing the Bayport site. In June, the City of Pasadena passed a resolution opposing the Bayport site. In July, U.S. Congressman Nick Lampson called for a supplemental draft EIS. In August and September, Shoreacres and Taylor Lake Village reaffirmed their opposition, in response to the port authority submitting two revised permit applications that both still failed to address the concerns of the cities.

The Texas Parks and Wildlife Department said the draft EIS was unclear, misleading, and biased. The EPA called for further analysis. Comments on the draft EIS by the U.S. Fish and Wildlife Service (2002) were the most damning of all: the agency said the Bayport site was *the most environmentally damaging* of the alternative sites under consideration for a container port and recommended that the permit application be denied. The USFWS would reiterate this in response to a revised permit application, again recommending permit denial because of significant cumulative loss of native coastal prairie habitat.

On August 13, 2002, four years after the saga had begun and three years after the scoping meeting, almost to the day, a delegation of mayors went to see the commanding colonel of the Corps of Engineers, Galveston District, to press again for a supplemental draft EIS. Accompanying them were Senator Jackson, staff members representing Congressman Lampson and State Representative Davis, Councilman Charlie Young of La Porte, two assistants to Pasadena mayor John Manlove, and officials of GBCPA and the Houston Yacht Club.

GBCPA suggested that biased actions by the port authority and the Corps of Engineers and insufficient disclosure of impacts in the Bayport EIS violated citizens' constitutional right to due process of law. Among the actions in question was the continuing flow of changes to project specifications. Under the National Environmental Policy Act, the public has a right to see and comment upon a draft EIS. The GBCPA position was that the draft EIS for Bayport was no longer valid because the plans had been materially altered in revised permit applications.

"The unfairness of these amendments is profound," GBCPA chair Jim Blackburn told the Corps in a letter. "The Port of Houston Authority had more than ample opportunity to get their proposal together. They have waited until after the close of the comment period on the draft EIS to make not just one but two major changes. That is simply unfair" (GBCPA 2002a).

The Corps of Engineers never did budge on the question of a supplemental draft EIS, despite the mounting public pressure. These are the custodians of our waterways, the federal guardians of environmental responsibility in projects affecting our ever-diminishing wetlands. By the time the mayors went to see the colonel, he was the third commanding colonel the Galveston District had had since the Bayport permit application had been filed. There would also be a sequence of three civilian project managers responsible for Bayport at the Corps.

Disregarding the widespread opposition by elected officials, which of course reflected opposition by the electorate, the Corps was simply unwilling to embark upon a supplemental draft EIS. It was difficult to believe. For five years, citizens and natural resource agencies had been identifying serious cumulative impacts on wetlands, water quality, and air quality, yet the port authority and the Corps were determined to proceed directly to a final EIS.

Texas City Gets Its Permit, 2003

Developments accelerated in 2003. In April, Col. Leonard Waterworth, commander of the Corps' Galveston District, issued a permit for a container facility to be built at Shoal Point in Texas City. This new port is designed to handle more containers than the proposed Bayport facility, guaranteeing that the region will remain competitive in container traffic. Moreover, some container traffic from Barbour's Cut is expected to move to Texas City, opening up capacity at the existing facility.

In May, the Corps of Engineers released the final EIS on Bayport, an enormous document running to six volumes (plus appendices on CDs) and weighing twenty-six pounds. In June, the opposition filed suit against the Corps of Engineers over serious inadequacies in the final EIS, charging that it violated the National Environmental Policy Act and Clean Water Act. Joint plaintiffs were the cities of Shoreacres and Taylor Lake Village, GBCPA, the Houston Yacht Club, and several conservation organizations, including the Houston Audubon Society; Seabrook and El Lago soon joined the suit. The biggest concern the plaintiffs expressed involved the assessment of alternatives to Bayport.

"Colonel Waterworth found that Shoal Point was the least damaging practicable alternative site for a container port on Galveston Bay," said Blackburn. "But now we have an EIS issued for Bayport that fails even to mention the issuing of the Shoal Point permit, let alone that the colonel found the Texas City site to be the best one for our bay system. Something is wrong here. That's why we are going to court" (GBCPA 2003a).

Would negative impacts be the same wherever a new container port was built? They would not. A key reason why Bayport is the wrong location is that a new container port so high up the bay is a recipe for further channel deepening. The Bayport opposition is convinced that if the port authority makes the enormous investment a new port requires, it will soon be back asking voters to support a bond issue to pay for deepening the Houston Ship Channel to fifty feet—claiming that newer container ships are larger and that we need the deeper channel to support our port investment and remain competitive. As we have seen, a deeper channel has major negative implications for the ecology of the bay. Long-term impacts of a port at Shoal Point in Texas City would be far lower because it is near the mouth of the bay, where a fifty-foot channel would not afflict the whole length of the estuary.

In response to citizen challenges, port spokespersons have repeatedly denied that channel deepening is planned, but history suggests we be wary of such denial. This is a promise waiting to be broken. For a hundred years, the channel has steadily been deepened. With wharves in the Bayport plans engineered to fifty-six feet, and Texas City already authorized to build a fifty-foot channel, the historical trajectory indicates that we are asleep if we imagine this pressure has gone away. There is even a standard phrase for the deepening mania—the "race to the bottom." All major ports are in the race.

A second respect in which Bayport is all wrong is that the number of people living in the immediate area is far higher than at any of the alternative sites. Shoal Point, in contrast, is remote from all dwellings. The health impacts of a concentrated source of diesel emissions and the traffic and noise and light problems are greatly worsened by having residential rather than industrial neighbors. A container port at Bayport would impact up to ten times more people than at other sites under consideration, according to the figures in the draft EIS.

Security issues arise as well. A spoil island such as Shoal Point constitutes an ideal port location in having just a single entry/exit route, notes maritime consultant Ricardo Fernandez of Indigo Services Corporation (GBCPA 2002b). Traffic going in and out can readily be monitored. In case of an alarm, the whole port can be isolated by shutting down a single route. Extremely tight security can be maintained as a matter of routine. Following the terror attacks of September 11, 2001, security became an even more prominent public concern.

Seeing how the Corps proceeded full steam ahead on the Bayport project regardless of events in Texas City makes it hard to shake the feeling that we could wind up with container docks every few miles along the western shore of the bay. Barbour's Cut is expanding into La Porte and Morgan's Point. Texas City is building a container port. The Port of Houston Authority already has control over a large portion of

Pelican Island. The only brake is citizen pressure. As earlier described, Houston leased portions of the Galveston docks during the years of the Bayport fight and tried to take over as owner; although the Galveston Wharf Board and City Council both agreed to this, voters rejected the idea in a referendum.

How many container ports are needed on Galveston Bay? Looking for a sense of national patterns, I found figures at the Web site of a citizens' group in Charleston, South Carolina, where people fought off a poorly sited container port and got it moved to a less damaging location (www.containtheport.com). The table showed calls at U.S. ports by container ships of all sizes in 1999.

The total number of container ships sidling up to U.S. docks that year was close to 15,000. New York City received almost 2,000. Next came Charleston with just short of 1,500. Four other U.S. ports had more than 1,000 container ships each, three of them on the West Coast serving the Asian trade—Long Beach, Los Angeles, and Oakland. The fourth was Norfolk, Virginia. Houston was down at number nine, with 623 container ships. Nothing has rearranged this broad distribution of container business since then.

The Port of Houston Authority likes to boast that Houston is the nation's "leading port in foreign tonnage," but the reason is not container shipping. It is bulk cargo, chiefly refined petroleum products and petrochemicals. These products are liquid cargo, and liquid cargo constitutes well over half of all cargo handled within the jurisdiction of the Port of Houston Authority, or within Harris County. Ours is a port with an established niche. Container traffic amounts to only a tiny percentage of the tonnage passing through the Port of Houston.

I have struggled to understand port, customs, and national maritime transportation statistics, and here is what I found. In 2001–2002, a total of some 118 million short tons of cargo went through the Port of Houston (about 88 million tons in imports and 30 million tons in exports). Nearly 80 million tons of the total consisted of liquid bulk cargo in tankers; only 10.8 million tons were containerized cargo— *less than 10 percent of the total* (U.S. Department of Transportation 2003; "Financial Reports and Trade Data" 2003).

Note, too, that almost all liquid cargo goes through private terminals, not public docks. Of the total 118 million tons, some 90 million tons went through private docks; only 28 million tons went through the public docks operated by the port authority, including the 10.8

"Light chocolate brown background with darker brown markings edged in black" is how Weis described the snake, noting that it was thirty-two inches long. It was probably a rat snake.

million tons in containers ("Financial Reports and Trade Data" 2003). Two other important kinds of cargo for Houston are bulk steel and "project cargoes," in which the entire load of a ship consists of materials and equipment all headed for a single project and destination. Most of the remainder is grains and intracoastal barge traffic—also not containerized.

Should the Bayport facility be built, then, we would be sacrificing air quality and wetlands, clogging roadways with horrible traffic problems, and drastically damaging quality of life in Galveston Bay communities, all for the sake of gaining a few percentage points in the amount of container traffic in our annual cargo figures. These are heavy costs to pay for questionable gain.

Casualties

A leading figure during the wrangle over Bayport has been Nancy Edmonson, mayor of Shoreacres. "They just don't get it," she observed one day of the port authority and the Corps. "They don't seem to understand that we aren't going to give up."

But people do give up, of course. One way and another, the energy cost of a fight like this is high, and it often seems as if the port is banking on exhaustion to make the opposition cave in. Several families I know have sold their homes and moved away—to the Hill Country, to

Spring, and deeper into Clear Lake City, away from the bay—partly because of the proposed Bayport project and fears of what it could do to savings caught up in home value.

My friend Dru Dickson did not quite make her move. She lived on a spacious property within a few hundred yards of the port authority's Bayport land. For five years she traipsed to public meetings as part of the opposition, wrote letters of objection to the Corps of Engineers, and collected press clippings that others in the Bayport fight needed to see. In 2002 she celebrated her birthday on the deck at the Point, watching ships and barges glide by on a hot summer evening. In 2003, as the Corps' scheduled date for a decision on the Bayport permit approached, she inexplicably died on the very morning she was setting out to explore Hill Country real estate for a new place to live, to get away from the Bayport mess. Properties on either side of hers were soon up for sale. Friends struggled to shake off the feeling that the port fight had killed her.

Glancing over more than thirty years of news articles about the Barbour's Cut container terminal reveals the same gloomy picture of overwhelming truck traffic, expanding container yards, decaying neighborhoods, and broken promises that Peter Brown found in Los Angeles. A sad little notice reports the death of John Grimes in 1992. He was the mayor of Morgan's Point and chairman of GBCPA. While riding his bicycle about 7:00 one morning on a quiet residential street near his bayfront home, he was hit by a heavy truck and killed. The truck was delivering cargo from El Paso to the container port when the accident happened.

Port commissioners are part of Houston's ruling structure, prominently concerned with ensuring that they have bond money to spend and large-scale construction contracts to award. City governments and citizens who get in the way are a nuisance to be conquered by manipulation of public opinion through paid advertising and a publicity machine. The Corps' failure to follow the spirit of federal environmental mandates is no great surprise. All over the nation, the Corps faces intensifying criticism for bending to development pressures.

The Corps of Engineers issued a permit to the Port of Houston Authority for the Bayport project early in 2004, while the opposition coalition's lawsuit against the Corps was in process. The judge upheld the permit, demeaning citizens' concerns as mere "quibbles." In June 2004 the coalition filed notice that it would appeal the judgment, moving the case to the Fifth Circuit Court of Appeals in New Orleans.

Luna moth, 1935.

The pending appeal, however, did not prevent the port authority from starting to dig. Thus, June also saw a groundbreaking ceremony at Bayport. A small airplane flew round and round in circles over the dignitaries towing a banner that read: "Be Informed—www.PortPork.com."

We can see what the future will be like if the new port is not stopped by looking at Barbour's Cut, where the sorry evolution is not over. Port-related facilities are trying to creep deeper into town. According to a mid-2002 report from Morgan's Point, "while a number of issues are addressed in the proposed new zoning ordinance, the two main focal points are the area south of Barbour's Cut Boulevard across from the Port of Houston Authority's Barbour's Cut Terminal, and the land owned by Boys and Girls Harbor" (*Bayshore Sun* 2002). Boys and Girls Harbor is a children's home—not a classic tough player in corporate negotiations—and it owns substantial acreage close to Barbour's Cut.

Right below this in the same issue of the paper is a second article about how Deer Park, Pasadena, and La Porte need to work together to achieve regulations preventing heavy trucks from using the fast lane along Highway 225 during certain hours so that commuters can travel in the fast lane without experiencing abject terror. This is how things go after a port comes in. Top-end new homes and prime businesses are not springing up nearby. Quite the reverse—thirty years later people are still struggling to soften the worst of the assault on their towns.

"La Porte City Council voted Monday night to table a request by the Port of Houston Authority for a special conditional use permit that would lead to construction of a 14-lane truck pre-check facility on 20 acres of and south of Barbour's Cut Boulevard," said a mid-2003 front-page lead (*Bayshore Sun* 2003). "Councilman James Warren [said] he was concerned about promises made to nearby residents by Port officials, but not included in the documents being approved by council." Promises not documented are promises waiting to be broken.

Many of us who live near the bay feel like lambs at the sacrificial altar of downtown power. Given the failure of the port authority and Corps of Engineers to give any of the alternative sites for a container port serious consideration, we feel as if the entire, long EIS procedure was more of a pro forma exercise than a good-faith environmental evaluation. We are faced with a steamroller of a port authority aiming to ram a destructive and ill-conceived project into place, and never mind the neighbors or the bay.

Two of my immediate neighbors are port pilots who carry the heavy responsibility of bringing ships safely up the channel from the Gulf to the docks, but theirs is not the only large responsibility here. The task of defending the bay falls to those who live near it. The people of Katy and River Oaks and the Woodlands, twenty or thirty miles away, are not going to be its voice. Civic leaders such as the Harris County commissioners and members of the Greater Houston Partnership are silent about the bay.

We are faced with questionable use of public funds by a port authority determined to build a port at the wrong place, at taxpayer expense, while we press for more intelligent use of tax dollars. By default and geography, we have become the advocates for the bay because the Corps is not fulfilling its environmental tasks. If we sit down and shut up, who will be left to stand up for the vast community resource that Galveston Bay represents for us all?

A Park at Bayport

The large green sweep of the Bayport site lies between the little community of El Jardin del Mar and the Bayport channel. The area holds historic interest in addition to its rarity as a large stretch of coastal prairie. John Richardson Harris and his brothers, William and David, all three born in the 1790s, were great-grandsons of the John Harris who founded Harrisburg in Pennsylvania in 1710. Shipowners and traders, the three brothers came to Texas and founded another Harrisburg, where Houston now stands. William Harris also had a ranch on Galveston Bay consisting of half a league (about 2,200 acres) and a labor (about 175 acres) at a place known as Red Bluff.

William Harris's grandson inherited the 175 acres on the bayshore that would become El Jardin. He had it platted and began to sell lots in 1924. His three children were born there, and one was still living there when Lucile Klopp wrote a history of the area in 2002. Like Frederick Weis, who made the sketches in these pages, many of the people who first bought El Jardin lots used them for a summer retreat to enjoy the bay. Similarly, Shoreacres on the north side of the Bayport channel was a residential community that began to develop in the 1920s.

The people of El Jardin and Shoreacres were not thrilled when the Bayport channel sliced between them; nor were the people who had to leave the tiny settlement of Red Bluff. Nancy Edmonson remembers old-timers planning to defend their property with shotguns because they had no legal recourse to fight the loss of their homes (pers. comm., 2003).

"We were there when the Bayport channel was dug and great bulldozers moved around on the prairie like dinosaurs. Our children found arrowheads in the wake of the diggers," says former resident Sylvia Jenkins (pers. comm., 2002). Bobcats used to frighten her horses, and she says there was a parade of night-herons, great blue herons, and green herons. Today all the houses of Red Bluff are gone. They were expropriated and razed or removed when the Bayport channel was built. "It was heartbreaking when the house was swept over the bluff," says Sylvia.

In January 1980 Agnes Skelly of El Jardin was pressing to get the bayfront where the homes of Red Bluff had stood set aside as a county park. The *Houston Post* said the county parks planner was authorized by the Harris County Commissioners Court to begin preparations to apply for funds from the Texas Parks and Wildlife Commission for acquisition of five hundred to a thousand acres for a state park in Harris County. "The Red Bluff area has been rated high for consideration as a park," said Skelly (GBCPA Minutes, March 1980).

The park idea did not bear fruit, but it keeps coming back again because a large bayfront park is an obvious use for the place. Metropolitan areas the world over have understood that greenbelts make cities more livable. "This site at Bayport is the last large tract of natural terrain on the upper west side of Galveston Bay," said Mayor Robin Riley of Seabrook in early 2003. "It does not take a lot of imagination to picture it as a park. A major new bayfront park in southern Pasadena would be an enormous asset to the people of Houston and other nearby cities as well as to Pasadena residents" (GBCPA 2003b).

Although the appeal by the citizens' coalition challenging the container port is still in progress at the time of writing, phase-one construction contracts have been awarded and the digging has begun. Neighbors were sickened to see a portion of the port land stripped bare of all vegetation, the prairie potholes gone. Spoonbills and ibises, owls and woodpeckers, deer and songbirds must find somewhere else to go.

As Blackburn has pointed out, however, a pattern in environmental fights like this is that "when you win, you win big." Examples already exist in the Galveston Bay watershed. Citizens fought for twenty-five years to prevent construction of the Wallisville Dam on the Trinity River, and there is now a nineteen-thousand-acre conserved area where that dam would have been. Virginia Point, where Interstate 45 crosses the causeway to Galveston Island, supplies a second instance. In the early 1980s Texas Copper was planning a smelter there. Marshes that had long been taken for granted were at risk from air- and waterborne pollutants deriving from the smelter. People fought successfully to keep it out. Today the property belongs to Scenic Galveston, and natural marshes at the approach to the island are securely conserved (GBCPA 2003c).

Stay tuned. The Bayport opposition is tired, but it is dogged. Federal laws now exist that were not on the books when the Bayport channel was cut or when Barbour's Cut first intruded upon Morgan's Point. The outcome may yet encourage us all.

CHAPTER 7

Destinations

To save the Texas coast, we must value it and we must defend it. The first step is to get to know it.

Jim Blackburn, *The Book of Texas Bays*

The distance from Buffalo Bayou or Allen's Landing in the heart of Houston to the far end of Galveston's South Jetty, or to remote Smith Point on East Bay, can be traveled by car in not much more than an hour. Yet to our collective shame, no guidebook exists for Galveston Bay. In its absence, this is a sampling of destinations. Places on the more heavily traveled western side of Galveston Bay are profiled first, followed by the Bolivar Peninsula, and then the wilder shores of West Bay and East Bay. To get out on the water, one can take boat tours and charter fishing trips, several setting out from Clear Lake and Galveston. Events on the bay follow in the next chapter, and additional resources are listed at the back of the book.

Clear Lake and Clear Creek

Clear Creek is among Galveston Bay's larger tributaries and remains in a natural state along much of its length, winding across the low terrain to flow into the bay between Kemah and Seabrook. One place to get onto the creek is at the public boat ramp under the bridge on Egret Bay Boulevard in Webster (take NASA Road 1 east from Interstate 45 and turn south onto Egret Bay; the boat ramp is where Egret Bay crosses the creek). Terns and ospreys fish the wide marsh here. From this put-in one can head upstream into wild stretches of the creek in Friendswood or downstream to Clear Lake.

Marsh grass restoration has been undertaken along some sections, and park plans in Webster and League City may allow substantial portions of the creek to remain natural for the long future. Home of NASA's manned space flight facility at the Johnson Space Center, the Clear Lake area mainly draws visitors who want to see Space Center Houston or who keep boats at marinas on the lake. Along the lakeshore a recreational atmosphere sets in, with waterfront condominiums and restaurants, boat yards, and bed-and-breakfasts (B&Bs).

Seabrook

The little town of Seabrook begins near where NASA Road 1 crosses Highway 146, becoming Second Street. Restored early houses in the heart of Old Seabrook, some of them built in the 1890s, are now charming antique stores and galleries in a nostalgic setting shaded by great oaks. Along the bayfront are little pastel houses up on stilts, once so typical of much of the Gulf shore. The local shrimp fleet plies the bay.

Seabrook has several B&Bs, among them the picturesque Pelican House (281-474-5295) nestled on a backwater cove; the Old Parsonage (713-206-1105); and Beacon Hill B&B (281-325-7643). For details on these and other B&Bs, hotels, and restaurants; for a Seabrook bird list; and for more about attractions in the area, visit the city's Web site at www.seabrook-tx.com.

HIKE THE TRAILS

Seabrook is proud of its green space and is promoting itself as an eco-tourism destination. In recent years the city has acquired sizable tracts of largely natural parkland and has connected its bayshore, bayou, and woodland parks with a network of hike-and-bike trails. All of Seabrook is designated a bird sanctuary, and it includes four sites on the Great Texas Coastal Birding Trail, plus one just outside Seabrook proper—Armand Bayou Nature Center.

Pine Gully Park is a good place to start. Stretching from the bayshore along the north bank of the bayou called Pine Gully, this park is large and wild enough to have armadillos and alligators in its woodlands and wetlands. A fishing pier attracts anglers. A Karankawa Indian shell midden hugs the shore where the bayou meets the bay, and the trail winds inland through native coastal oak forest. Watch for herons of several species, shorebirds, and loggerhead shrikes.

The trail proceeds southward to Robinson Park and the Seabrook Wildlife Refuge, and then on south to Hester Garden Park, also heavily wooded. Both Hester and Pine Gully parks were acquired from families who wanted to avoid seeing their leafy holdings subdivided. Deer persist in the northern part of town, as do great horned and barred owls and the large, dramatic pileated woodpecker with its sheeny black plumage, red crest, and Woody Woodpecker laugh. McHale Park near the south end of Seabrook, close to the Kemah Bridge, has a viewing platform from which to enjoy watching resident pelicans, and visitors may be rewarded with an osprey in flight or perched on a tall piling.

A comprehensive wetlands conservation plan has been drawn up to avoid damaging wetlands through future development. The city's eco-tourism committee also has a habitat conservation plan to ensure preservation of representative coastal prairie and woodland habitat types.

ARMAND BAYOU NATURE CENTER

Established in 1975, the nature center takes in twenty-five hundred acres of coastal prairie, woodlands, and bayous—enough terrain so that coyotes can be heard yipping at night. Conservationists set about acquiring this lovely bayou tract as they watched the population of the Clear Lake area booming and the pumping of groundwater drowning the marshes through subsidence of the land surface. Aerial photos shot in 1953 and 1993 dramatically illustrate the loss of marshland flanking the waterway. Marsh and prairie restoration began.

Today Armand Bayou has a prairie viewing platform and some nine hundred acres of tallgrass prairie; raptor and reptile exhibits and a bird blind; some bison; three trails; and a boardwalk through wetland habitat. Deer, snakes, turtles, and armadillos are commonly seen, in addition to numerous birds. Volunteers conduct guided hikes, including magical night walks, and evening boat trips on the bayou. Night visitors often hear and see barred owls and screech-owls and learn to spot spiders by their prominent eye shine. To get there, go east from Interstate 45 seven miles on Bay Area Boulevard. Armand Bayou is on the right, just beyond Bay Area Park. For more information and to reserve guided trips, call 281-474-2551 or visit www.abnc.org.

Kemah

The name *Kemah* is an Indian word meaning "wind in my face," an idea neatly captured in the city's promotional slogan: "Breeze into Kemah." Kemah has long been a seafood stop, and for a time after World War II it was a gambling town as well. When hurricanes ravaged the waterfront in 1961 and 1983, Kemah rebuilt, but it would not see major traffic until the 1990s, when its waterfront was transformed from a ramshackle assortment of seafood restaurants to the amusement-park ambiance of the Kemah Boardwalk today. Restaurants have multiplied, attracting enough people to support a shopping district.

KEMAH BRIDGE

The sweeping Kemah Bridge is the fourth-generation crossing of the channel. Until 1929 the way to get across the mouth of Clear Creek was on a hand-cranked ferry. The first bridge was a swing bridge built in 1930. By the late 1950s traffic was straining the old bridge, and sailors wanted something higher. The famous drawbridge that turns up in local photos and paintings was bridge number two, built in 1959. At low water many boats could go under it, but when the water was high, the bridge had to be opened whenever a boat blew its horn to go through. On busy Sundays motorists sat in long, hot lines of cars while the bridge eased upward for sailboats to pass.

Eventually the inconvenience of a drawbridge grew too great. Bids were let in 1983 for construction of a new fixed-span bridge, 3,745 feet long and 75 feet wide, with 75-foot clearance, to allow both road traffic and sailboats to pass without delay. It was officially opened on May 16, 1986. The gated structure near its base, a later addition, is to allow increased flow of floodwaters out of Clear Lake into the bay when the lake is high. The gates are usually closed but can be opened as a second outlet in addition to the narrow Kemah channel.

Texas horned lizard at El Jardin, 1956. In the last thirty years the species has disappeared from much of its former range in East and Central Texas, for reasons believed to include the spread of fire ants, collection for the pet trade, environmental contaminants, and changing land use.

Tucked away on an island on the lake side of the Kemah Bridge is the Seabrook Shipyard, and within this complex, the Sundance Grill (281-474-2248) offers waterfront and outdoor dining in a peaceful setting just right for watching evening wane and lights twinkle on around the lake. Exit Highway 146 on the north slope of the Kemah Bridge, go east, and follow the signs inside Seabrook Shipyard.

KEMAH BOARDWALK

Within a few years from the time that entrepreneur Tilman Fertitta first approached the Wiggins family, who ran the old Jimmie Walker's restaurant, to sell, all the privately owned restaurants along the Kemah side of the Clear Creek channel disappeared under the makeover into the Kemah Boardwalk. In 1998 Fertitta opened a new drawing card: the Aquarium, with its fifty-thousand-gallon tank of exotic fish and its "underwater dining adventure." The complex also features a Ferris wheel, carousel, miniature train, games arcade, Stingray Reef where visitors can feed and pet the stingrays, and walk-through "dancing fountains" in the central plaza.

To reach the Boardwalk, take Interstate 45 south, exit at NASA Road 1, go east to Highway 146, and turn south on 146 to cross the Kemah Bridge. The Boardwalk entry is on the left, just south of the bridge. For information about its many restaurants, visit www.kemah-boardwalk.com; for detail about accommodations, contact the City of Kemah Visitor Center at 281-334-3181 or www.kemah.net, or call the Boardwalk's information line (281-334-9880).

The Houston Ship Channel and Baytown

Showcasing the natural world among the industrial towers lining the upper Houston Ship Channel are two newly created waterfront destinations. A marsh placed back in service at the San Jacinto Battleground is the reinstatement of a natural landscape, and the Baytown Nature Center is a case of nature reclaiming terrain that was temporarily tamed. Like irrepressible dandelions sprouting through cracks in a sidewalk, these are places where wildness is bouncing back, and the birds rejoice.

SAN JACINTO MARSHLAND TRAIL

At the site where the Battle of San Jacinto was fought in April 1836, when Gen. Sam Houston and the Texas army prevailed over General Santa Anna's much larger Mexican force to garner Texas independence, an extensive restored marsh now invites attention. Covering more than a hundred acres, with parts of it accessible on a boardwalk trail, the marsh is an asset for educators wanting to show students how wetlands work. The original marsh barred the escape of Mexican troops in 1836, and the new one is part of an effort to restore the whole site to its appearance at the time of the historic battle.

There is no admission fee for the park, trail, or San Jacinto Museum of History—an understated and old-style display. For a fee, one can watch a multiprojector slide show about the Texas Revolution; take an elevator to the viewing platform at the top of the great commemorative obelisk of the San Jacinto Monument for a panorama of the ship channel and surrounding industry; or visit the battleship *Texas* at its permanent mooring nearby. For park and battleship information, call 281-479-2431; for museum and other information, call 281-479-2421.

LYNCHBURG FERRY

Next to the battleground park is the picturesque little Lynchburg ferry often mentioned on Houston weather and traffic broadcasts, crossing the Houston Ship Channel from Pasadena to Baytown. Nathaniel Lynch established a settlement there in 1822 and started the ferryboat service across the San Jacinto River. Lynchburg was on the main route to San Antonio from New Orleans, and the ferry was a flatboat powered by hand by pulling on cables. Because of the slowness of crossings, the place was a bottleneck for settlers retreating from the advancing Mexican army in 1836 (Handbook of Texas Online 2002).

The diesel ferries in modern service are still diminutive, the sixty-one-foot *William P. Hobby* and *Ross S. Sterling*, built at Todd Shipyard in 1964. Each has a capacity of just twelve vehicles, and they take ten minutes or so to make the crossing. The ferry ride is free as part of the highway system. Thirsty or hungry riders can pause for some sustenance nearby at the Ferry Inn. The views are oddly captivating: serene scenes of foraging herons and egrets on the mudflats lining the approaches to the ferry yield to busy ship and barge traffic on the channel itself, backed by an intimidating skyline of chemical plants. Whatever would Sam Houston say if he could see the place now?

BAYTOWN NATURE CENTER

One of two Baytown stops on the Great Texas Coastal Birding Trail, the Baytown Nature Center is a large wetlands preserve established where subsidence compromised the Brownwood subdivision on a peninsula jutting out into the bay. It has marsh and pond habitats, a pleasing butterfly garden, and miles of trails into areas of native plants, freshwater ponds, and abundant bird life. Naturalist-guided walks are offered on the weekends. Much of the area has no shade—bring a sun hat, sunscreen, and mosquito repellent. Call 281-420-5360 for details (you may need to dial 1 before the area code).

To reach the Baytown Nature Center from Houston, go east on Interstate 10 and take the first Baytown exit, Decker Drive (Spur 330). Almost immediately take the first exit and remain on the access road until turning right onto Bayway Drive at the first traffic light. Continue for a mile and a half on Bayway, and then turn right onto West Shreck, at the brown-and-white Great Texas Coastal Birding Trail sign. The entrance to the nature center is just beyond the West Little League Park, at 201½ West Shreck.

MV *SAM HOUSTON*

The Port of Houston Authority offers narrated tours of a portion of the Houston Ship Channel on a pleasantly appointed vessel with a comfortable cabin. There is no charge, but reservations are needed. Call 713-670-2576 for bookings. To get there, exit East Loop 610 at Clinton Drive and go west for several blocks through the tired townscape of decaying dockland, warehousing, and empty lots. The embarkation point is across the railroad tracks on the left. Close by is the Athens Bar and Grill (8037 Clinton Drive; 713-675-1644), noted for live Greek music on the weekends and vigorous dancing and belly dancing. As the night wears on, sailors often arrive and get the place hopping.

BRADY'S LANDING

The appeal of this large restaurant, built on the upper Houston Ship Channel in 1984, lies in its unlikely setting in the heart of port and industrial installations. Diners are right in the middle of major petrochemical and port facilities. The place is notable for its outstanding Sunday champagne brunch buffet. Call Brady's Landing at 713-928-9921. Its address is 8505 Cypress Street, but it is not easily found by following street numbers. To get there, take Highway 225 west from where it meets with Loop 610; it soon ends. At the first light go right on Broadway, and after a few blocks turn right again onto Cypress. Brady's Landing is on the left. It has a series of rooms suitable for private gatherings and is a popular spot for weddings.

THE POINT

For close views of ships and barges passing in the Houston Ship Channel, but with a natural backdrop, the deck flanking the funky Texas ice house called the Point (281-471-1418) is the ideal location, scenic in its own authentic sort of way. Take Barbour's Cut Boulevard east from

Waterfront, 1941.

Highway 146 in La Porte, past the yards and docks and giant cranes of Houston's container terminal. Almost at the end of Barbour's Cut Boulevard, turn right on Vinsonia, go left at the T junction after one block, and then plunge down from the high bank of Morgan's Point into a stand of cane. The road turns to gravel and widens out into the parking lot of the Point.

San Leon and Texas City

Two places usually bypassed en route from Houston to Galveston are the free-and-easy community of San Leon and the industrial center of Texas City. Between them lies a preserve of special note on the Galveston Bay shore.

TEXAS CITY PRAIRIE PRESERVE

Watch for the sign on Highway 146 for this conservation area operated by the Nature Conservancy. The distinction of the place is that it is one of only two sanctuaries protecting the tiny population of the severely endangered Attwater's prairie-chicken. The preserve has a coastal prairie trail good for birding or "butterflying." Hours are variable, and public access is mainly through volunteering; call 409-945-4677, fax 409-943-5056, or visit the Nature Conservancy Web site at http://nature.org/ (click on Where We Work).

APRIL FOOL POINT

For a wide-open bay view with wheeling gulls, consider the Topwater Grill at April Fool Point in San Leon (281-339-1232), between Kemah and Texas City. Shrimp boats are moored in its small harbor, and other small craft ply the nearby waters of Dickinson Bay. Take Highway 146 south from Kemah, past Highway 646. Turn left onto FM 517, stay to the left at the Y junction, and keep going for about five miles; the road becomes Grand Avenue. Turn right on Ninth Street at the flashing red light, and this little road eventually goes right into the April Fool Point/Topwater Grill parking lot.

TEXAS CITY

Texas City is famous for the fire that qualifies as the worst industrial disaster in the United States. Almost six hundred people were killed and nearly four thousand injured. Elizabeth Lee Wheaton (1948) gives a full account of the calamity in her *Texas City Remembers.* The first fire broke out one morning aboard the French ship SS *Grandcamp,* which was in the harbor loaded with ammonium nitrate fertilizer. The Texas City Volunteer Fire Department was summoned, and a crowd of spectators gathered. At 9:12 A.M. on April 16, 1947, the *Grandcamp* blew up.

The explosion threw up a wave that sent a thirty-ton barge a hundred feet inland and drowned a number of people who had survived the initial blast. It also triggered a series of blasts at nearby chemical plants as pieces of the ship became deadly missiles, and fires burned out of control for four days. Under a sky thick with black smoke, at 6:00 P.M. the Coast Guard reported that the SS *High Flyer* was on fire. The city was ordered to evacuate, and the second ship blew at 1:10 A.M. on April 17.

The *Grandcamp* could not be moved out of the harbor under its own power because it was in for engine repairs. The first mistake was the captain's attempt to smother the fire by sealing the hold and filling it with steam, instead of using water to douse the blaze—he feared water would ruin the cargo. "The resulting combination of heat and pressure was the very condition that wartime studies had indicated could destabilize ammonium nitrate and make it explosive. Apparently, neither the captain nor anyone else on the scene was aware of that" ("The Explosion" 1997, 4–5). The second mistake was not dispersing onlookers.

Ammonium nitrate—an estimated two and a half tons—was used to blow up the Murrah Federal Building in Oklahoma City in 1995; the Texas City blasts were many times more powerful, involving some 880 tons. Monuments include the anchor from the *Grandcamp* at the landward end of the Texas City Dike and the propeller of the *High Flyer* at Mikeska–Sandburg Park on Loop 197 at the entrance to the Port of Texas City. Farther down the loop is a memorial where sixty-three unidentified bodies rest in numbered graves, and a small pavilion chronicles the disaster.

Galveston Island

Galveston's main attractions for visitors are its many miles of beaches; the historic district on the Strand, effectively promoted by the Galveston Historical Foundation (409-765-7834; www.galvestonhistory .org); and the Moody Gardens tourist park. The city hosts numerous activities to draw the visitors who sustain its economy (see www .galveston.com).

Several of Galveston's old homes are open to the public. On Harborside Drive at Pier 21, the GHF operates the Texas Seaport Museum and the restored 1877 iron barque *Elissa,* a merchant sailing ship that first called at Galveston in 1884. A less nostalgic, more topical spot is the nearby Ocean Star Offshore Drilling Rig and Museum. Built in 1969 at the Bethlehem Steel Shipyard in Beaumont, this rig drilled some two hundred wells before being retired, and since 1997 it has served as a museum depicting how oil and gas are produced offshore.

Among the island's ventures into ecotourism, dolphin watching is a favorite. Ninety-minute harbor ecotours on Saturday mornings aboard the fifty-foot catamaran *Seagull II* offer a chance of excellent viewing of the resident Atlantic bottlenose dolphins. They may not be fed or approached more closely than fifty feet (although they may approach the boat more closely). Tours leave from Pier 22; call 409-765-1700.

In spring and summer, weather permitting, Harbour Tours conducts two-hour Saturday morning visits to some of the bay's spectacular colonial waterbird nesting islands, such as Little Pelican Island, the site of a brown pelican colony, and the very busy North Deer Island, used by some thirty thousand pairs of birds of more than a dozen species. Birding is burgeoning on Galveston Island thanks to its series of sites on the Great Texas Coastal Birding Trail (see the resources to order maps) and its proximity to birding destinations on the mainland and the Bolivar Peninsula.

The Kemp's Ridley Sea Turtle Research Center operated by the National Marine Fisheries Service is just off the seawall near Fifty-third Street, at 4700 Avenue U. It is open to the public at certain times and admission is free (call 409-766-3670 or check www.galveston.com/museums/turtle.shtml for details). In winter, consider a shelling expedition to Galveston Island State Park. A fine time to collect shells on Gulf beaches is just after the cold front of a winter norther has passed through. The winds produce strong wave action that can toss treasures up onto the beach, and severe cold may kill some of the slow-moving animals before they can escape into deeper water.

Bolivar Peninsula

The intersection of Galveston Bay and the Gulf Intracoastal Waterway is called the Bolivar Roads. An easy way to get out on the waters of the bay is to ride the free ferry from Galveston over to the Bolivar Peninsula—a pleasure, rain or shine. The peninsula can seem windblown and featureless, but it has a strategic position, and it has gained fame in the birding fraternity.

BOLIVAR FERRY

Departing from Galveston, ferry passengers may spot dolphins or frigatebirds and are likely to see several species of ducks during migration. The ferry passes the headquarters of the U.S. Army Corps of Engineers, Galveston District, which is responsible for a thousand miles of navigation channels, including the Intracoastal Waterway. Ferries pass the U.S. Coast Guard's local base, which carries responsibility for aids to navigation, law enforcement, and search-and-rescue operations. Opposite is Seawolf Park on Pelican Island with its World War II submarine and destroyer. The park is on a site that was once a quarantine station operated by the U.S. Immigration Service.

Off to the north, ferry passengers can see the hulk of the SS *Selma*, a reinforced concrete tanker ship damaged soon after its launching in 1919 and abandoned in 1922 where it now lies. A succession of private owners failed to make a go of using the *Selma* as a fishing pier or bait camp, though it is a favored fishing spot. Hermits have occupied it more successfully from time to time.

Port Bolivar today is a sleepy little town, but at one time it was the scene of ambitious plans. After railroad service from Beaumont to Port Bolivar was completed in 1896, barges ferried railcars across to Galveston and also carried passengers. The Great Storm of 1900 damaged the new railroad, but it was rebuilt, and then the Santa Fe Railroad bought it and added major investment in piers and warehouses. "On June 9, 1909, the first deep sea vessel, the *Margaret M. Ford*, docked at Port Bolivar with a load of granite. Two weeks later the *Penrith Castle*, an English steamship, loaded the first lumber shipment from the port. Lumber shipments developed rapidly, increasing to 15 million board feet in 1911 and 23.8 million in 1912. For a few years the Port of Bolivar flourished" (Daniels 1985, 29–31). A huge iron ore dock, 325 feet long and standing 58 feet above high tide, was completed in 1912, part of a grand plan to ship iron ore from East Texas via Bolivar.

But it was not to be. The 1915 hurricane wrecked the ore dock and the railroad. The rail line was again rebuilt, farther from the beach, and rail service continued into the 1940s, but the momentum of the port was gone.

Two ferryboats, the *RS Sterling* and *Cone Johnson*, plied the Bolivar Roads for more than fifty years. They came into service in 1950, followed by the *E. H. Thornton Jr.* in 1959, *Gibb Gilchrist* in 1977, and *Robert C. Lanier* in 1991. All but the *Gibb Gilchrist* are named for men who served on the Texas Highway Commission. Sterling became governor of Texas; Lanier was mayor of Houston; and Gilchrist, an engineer with Santa Fe when the Bolivar line was rebuilt after the 1915 storm, was the first chancellor of Texas A&M University. The *D. C. Greer*, *Ray Stoker Jr.*, and *R. H. Dedman* are new additions.

OLD FORT TRAVIS

The peninsula is named for Simón Bolívar, the great liberator in the fight to free South and Central America from Spanish colonial rule. The first fortifications date back to the early 1800s, when rebels were challenging the Spaniards in Mexico. Col. Henry Perry had an encampment at Port Bolivar in 1815. Francisco Xavier Mina built earthworks there in 1816 and joined forces with the Galveston pirate Luis

Aury to challenge the Spanish government. In 1819 James Long headed an ostensibly independent Texas government and later erected a mud fort at Port Bolivar. The Confederate army had an outpost there in the 1860s (Daniels 1985).

The federal government purchased Fort Travis in 1898 for coastal defense. A fort completed in 1899 suffered storm damage in 1900, and the installations now to be seen were built later. Gun emplacements housed artillery batteries in World War I and again in World War II, when twenty-five hundred troops were stationed there. Now a Galveston County park and campground called Old Fort Travis, the place also has modest accommodations and has become a base for birding visitors. Call 409-934-8126 for reservations; 409-934-8100 for information.

BOLIVAR FLATS

Among the several properties purchased by the Houston Audubon Society to ensure protection of critical habitat for many thousands of shorebirds and migratory waterfowl and songbirds is a large beach and marsh sanctuary on the Bolivar Flats. Here and near the North Jetty, birds gather to feed on the flats and in the shallows, and people in search of wild beaches come to see the birds. Detailed instructions for reaching birding areas are on the Great Texas Coastal Birding Trail map of the upper Texas coast.

ROLLOVER PASS

A favorite fishing spot, Rollover Pass is an old natural pass between the bay and the Gulf. In the 1940s, when it had been closed for a long time, anglers began urging the Texas Game and Fish Commission to reopen in pass. In 1955 a cut was made about a quarter mile long, some two hundred feet wide, and four to six feet deep. The flow of water has since gouged its depth down to about thirty feet in places. As the commission marker declares, the pass was reopened to "introduce into East Bay sufficient quantities of sea water to increase bay water salinity, and to provide additional opportunity for the travel of marine fish to and from spawning and feeding areas of the bay."

The pass quickly became a major migration route for marine life and hence a focal point for fishermen and birds. It was called Rollover long before the 1950s cut was made, and one explanation is that in the bad old days of smuggling, barrels of contraband could be transshipped

Passionvine flower.

by rolling them over this narrow section of the peninsula between the Gulf and East Bay, so as to avoid customs inspectors at Galveston.

HIGH ISLAND SANCTUARIES

In the late 1840s Robert Cade purchased some thirteen thousand acres near High Island and established a ranching empire that has kept the peninsula largely wild between High Island and Crystal Beach. His great-great-granddaughter Melanie Wiggins recorded the stories of its inhabitants in her 1990 *They Made Their Own Law.*

In recent years, as the importance of the oak and hackberry woods at High Island to migrating birds has become ever clearer, the Houston Audubon Society has been buying property to set aside as sanctuaries. At the village of High Island are two sanctuaries where admission operates on the honor system of donations. During spring migration when songbird concentrations are highest, birders are much in evidence, but for much of the rest of the year, visitors may have these places to themselves. An observation platform offers fine viewing of the colonial waterbird rookery in the Smith Oaks sanctuary—nesting herons, egrets, spoonbills, and cormorants in spring—plus a year-round show of thousands of birds coming in at sundown to roost. Directions to the sanctuaries are to be found on the Great Texas Coastal Birding Trail upper coast map.

West Bay and Christmas Bay

SAN LUIS PASS

At the western end of Galveston Island on the southern shore of West Bay lies San Luis Pass, noted for its abundance of shorebirds and white pelicans. Crossing the toll causeway over this pass between bay and Gulf takes one from Galveston County into Brazoria County, where the rest of the run south to Surfside is called the Blue Water Highway. At this southwestern extension of the Galveston Bay system are Bastrop, Oyster, Drum, and Christmas bays.

On the Galveston Island side of the causeway, visitors can drive down to the beach to nose around. Peak shelling season is December though February. On the Brazoria County side, facing the bay rather than the Gulf, lies San Luis County Park, which offers camping (1-800-372-7578). Brazoria County has eighteen miles of accessible sandy beaches and more than twenty public boat ramps, five of them on the bay side of the coast highway between San Luis Pass and Freeport, as shown in GLO's 2002 *Beach and Bay Access Guide.*

Among the birding spots profiled on the Great Texas Coastal Birding Trail map, one that warrants special mention is the Quintana Bird Sanctuary beyond Freeport, adjacent to Quintana Beach County Park, which offers camping (1-800-872-7578). As at High Island, the sanctuary is a prime site to see songbirds during spring migration, and the area has a small population of brown pelicans and great diversity of wildlife and habitat.

MIDCOAST NATIONAL WILDLIFE REFUGE COMPLEX

The unwieldy name belies an underexposed natural treasure within easy striking distance of Houston. The complex consists of the Brazoria, San Bernard, and Big Boggy national wildlife refuges (NWRs), all jointly administered from offices in Angleton (979-849-6062; http://southwest.fws.gov; see also www.refugefriends.org, Web site of the assisting volunteer group). Together they offer exceptional winter waterfowl watching and excellent birding the rest of the year as well. The bird list for the complex includes 320 species.

Brazoria NWR is the largest, at more than forty thousand acres. Established in 1966 specifically as a refuge for wintering waterfowl, it lies along the shores of Chocolate, Bastrop, and Christmas bays. It has saltwater, freshwater, and brackish marshes, lakes and streams, prairies, woody thickets, and sand flats and mudflats. At its maximum tip-to-tip extent, the Brazoria refuge is almost as long as the distance from Clear Lake to the Galveston causeway. The San Bernard NWR, about half as large but nevertheless a sizable refuge, is farther down the coast, ten miles south of Freeport on the inland side of the Gulf Intracoastal Waterway. And the smallest component, Big Boggy NWR, is farther south yet.

Birding on the refuge complex is most interesting during winter because these wetlands along the Texas coast are a primary wintering area for Central Flyway waterfowl, most notably lesser snow geese, with smaller populations of Canada and white-fronted geese. The waterfowl numbers peak in December and January. This is the place to view spectacular concentrations of a hundred thousand geese and eighty thousand ducks of two dozen species, including pintail, mallard, teal, gadwall, mottled duck, and widgeon. In addition, thirteen species of sparrows winter on grassland sections of the refuges.

Spring brings a spectacle of its own. The three-refuge complex has been designated as an internationally significant shorebird site by the Western Hemisphere Shorebird Reserve Network because it hosts more than a hundred thousand shorebirds during spring migration. Dowitchers, dunlins, lesser yellowlegs, and semipalmated and western sandpipers are best observed during migration, from mid-March to mid-May and again between July and September.

Bird-watchers may also see up to fifty different kinds of migrating songbirds, including thirty warbler species. During a spring "fallout," typically after a rainy cold front when the birds are exhausted from a difficult Gulf crossing, it is sometimes possible to see dozens of species of neotropical migrants within a few hours. The sheltering woodlands and canebrakes are important resting and feeding habitat for trans-Gulf migrants. More than a thousand square miles of bottomland hardwood forest once stretched from the Gulf inland along the Brazos, San Bernard, and lower Colorado rivers. Today the woodland is vanishing under development pressures, hence the importance of these refuges.

The Brazoria and San Bernard refuges are open from sunrise to sunset daily from September through May. Summer opening times are more limited (call 979-849-7771 for details). Brazoria NWR is in the Freeport Christmas Bird Count circle, which consistently produces more than 210 species and is usually number one or two in the nation in number of species sighted (USFWS 2000b). Big Boggy NWR (979-849-6062) is not routinely open to the public, but tours can be arranged.

CHRISTMAS BAY

Wild and beautiful, Christmas Bay covers some six thousand acres between Galveston and Freeport. It is shallow, most of it just a foot or two in depth, and conservationists and resource personnel recognize it as presenting a significant opportunity: if Christmas Bay can be kept relatively unpolluted and pristine, with its wetlands and sea grass beds intact, it can serve as a natural laboratory for learning about estuary dynamics and as a reservoir for restocking during restoration efforts in other sections of the bay system.

One reason it has remained relatively unscathed is that it is isolated from the main part of the estuary by an island and a promontory. Another is that the whole northern shore of Christmas Bay lies within the Brazoria NWR. Thus, the area has escaped fouling by urban runoff and industrial pollution, and it still has extensive areas of the submerged sea grass meadows so important to marine life, where tiny marine organisms find shelter and food. Bastrop Bayou feeds fresh water into Christmas Bay, and its circulation of salt water is via San Luis Pass and Cold Pass farther south.

In the 1980s biologist Robert McFarlane undertook a major wildlife inventory of Christmas Bay, finding there 140 mollusk species, almost 100 fish species, and 68 crustacean species. Eight endangered and threatened species occur, among them the green sea turtle, bald eagle, brown pelican, piping plover, and whooping crane. The sea grass meadows are more varied than elsewhere in the estuary, with four species of grasses, by contrast with only a single species in most of the rest of the bay system.

McFarlane's findings matched what fishermen and bait camp operators knew: Christmas Bay was not what it had once been. About a third of the sea grass beds disappeared between 1956 and 1987, McFarlane noted, possibly as a result of damage done by boat traffic. Clams had grown rarer. A hundred fishing cabins had sprung up. Still, a successful fight to prevent issue of a permit for wastewater discharge helped focus attention on the place, and that momentum helped lead to congressional designation of Galveston Bay as a nationally significant estuary in the federal Clean Water Act in 1987, which made the bay part of the National Estuary Program (Dawson 1991).

SEA CENTER TEXAS

The way to get a close look at a 250-pound grouper or an artificial reef without learning to dive is to pay a visit to Sea Center Texas at Lake Jackson, down at the southwesternmost corner of the Galveston Bay system. Dow Chemical Company, the Coastal Conservation Association (CCA—see the resources), and the Texas Parks and Wildlife Department were partners in developing Sea Center Texas, a marine fish hatchery and visitor center occupying seventy-five acres within the boundaries of Dow property.

Separate aquaria depict different coastal habitats. The centerpiece is a fifty-thousand-gallon Gulf of Mexico offshore exhibit, cruised by sharks, red drum, blue runner, jack crevalle, and snapper, as well as the giant grouper. Smaller tanks showcase the marine life of the artificial reefs, salt marshes, and coastal bays. The hatchery building next door is tailored for production of red drum and spotted seatrout.

CCA was formed in 1977 when anglers grew alarmed over the decline in game-fish populations along the Texas coast. Both redfish and speckled trout were being overfished by commercial interests. The group helped establish the state law that extended game-fish protection to these species so that they could not be commercially harvested in state waters. Members of CCA and TPWD formed an alliance with Dow to try to avert the decline of these game fish; CCA chapters provide fund-raising and volunteer support.

Today Sea Center Texas is the largest red drum hatchery in the world. Millions of larvae have been raised to inch-long fingerlings in the Dow ponds and released into coastal bays. Studies have shown that more than 20 percent of the redfish living along the coast were born in hatcheries like Dow's. In addition, there is a five-acre marsh area of shallow ponds and fresh- and saltwater marsh areas, with boardwalks and viewing decks. To get there, take Highway 288 and turn right at the Sea Center Texas sign on Medical Center Drive. The center is open Tuesday through Sunday. Admission is free, but reservations are required for hatchery tours (call 979-292-0100).

Trinity Delta and Chambers County

The floodplain of the Trinity River reaches some twenty miles northward from Interstate 10 and up to six miles from east to west, its northern two-thirds consisting mainly of cypress swamps and the southern third made up of marshes and lakes. Old meanders of the river are easy to see, preserved by their own natural levees rising a few feet above the general level of the floodplain.

At Wallisville on Interstate 10, the floodplain flares out into the Trinity delta complex, consisting of the three-mile-wide modern delta at Anahuac and three abandoned deltas to the west (Freedenberg and Rica 1990). About three thousand years ago when sea level reached its present elevation, Trinity Bay still extended inland about six miles farther than it does today; the river has been actively depositing sediment and filling in the floodplain.

The Trinity is the largest Gulf Coast river, more than five hundred miles long and draining an enormous watershed reaching all the way up to the Dallas–Fort Worth area. Its sediment load upon reaching Trinity Bay is small today as a result of dams upstream trapping the suspended silt. Most of the time the Trinity delta is a beautiful, varied, and peaceful place for canoeing, kayaking, fishing, and birding.

In May 1990, however, the Trinity showed its power. Huge floods surged down the river following heavy rains in North Texas. In some areas between Dallas and Lake Livingston, the water was ten miles across, and parts of the floodplain were under fifteen feet of water (Freedenberg and Rica 1990, 27).

WALLISVILLE

On the south side of Interstate 10 near the Anahuac exit, at a big bend in the Trinity River, is a cluster of buildings called Wallisville Heritage Park (409-389-2252). Established in 1979, the nonprofit body is devoted to local history. The Wallisville town site and the El Orcoquisac Archeological District are both in the National Register of Historic Places.

The Orcoquisac were a subgroup of the Atakapan, the native inhabitants of the lower Trinity River basin at the time of European contact. They moved seasonally with food resources, depending on oysters, fishing, hunting, and plants they gathered. French traders from Louisiana were active in the area in the 1740s, and a French trading post was established there in 1754 by Joseph Blancpain (Fox, Day, and Highly 1980). In an effort to secure the area against the French, the Spaniards established a mission and presidio on the lower Trinity in 1756. Isolation, swampy terrain, and hurricane flooding resulted in abandonment of these settlements.

Moored boats.

It was a confusing area, with portions of the New World changing hands as spoils of war in Europe. In 1762 France ceded Louisiana to Spain, but this was destined to be a short-term switch. In 1803 Spain returned Louisiana to France, and then within a month the United States purchased Louisiana from France. Spain still held Texas as part of New Spain and saw the United States as a threat to Spanish control of this far province (Fox, Day, and Highly 1980).

Mexico gained independence from Spain in 1821, further confusing immigration procedures. All this flux notwithstanding, Wallisville was founded in 1824 at an important Trinity River crossing, and in 1830 a Mexican military post and customhouse were built at nearby Anahuac, which would become the main center of local commerce. Sawmills were the major early industry. Several flourished in the 1890s and early 1900s, the largest being Cunningham Mill and Shipyard, jointly employing some two hundred people. That mill and much of the town of Wallisville were devastated by the 1915 hurricane.

By the late 1950s Wallisville had only twenty-five homes, and in the 1960s the land was purchased by the U.S government for the construction of the Wallisville Dam by the U.S. Army Corps of Engineers (see chapter 5). Most of the buildings were moved. The first courthouse, built of wood, had been destroyed by fire, and its brick replacement commissioned in 1886 had been demolished in the 1940s, but sufficient records were available for its reconstruction through the efforts of the Chambers County Historical Commission and Wallisville Heritage Park Foundation. This and the nearby 1895 jail are central features of the heritage park.

ANAHUAC

Chambers County, with its county seat at Anahuac, feels worlds away from Houston. The names of the pioneer families who established dynasties there still hold sway—the Wallises, Winfrees, Barrows, Barbers, Jacksons, Dunmans, Lawrences, and Tiltons. "One reason behind this clannish atmosphere is a simple matter of geography," note Margaret Henson and Kevin Ladd in *Chambers County: A Pictorial History*. "No major highways pierced the county until 1955, when Highway 73 (now Interstate 10) connected Houston and Beaumont. The only railroads passed through the county's eastern and western borders. Thus the area depended on water transport to Galveston, and many areas of the county remained relatively isolated" (1988, 21). Before Interstate 10 opened, people either drove to Liberty to get to Houston or had to take six ferries to get across the Trinity River and its delta; it was farther but easier to cross the bay to Galveston (Evans 2000a).

Anahuac was named by the Mexican commander Manuel Mier y Teran in honor of the Aztecs' ancient capital city, and it was the site of the initial skirmishes in 1832 and 1835 that culminated in the Texas Revolution in 1836. Today Lake Anahuac has a prime site on the Great Texas Coastal Birding Trail, on the levee impounding Lake Anahuac, and people go out onto Trinity Bay in the *Smith Point* and the *Moss Bluff*, two renovated Coast Guard buoy tenders operated by the Chambers–Liberty County Navigation District. The boats take groups of up to thirty people—mainly teachers and students—into the marshes on environmental and historical trips (Evans 2000b). Chambers County has a considerable population of alligators, which play their part in keeping Anahuac from obscurity via the annual Gatorfest celebration in the town (see chapter 8).

ANAHUAC NATIONAL WILDLIFE REFUGE

Some eighteen miles south of the town of Anahuac lies the large
Anahuac National Wildlife Refuge, established in 1963. It covers more
than thirty thousand acres, most of it coastal marshland. It is not easy
to miss the alligators. The refuge was created to supply habitat for
wintering waterfowl on the Central Flyway as well as for other migratory bird species, from raptors to rails and shorebirds to songbirds. The
refuge bird list contains 279 species, including 28 kinds of geese and
ducks, and another 20 species considered "accidental" (USFWS
2000c). The Friends of Anahuac Refuge have established a butterfly
and hummingbird garden beside the gift shop and information station,
using native prairie host plants and nectar plants.

SMITH POINT

Driving into the oystering town of Smith Point feels like driving into
the 1950s—a forgotten little settlement at the end of the road. A
Cherokee princess named Sarah Ridge Pachal Pix lived here from 1850
until her death in 1891, and among her heirs are brothers Joe and Ben
Nelson, who operate oyster leases in the bay—relying on the bay for
their livelihoods, as their father and grandfather did. Ben Nelson has
been the largest oyster producer along the Texas coast for more than a
decade, and the Nelsons oversee more than nine hundred acres of
leases. They contend that fishermen are too often blamed for deplet-
ing fisheries, when industrial pollutants, pesticides, and fertilizers
flowing into the bays do far more harm (Evans 2000a).

Two Great Texas Coastal Birding Trail sites are at Smith Point,
which juts out at the southern end of Trinity Bay, and one of these sites
has gained fame as a location for annual counts of migrating hawks (see
chapter 8). Just north of Smith Point lie the Vingt-et-Un Islands, a favored haunt of roseate spoonbills. The renowned artist and ornitholo-
gist John James Audubon may have visited these islands during his
1837 sojourn in Texas. The birds came close to disappearing altogether
during the heyday of the plume trade around 1900. A 1920 survey team
found only 179 spoonbills along the upper Texas coastline.

"A rather remarkable recovery was evident by 1941 when another
survey team counted over 5,000 roseates. This report indicated that
the islands off Smith Point were one of five large active breeding sites

along the coast" (Henson and Ladd 1988, 265). Thus, it is fitting that accommodation at Smith Point is called the Spoonbill Lodge.

A Metaphor

During the far-off 1930s, the Dickinson Fuel and Ice House was a landmark meeting point at what is now the junction of Highway 146 and NASA Road 1, just north of the Kemah Bridge. Most people approaching the Kemah Boardwalk from Houston today pass the tiny triangular structure that is the successor to the ice house. It was a good spot for one of the few ice houses between Pasadena and Galveston: ideal for thirsty fishermen and for motorists trapped in a hot waiting line when the swing bridge opened for boats to pass through the Kemah channel. In the 1950s the place came to be called Doc's Ice House, and its next incarnation was as Curly's Corner, as it is still known by Seabrook old-timers ("Curly's Corner" 2002).

When Highway 146 was to be widened, Alan Thayer of Seabrook Construction Company reworked the modest building with whimsical additions of Mexican folk art. He added mission-style bells and lanterns, Talavera plates, a *santo* in a niche, decorative plants, beams, tile on the roof, and a small upper deck. It became a lawyer's office, then a tax office, and has since undergone another bout of remodeling and ornamentation.

Not quite a mile from Curly's, on the bayfront on Todville Road, is a house built almost completely out of recycled materials—recognizable by a small lighthouse-like tower. The wood flooring came from other homes; the air conditioner was a discarded unit; lumber from older boats was used; and the electrical wiring came from a demolished building ("Another Man's Treasure" 1997).

One might consider the recycled house and the reincarnation of Curly's Corner as metaphors for Galveston Bay's own transformation. They depict the shift from a sprinkling of fishing outposts and summer homes to being part of the busy outskirts of a booming metropolis, one structure a modern reflection of the era of Spanish rule and the other expressing the new surge of environmental concern. And around them, all the changes notwithstanding, much has stayed the same: pelicans and ospreys still come for the fish in the bay and bayous, geese and cranes come for the winter bounty of the surrounding coastal prairie, and people come to enjoy being by the bay.

CHAPTER 8

Events

*Make no mistake about it, the spring bird migration
on the upper Texas coast is unparalleled anywhere,
any time.*

Jim Stevenson, *Wildlife of Galveston*

Several communities make the most of their situation near Galveston
Bay by holding festivals and activities open to everyone. Most of the
selections that follow are established annual events. In addition, the
Texas Parks and Wildlife Department (1-800-792-1112) hosts seasonal
gatherings at several parks, and the Brazoria County Parks Department (979-233-6026, 979-233-1461, 979-864-1541) holds a series of
beach and bay activities each year. In 2002 these included Dunes Day;
spring and fall beach cleanups; Christmas Tidings on the Gulf at Quintana Beach; and Discover Nature's Wonders at San Luis Pass.

Inevitably, telephone numbers and Web sites change, and new options come into being. Newspapers distributed at bay area convenience stores advertise other current activities and guided trips. Fishing tournaments and sailing competitions are well publicized in
special-interest magazines. The natural events following the name of
each month are from the Galveston Bay Foundation's *1999 Calendar*
and serve as a reminder of the ongoing cycles on the bay that are not
publicized by chambers of commerce.

January

Blue crabs burrow in muddy substrate to escape the cold and predators.

The State of the Bay Symposium is a forum for formal public exchange of information about the bay and generally takes place in January of odd-numbered years. Chiefly intended for scientists and agency staff, it is nevertheless open to anyone interested, at a conference registration fee of around one hundred dollars. Papers presented have later been published as proceedings, which by now constitute a major information source. The sixth symposium was in 2003 on the theme "The Future of Galveston Bay: Local Communities Leading the Way." Information is available at http://gbep.tamug.edu.

February

Endangered Attwater's prairie-chickens begin "booming" (mating dance) on the Coastal Prairie Preserve near Dickinson Bay.

CLEAR CREEK CLEANUP

Since the launch of the Clear Creek Environmental Foundation (ccefsec@houston.rr.com; www.clearcreekcleanup.org) in 2000 by the energetic Rex Ward, hundreds of people have gathered annually on the third Saturday of February for a ferocious one-day cleanup along the creek upstream of Clear Lake. The volunteers have relieved the creek of thousands of junked tires, among other debris. They meet at Walter Hall Park in League City to be assigned to boats, and trucks haul off the trash they collect. In the afternoon, somewhat the worse for wear, everyone gathers back at the park for a celebratory barbecue.

MARDI GRAS, GALVESTON AND CRYSTAL BEACH

In addition to the widely known annual Mardi Gras madness in Galveston, including everything from wild street shenanigans to formal balls, a kind of little-sister Mardi Gras celebration takes place each year at Crystal Beach on the Bolivar Peninsula. This neighborly day-

From the bold facial markings of the lowest bird, it appears that Weis was observing longspurs.

time parade is suitable for those not attracted to the sometimes rowdy Galveston celebration. Visit www.lighthousekrewe.com for details.

March

Post-larval brown shrimp wash through the passes and into the shallow marshes of the Bay known as nursery grounds.

TRASH BASH

The rivers, lakes, and bayous cleanup called Trash Bash takes place at a dozen or so locations around the Galveston Bay watershed—for details, see www.trashbash.org. In return for the grubby work of cleanup, volunteers get a T-shirt and a community gathering with some exhibits and refreshments. The Seabrook location, for example, has been cosponsored by CK Productions, Watermark and Kayak Adventure Quest, the City of Seabrook, Seabrook Rotary Club, and Seabrook Sailing Club and usually includes a cadre of committed trash pickers from the science magnet program at Seabrook Intermediate School.

April

Larger concentrations of neotropical migratory songbirds reach the woodlots along the shore after their long flight across the Gulf of Mexico.

TEXAS ADOPT-A-BEACH SPRING CLEANUP

One Saturday in April each year, the Texas GLO and Keep Texas Beautiful coordinate beach cleanups at more than two dozen sites along the coast, literally from the Louisiana border to the Mexican border—from Sabine Pass to Boca Chica at the mouth of the Rio Grande. Six of the sites are on or near Galveston Bay: Bolivar Peninsula, Dickinson Bay and Bayou, John M. O'Quinn I-45 Estuarial Corridor in Galveston County, Galveston Island, and at Surfside and Quintana in Brazoria County.

The idea is to choose the beach you fancy, contact the local coordinator for details, and then round up some friends to come and help. For contact phone numbers or e-mail addresses and locations of the various check-in sites so that you can participate, call the Texas GLO Adopt-A-Beach program at 1-877-TXCOAST (1-877-892-6278) or visit www.glo.state.tx.us. A second beach cleanup day takes place up and down the coast in the fall, with thousands of volunteers again scouring the beaches (see September).

GREAT TEXAS BIRDING CLASSIC

Every spring teams of birders set out for a week-long birding tournament, to see how many kinds of birds they can spot. The Texas Parks and Wildlife Department launched the event in 1996 to focus interest on the Great Texas Coastal Birding Trail and, more generally, to promote an interest in birds and bird conservation (Koeppel 2003). It is a sporting event governed by the American Birding Association.

Forty-four teams of three to five people each competed in 2002, either over the whole week or in twenty-four-hour counts (called Big Days) on the three sections of the trail—the upper, central, and lower coast. Two-thirds of the participants were youth teams. Members of the winning team get the right to donate a purse of fifty thousand dollars to conservation projects of their choice. The five-day winning count for 2003 was 325 species, with 321 species for the team placing second (Banks 2003). For information about the Great Texas Birding Classic, call Texas Parks and Wildlife at 1-888-TX-BIRDS (1-888-892-4737) or visit www.tpwd.state.tx.us/gtbc.

During an unrelated Big Day in April 2001 during one of the sectional counts, a team led by Ron Weeks of Lake Jackson tallied 258 species; no other team of birders in any state had ever tallied so many species in a single day. South Texas and southern California had previously been the settings of the top Big Days because of their mix of resident and migratory birds during the springtime. The new 2001 record was set by including time in the Hill Country as well as along the central Texas coast. The team of experienced birders planned for months and scouted for weeks before starting their Big Day in the western Hill Country.

Once out searching, they soon got a surprise: a sheriff pulled them over at 3:00 A.M. "Unbeknownst to the upstanding citizens of the team, they were traveling on a back road frequented by less than lawful people. The sheriff was surely relieved and no doubt amused to find five grown men looking for birds in the dead of night," records Gary Clark (2001, 3) in a report about the excitements of that Big Day. No spotlights are allowed under the rules; nighttime birding is by ear.

FEATHERFEST

Galveston's new birding festival began in 2003 at the Hotel Galvez on the waterfront, coinciding with spring migration. It includes nature art and photography exhibits, demonstrations, seminars, children's events, and field trips. The 2004 FeatherFest was considerably larger, and the event looks likely to take place each year. In 2005 it moved to the Strand. For information, call 1-888-425-4753 or visit www .galvestonfeatherfest.com.

CRAWFISH FESTIVAL

Held at Clear Lake Park on NASA Road 1, this is a charity fund-raiser featuring a gumbo cook-off, crawfish-eating contest, crawfish races, and the five-kilometer walk known as the Crawfish Crawl. Call 281-488-7676.

SAN JACINTO DAY CELEBRATION

The anniversary of the Battle of San Jacinto, where Texas independence was won, is April 21. Late April sees a commemorative reenactment of the 1836 battle at the San Jacinto Battleground and Monument, a state historical park beside the Houston Ship Channel, with cannon and musket fire and a ceremony aboard the battleship *Texas*. Call 281-479-2431; no admission fee is charged.

OTHER APRIL EVENTS

Flags in the area fly at half-mast on April 16, the date of the Texas City fire in 1947. Texas City has held commemorative occasions of various kinds over the years. April is also the month of some local events not related to the bay but good for getting Houstonians out to enjoy the spring weather in surrounding towns—the Galveston County Fair and Rodeo at Santa Fe (409-986-6010); and Deer Park's Totally Texas Festival (281-478-2050), celebrating Texas independence.

May

Oyster transplanting season begins for leaseholders.

MARSH MANIA

Hundreds of Galveston Bay Foundation marsh restoration volunteers set out on May 1, 2004, for their sixth annual day of marsh grass planting. Appropriate sites are selected each year in an ambitious plan to restore thousands of acres of lost marshland habitat on the bay and bayous. Call 281-332-3381 to register, or visit http://www.galvbay.org for details.

Winter woods, 1940.

HISTORIC HOMES TOUR

Owners of some of the historic homes in Galveston open their doors to guests during the first and second weekends of May each year for tours hosted by the Galveston Historical Foundation (409-765-7834; www.galvestonhistory.org).

KEELS AND WHEELS

Lakewood Yacht Club in Seabrook hosts an annual gathering to showcase vintage wooden boats and yachts and classic and exotic cars (713-521-0105; www.keels-wheels.com). Admission is charged, and the show was in its tenth year in 2005.

BUFFALO BAYOU REGATTA

This has been an annual bayou celebration for more than thirty years. One component is a race for canoes and kayaks, with a category just for fun. Another weekend features the Anything-That-Floats Parade—what one might call art boats—on the downtown stretch of Buffalo

Bayou from the San Felipe bridge to the Sabine Street bridge, concluding with a celebration of the winners. In 2003 there was also a Dragon Boat Festival, with a Hong Kong–style dragon boat race on a 250-yard course, and Asian food and entertainment. For details, contact the Buffalo Bayou Partnership at 713-752-0314 or www.buffalobayou.org.

TEXAS CRAB FESTIVAL

Held at Crystal Beach on the Bolivar Peninsula, this was in its eighteenth year in 2003. It features a crab cook-off, crab race, and a crab-legs contest, plus music and a carnival. Call 409-684-5940.

EARTH DAY FESTIVAL

Exhibits by forty or more environmental groups, outdoor activities for children, and a rock concert take over Buffalo Bayou Eleanor Tinsley Park at this event, sponsored in 2003 by Green Mountain Energy and the radio station KRBE 104. Contact 713-524-4232 or www.houston-earthday.org for information.

June

Adult brown shrimp migrate out to the Gulf; post-larval white shrimp migrate into the Bay nursery grounds.

AMERICAN INSTITUTE OF ARCHITECTS SAND CASTLE COMPETITION

More than eighty teams hit Galveston's East Beach to challenge one another in architectural exotica during the annual sand castle design competition, in its twentieth year in 2005. The result is a half-mile stretch of astounding creations in sand. Call 713-520-0155 for details.

July

Speckled trout spawning reaches its peak in the calm shallows of East and West Bays.

FIREWORKS DISPLAYS

Fourth of July fireworks over the water are an obvious way to celebrate Independence Day. Annual fireworks displays are held over Clear Lake, over the bay at Shoreacres, and at Sylvan Beach in La Porte, among other places. These are some of the last great bargains any-where—free to everyone who can find a suitable spot to park and watch the show. Parks and restaurants on the Clear Lake shore and bay waterfront are prime watching points.

August

White pelicans begin to arrive and join the non-breeders that remained through the summer months to feed on the abundant supply of fish.

BLESSING OF THE FLEET

For more than thirty-five years, Kemah's annual parade of decorated shrimp boats along the Clear Creek channel has celebrated the local shrimp fleet with entertainment and food and crafts booths open all through the first weekend of August. There is usually a dance on Friday night, a land parade on Saturday, and the boat parade and for-mal Blessing of the Fleet on Sunday afternoon. A major sponsor is the Clear Lake (Kemah) Elks Lodge No. 2322. Admission is free. Call 281-334-9880.

September

Thousands of hawks and other migrating birds of prey ride cold fronts to Smith Point.

GATORFEST

The sleepy little town of Anahuac in Chambers County wakes up in September for a memorable party. Almost the whole place, with its population of about two thousand, is given over to the annual charity

fund-raiser called Gatorfest, which draws in more than ten times that
many people. Alligators outnumber people by a considerable margin
in Chambers County, as residents are proud to point out. In 1989, the
year of the first Gatorfest, Anahuac was named "Alligator Capital of
Texas" by the state legislature, and gators entered the limelight at the
spacious Fort Anahuac Park (see chapter 7 for more on local history).

The festival includes music from zydeco and gospel to blues and
country; street dances; food booths where the adventurous can sample
alligator meat; and the Great Texas Alligator Roundup. For a time, alligator numbers were down across the southern United States, and
hunting seasons were closed in 1972. But gators are prolific—they lay
lots of eggs. The population quickly regenerated. In the late 1980s
Texas reopened its alligator hunting season, and Gatorfest is timed to
coincide with the opening weekend. Hunters haul in trophy specimens to compete for cash prizes. Winning specimens have reached almost thirteen feet in length. When someone brings in a big gator, a
Klaxon sounds across the park to draw people to the block and tackle
where the trophy is weighed, measured, and admired.

For information, call the Anahuac Area Chamber of Commerce at
409-267-4190 or visit www.texasgatorfest.com.

BAY DAY

During the 1990s the Galveston Bay Foundation's annual Bay Day celebration at Sylvan Beach County Park in La Porte was a premier way
to find out about organizations, events, artists, and resource agencies
devoted to the bay. Usually held in June, it evolved into a two-day festival staged jointly by GBF and the Galveston Bay Estuary Program.
After two difficult years when bad weather compromised it, and following GBF reorganization, the event was switched to September for
2004, and plans are for it to be held each fall.

HAWKWATCH

One place to watch birds as fall comes on is from the thirty-foot
watchtower in the Candy Abshier Wildlife Management Area at Smith
Point in Chambers County—the point that juts farthest into the bay
from its unpopulated eastern shore, across from San Leon. "Many migrating birds are hesitant to cross water, and Smith Point acts like a
large funnel for those hesitant southbound travelers. It is famous for

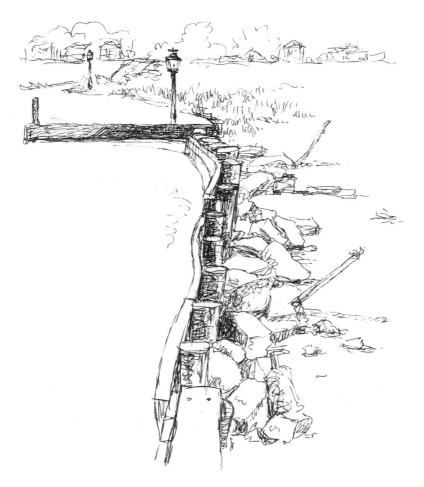

Bulkhead.

the spectacular numbers of hawks that migrate through, but large numbers of swallows also fly by from August to November, along with warblers, buntings, orioles, gnatcatchers and even frigate birds," reports the Houston Audubon Society (2001, 3). Hummingbird feeders may be surrounded by whirring hosts of hummingbirds, and there are also dragonflies and butterflies to be seen.

Hawk-watchers from Hawkwatch International staff the tower through mid-November, and visitors are welcome. Hawkwatch began in 1991, covering a more limited period, as a way to monitor trends in raptor populations. For more details, call the Gulf Coast Bird Observatory (979-480-0999). To get to the Candy Abshier Wildlife Management Area from Houston, take Interstate 10 east to the Hankamer exit (Route 61), turn right onto 61, follow it to Route 562, and then take 562 to Smith Point. The tower is on the left just before the end of 562.

ADOPT-A-BEACH FALL CLEANUP

According to Adopt-A-Beach literature, by 1994 some 140,000 volunteers had picked up more than twenty-eight hundred tons of garbage since the cleanups began in 1987; they are now held twice a year, in April and September (see April for contact detail). Pickers are invited to turn in data cards reflecting what they have collected, and from this a listing of the "Dirty Dozen"—the twelve most common debris items— is compiled. Eight of the twelve items in the 1993 compilation were plastic: plastic pieces, container lids and caps, food bags, rope, foam plastic, bottles, straws, and other miscellaneous items. The largest two categories that year were "plastic pieces," almost forty thousand, and plastic caps and lids, just over twenty-eight thousand items.

Overall, by far the greatest share of beach trash picked up in 1993 was plastic—just short of 70 percent. No other category of items tallied more than 10 percent. Metal objects amounted to 9.8 percent; glass, 8.9 percent; paper, 6.5 percent; and wood, rubber, and cloth items, about 2 percent or less each (Texas GLO 1994).

In addition to calling attention to the problem of marine debris along the Texas coast, data collected during the cleanups showed that more than half of the trash ending up on Texas beaches is dumped from ships. This information was instrumental in convincing the U.S. Senate to join other nations of the International Maritime Organization in ratifying the treaty that prohibits dumping of plastics anywhere in the world's oceans.

October

Arrival of geese and other migratory waterfowl intensifies.

INTERNATIONAL IN-THE-WATER BOAT SHOW

This is a major annual event for the boating trade on Galveston Bay. Powerboats and sailboats are gathered both in and out of the water at Watergate Marina in Clear Lake Shores. Booths showcase nautical products and services. Call 713-526-6361; admission is charged.

Pier.

ANAHUAC SMALL-CRAFT FESTIVAL

All about boats, this event is held at Anahuac on the fourth Saturday of October as part of the Scow Schooner Project. The objective is to create a Galveston and Trinity bays marine museum and education center. The festival opens with a seafood dinner, with a silent auction and entertainment. Activities the next day include boat rides, rent-a-rowboat, boat building for kids, and a boat junkyard sale. The organization is building a full-scale replica of an 1890s Galveston Bay cargo schooner. By late 2004 the hull was complete, and the schooner's tender, a replica skiff, had been built and launched. Call 409-267-4402 or visit www.scowschooner.org to check on upcoming events.

November

Mullet begin to congregate at the passes and begin their annual spawning activities.

MARTYN FARM FESTIVAL

An annual showcase of turn-of-the-century lifestyles on the coastal prairie takes place around the Martyn farmhouse at Armand Bayou Nature Center, featuring crafts, demonstrations, food, wagon rides, and pie-eating contests. Call the nature center at 281-474-2551.

December

Growth rate of fish and invertebrates slows with the cooling temperature as winter begins.

DICKENS ON THE STRAND

This wonderful Victorian Christmas festival in the historic district of Galveston is a spectacular holiday event that celebrated its thirtieth anniversary in 2003. Over the years it has grown from a small gathering of Galveston Historical Foundation members into an event of worldwide renown, acknowledged in travel guides and attracting winter cruise ships. For details, call 409-765-7834 or check www.dickensonthe strand.org. It is held on the first full weekend in December.

Every effort is made to cultivate a setting that evokes the era of Charles Dickens, from food and vendors to street entertainers and acts on stage. Vendors are required to wear Victorian garb, and festival-goers are also encouraged to do so: a costume gains one free admission. There are no hamburgers—but there are roasted chestnuts. The several processions contain no motorized vehicles; horses, coaches, unicycles, and penny-farthings convey participants who are not on foot. London bobbies and red-uniformed Beefeaters are on patrol among handbell choirs, jugglers, and sword swallowers, all contributing to the magic. Seagull cries yield to the haunting wail of bagpipes, from well-drilled and championship-winning high school pipe bands to casual musical adventurers like the Scottish Rogues, who duck for a watering hole between sets. In short, the Galveston townscape is transformed.

Live entertainment includes plays and musicals, concerts, and balls. Offerings differ from year to year but have included a snowy playground; the Budweiser Clydesdales; a costume contest; elephant rides; and showing of llamas and alpacas and the beautiful clothes, fabrics, and knitted goods made from their soft wool. Civil War reenactors sometimes join the festivities, Santa Claus may put in an appearance, and there have been book-signing events featuring Charles Dickens's grandson Mark Dickens.

Many of Galveston's historic houses are employed for what they do best—host public events—during Dickens on the Strand. Offerings in 2002 included evening functions for every budget, from the Dickens Holiday Ball in the elegant ballroom at Ashton Villa to the Christmas by Candlelight evening at the home of Stephen F. Austin's secretary, Samuel May Williams.

This is a time to be glad that the combined effects of the Great Storm of 1900 and the oil strikes near Houston slowed Galveston's economic engine to idling speed, with the result that the city never replaced its graceful Victorian downtown buildings. They still stood, eighteen-foot ceilings and ornamentation intact, when townspeople hit upon the inspired idea of a wintertime tourist event taking advantage of this architectural heritage.

CHRISTMAS BOAT PARADE

The splendidly festive lighted boat parade is a treasured Christmas tradition on Clear Lake—in its forty-fifth year in 2005. Usually held the second weekend in December, it ushers in the Christmas season with a beautiful show for onlookers and is a lot of fun for participants.

There were just five entries in the first parade. Today there are routinely more than a hundred boats entered, ranging from tiny canoes to hundred-footers, and they compete for awards in several categories: sail, power, sponsored sail, sponsored power, and human-powered. Some boat owners develop creative new designs each year, coordinating their light decorations with music. Others focus on quiet elegance or topical or Christmas themes.

The boats assemble at a marina on Clear Lake, and the parade begins about 6:00 P.M., the first boats reaching the judges at the Clear Creek channel into the bay by about 7:00. Awards are presented by category and for the most artistic, most original, and most beautiful boats, plus an overall winner. For more information, call the Clear Lake Chamber of Commerce at 281-488-7676 or 281-844 LAKE.

CHRISTMAS BIRD COUNTS

The first Armand Bayou Christmas Bird Count was on December 22, 1982, part of the great national network of bird population monitoring begun in 1899 and coordinated by the National Audubon Society. Everyone is welcome to participate and learn. Contact Armand Bayou (281-474-2551) or the Houston Audubon Society (713-932-1639; www.houstonaudubon.org) for details about local count circles, or find one near you through www.audubon.org/bird/cbc/.

Christmas Bird Counts take place all over the nation, but I hope I have made it clear that the birdlife on and near Galveston Bay far out-strips that of most other places. We can borrow winter holiday rituals from elsewhere—door-to-door caroling, or draping trees with cranber-ries and popcorn for wildlife—and we can add our own. Dickens on the Strand and the Christmas Boat Parade are special holiday season highlights unique to the communities around Galveston Bay.

CHAPTER 9

Hopes and Fears

*The trouble is that once you see it, you can't unsee it.
And once you've seen it, keeping quiet, saying nothing,
becomes as political an act as speaking out.*

Arundhati Roy, *Power Politics*

This portrait of Galveston Bay is a catalog of ambiguities. Although parts of the bay are subject to the taming and damaging forces of urbanization, industry, and commerce, much of it remains wild and beautiful. Although it suffers immense legally permitted contamination every day of the year, it continues to serve as a major nursery for aquatic life and to produce large volumes of fish and shellfish. Boaters, fishermen, and birders know and love the bay, but millions more people who live nearby simply ignore it. Solutions to its problems are possible but hardly straightforward.

Suggestions of places to go and things to do in the preceding chapters showcase the range of recreational opportunities on the bay. There is much more to tell than space allows about the conservation achievements of the birding fraternity and about innovations such as creating productive artificial reefs with old oil platforms. The historical and political discussion indicates increased scientific understanding of bay dynamics and growing public pressure for more thoughtful approaches to conserving bay resources. And yet right alongside these positive developments, unknowns remain and threats intensify.

Is the Seafood Safe?

The short answer to the question of whether fish and shellfish from Galveston Bay are safe to eat is yes, mostly. Because of their short lives and migratory habits, shrimp are among the safest. Oysters are monitored more closely than other seafood species, and commercial oyster harvesting is prohibited in areas where they may be unsafe. As oysterman Joe Nelson has said: "The state can't control floods, they can't control drought, can't control predators, can't control parasites, but they can control fishermen" (in Racine 1999, 14).

The Texas Department of Health (2001; hereafter cited as TDH) says that fish and crabs from areas of the bay where most recreational fishing occurs are "safe for unlimited consumption." TDH advises that women of childbearing age and children should avoid eating any fish or crabs from the lower San Jacinto River, the upper Houston Ship Channel, or the upper western lobe of the bay where the ship channel lies, and that no one should eat more than a single eight-ounce serving per month of seafood from those places.

The long answer is more complicated. Thousands of people eat Galveston Bay seafood regularly with no sign of trouble. Yet there are no guarantees. Beyond the areas covered by advisories and oyster closures, there can be no definitive statement of safety because there is no comprehensive monitoring of seafood safety on the bay.

As Robert McFarlane and Frank Shipley note in their preface to the *State of the Bay* (2002, xii), serious questions remain unanswered. "The Texas Department of Health has been hampered for years by inadequate funding to determine the accumulation of toxic substances by seafood organisms. Although the public identified this issue as a priority problem, high analytical costs have placed constraints on this type of work. A full-scale detailed survey . . . would have consumed the entire Galveston Bay National Estuary Program scientific budget."

Based on the results of the more limited sampling and surveys that have been feasible, regulations prevent harvest and sale of oysters and crabs from areas known to have toxicity problems or to have high bacteria counts, and warnings are issued when special conditions apply, such as when floodwaters raise fecal coliform bacteria counts in the bay.

In the Chesapeake Bay the breeding stock of the Atlantic blue crab, Callinectes sapidus, *has crashed since 1990. Captive-bred young are now being released.*

For recreational anglers, details of the warnings and restrictions are available from the Seafood Safety Division of the TDH (call 512-719-0215 or 1-800-685-0361, or visit its Web site at www.tdh.state.tx.us/bfds/ssd/). Since 1990 an advisory against eating blue crabs and all species of catfish has been in effect for upper Galveston Bay and the Houston Ship Channel from the Lynchburg ferry down to a line from Red Bluff Point across the bay to the Five Mile Cut marker (at the south end of Atkinson Island) and Houston Point (south of Cedar Bayou in Chambers County). Since 2001 an advisory has covered the San Jacinto River below the Highway 90 bridge, also for crabs and catfish.

The main toxic compounds of concern in the channel and upper bay are dioxins and polychlorinated biphenyls (PCBs)—highly toxic byproducts of chemical manufacturing—and organochlorine pesticides. Sediments in the ship channel and in dredge spoil disposal areas show reduced diversity of sediment-dwelling organisms and high levels of some heavy metals and polycyclic aromatic hydrocarbons (PAHs), which are toxic organic compounds derived from fossil fuels and their combustion. These substances can accumulate in living organisms. Crabs, oysters, fish, and fish-eating birds sampled at these sites (and various other sites in the bay system) have shown contamination with metals, PAHs, PCBs, and dioxins (GBF, "Galveston Bay Sediments," n.d.).

Offshore, a 1997 Department of Health advisory suggests not eating any king mackerel larger than forty-three inches in length taken along the Texas Gulf shore, including Galveston and Chambers counties. The contaminant in this case is mercury. Meals of king mackerel thirty-seven to forty-three inches long should be restricted to one per week. King mackerel smaller than thirty-seven inches are considered safe for unlimited consumption (TDH 2001).

Oysters are fixed in place and therefore more subject to bioaccumulation than many other seafood species. The monitoring of oysters and oyster waters has equipped us with better information about them than about most other denizens of the bay. Waters known for problems with fecal coliform bacteria and industrial contaminants are closed to commercial oyster harvest. Other areas have restrictions whereby oysters may not be harvested for market, but at certain seasons they may be transplanted to commercial leases, where within weeks they purge themselves of contaminants and may be harvested for sale. Again, details are available from the Department of Health at the Web address already given and from the Texas Parks and Wildlife Department at www.tpwd.state.tx.us.

Even so, there are surprises. No one had any idea there was reason for particular unease about the gastrointestinal infection from *Vibrio parahaemolyticus* until Galveston Bay oysters suddenly caused quite an extensive outbreak in 1998. In June and early July, 416 people in thirteen states reported cases of gastroenteritis after they had eaten raw oysters taken from the bay. "At the time, oyster beds met bacteriological standards and fecal coliform levels were within acceptable regulatory limits. This suggests that current policies regarding water quality testing associated with oyster harvests may need to be reevaluated" (*State of the Bay* 2002, 116).

Contemplating an oyster on your plate, you are essentially on your own. Tagging and reporting systems in place mean that its source can be traced if a diner falls ill, but at the time of dining, it is next to impossible to know where that oyster was dredged. Restaurant staff may not know or may hedge to allay patrons' concerns about local seafood—"We're getting great Louisiana oysters this week." Whether a given Louisiana oyster has suffered less of a buildup of toxic substances than your average Texas oyster is a moot point, of course. The likelihood, however, is that oysters in a restaurant near Galveston Bay are probably not far from home.

In the absence of more comprehensive testing, we cannot know

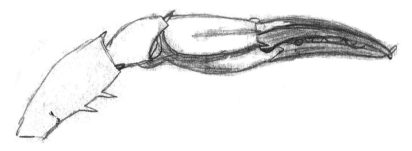

Crab claw.

much more. "Science cannot currently determine the true risk to bay users or seafood consumers resulting from contamination by bacteria, viruses, or toxic materials. Risk varies among different segments of the population. Some risk estimates are available as guidelines, but decisions about tolerable risk are a matter for the individual" (*State of the Bay* 2002, 127).

I submit that risk cuts both ways. The oysters do not create the buildup of fecal coliform bacteria—this derives from our own wastes. Crabs and catfish do not create the toxic substances that accumulate in their tissues—we produce those toxins with our industry. We blame the seafood and think of it as risky, but much of the risk in seafood comes from contamination that *we ourselves create.* Possibly we should be asking not whether the seafood is safe to eat but whether it is safe from our own dangerous actions.

As noted in chapter 2, crab, shrimp, and oysters all have special salinity requirements during different life stages, and much the same is true for many finfish species. Increasing salinity in the bay with ever-deeper channels can create significant problems. The primary oyster disease in Galveston Bay is a parasite called dermo (*Perkinsus marinus*), known to flourish during periods of high salinity. Its most pronounced effects are on the larger oysters, and it can kill up to half of all the oysters in the bay each year. Oyster researchers, including the renowned Sammy Ray, started the DermoWatch monitoring program (see http://www.dermowatch.org) to try to curb losses. This disease has crippled the Chesapeake Bay oyster fishery.

The conch drill (*Thais haemastoma*), which is our main oyster predator, also favors water of relatively high salinity. Thus, if the water stays too salty for too long, oysters face a major struggle on two fronts. And if enough oysters are not filtering the bay waters, turbidity increases, which in turn slows the sea grass growth that supports so much other life, and the negative effects multiply.

These complex dynamics are among the reasons why conservationists resisted further deepening of the Houston Ship Channel and resisted the reduction of freshwater inflows in the Wallisville fight. Obviously, everything we can do to promote the ecological health of the bay also helps to produce safer seafood—and to keep the marine organisms safe from us.

The Shot Glass

The notion of compromise, applied in both the ship channel and Wallisville cases, enjoys a reputation as a civilized way to go about problem solving and decision making. In theory, everybody wins. But it also carries risks. A difficulty with compromise is that it often constitutes the thin end of the wedge. The end point of compromise one tends to be the starting point of compromise two, and so on. In a short piece tellingly titled "Compromise and Deceit," outdoor writer John Swinton cites the analogy of halving a quart jar of water until one is left with only a shot glass. Although a variable quantity in our imperfect world, a shot is supposed to be a single fluid ounce. Even the most generous of shots is a sorry contrast to the thirty-two fluid ounces it takes to fill a quart jar (Swinton 2003, 21).

Compromise works reasonably well for traffic in intangible forces like love or hope. Having a second child does not mean that the amount of love previously showered upon the first must now be divided between them; more love comes into play. Similarly, the hope of one person can expand if it becomes the hope of many and the impulse to action. Natural resources, however, are finite. They do not increase with the number of subscribers. Division applies. The plants and animals and working chemistry that make up an ecosystem can often adapt to changing conditions sufficiently well for us to lose sight of the extent of changes until a crisis pulls us up short.

Creatures reliant on submerged aquatic vegetation decline when sunlight cannot penetrate Galveston Bay and the sea grass meadows are halved. It does not matter whether the turbid conditions killing sea grass meadows result from channel maintenance or from a nutrient overload that turns the water cloudy with algal blooms. Whether turbidity derives from compromise on dredging or from compromise on

Cattle and a pair of horses still occupy the Harris Ranch in 2004.

wastewater treatment, the fact is that the meadows can be destroyed by compromise.

Small life-forms dependent on a certain amount of dissolved oxygen in the water may get by for a time at reduced oxygen levels, but they cannot survive if the dissolved oxygen keeps being halved. Some may be able to move away, but the time comes when they have nowhere else to go. The quart jar becomes a shot glass. At some point compromise represents only a light brake on an accelerating downhill run—an essentially useless procedure. Worse than that, compromise can produce the illusion of making a difference.

A transporting moment for me was the day I realized I was watching an osprey less than half a mile from my home. Its gleaming white undercarriage was the predominant view as the bird landed on top of a utility pole, bearing a good-sized fish in its talons. By the time I had done a U-turn and pulled off the road beside the pole, the osprey was ripping and eating the fish. When it lowered its head for the next chunk, I could clearly see the diagnostic dark Cleopatra eye stripe. Knowing that osprey populations had taken a serious hit in the worst days of pesticide pollution, I was thrilled to see one, and it provided my own point of engagement with the large phenomenon of migration.

For three or four years I saw ospreys only during the weeks of spring and fall migration. Later I began to see them all through the winter months, and then in May and occasionally even June. I learned what their call sounds like, and it has sometimes drawn me outside to see one from my own front yard. As far as I know, they do not breed on the Galveston Bay shore, and individuals present in summer are probably young birds, not yet of breeding age. To me, every one of these elegant fish-eating hawks is a thrill.

Watching migrating birds also carries tension. The long-distance champions, such as some terns and sandpipers, may have come all the way from the high arctic and may be headed to the far limits of South America, with hazards at every point. Banding records show some individuals turning up in exactly the same places year after year—what are they to do if "their" stretch of beach or sandbar or prairie or marsh suddenly becomes a subdivsion, parking lot, or bulkheaded straight edge? Is a substitute available? Will the birds find it? Will the hiccup compromise the menu or the delicate timing of the great journey?

It pays to keep an eye peeled for surprises. In the bayous one may see the large alligator and longnose garfish that have occupied these waters for millions of years, equipped to survive in conditions of low oxygen by gulping air. Far out beyond the youngsters tossing skimboards into inch-deep water at the El Jardin bayfront, dolphins may be moving by in the bay. One spring afternoon in 2004 I was astonished to see a clapper rail—a secretive and rarely seen marsh bird—ducking behind riprap right on the Galveston beach near the Flagship Hotel, scarcely twenty feet from a boisterous party of kids and dogs. In the early 1990s I heard from friends living beside Offat's Bayou in Galveston that they had sometimes seen otters in the marsh grasses.

I was not sure whether to believe them. Most of the time, seeing an otter means seeing a head breaking the water surface into a wake. Had they really seen otters? The question was answered when a 1994 issue of the Galveston Bay Foundation newsletter *Soundings* led with a report of river otters photographed in the Galveston Ship Channel near the Pelican Island bridge: two adults and two youngsters (Fertl, Jackson, and Yin 1994). The observers reported seeing four otters in the same area two weeks later, and once they began to talk about their sightings, they learned that others had seen otters at Offat's Bayou, at the west end of Galveston Island, and on the Bolivar Peninsula.

They reported that the river otter population along the coast was apparently restricted to the area from Galveston County northeast to the Sabine River on the Louisiana border. I once watched a film showing that in the ocean, sea otters eat the urchins that eat the kelp. Remove the otters, and the urchins proliferate to such a degree that they can mow down kelp "forests" like a line of combine harvesters mow-ing a field of grain, radically altering the habitat. One wonders what role river otters might play in coastal bayous. Might otters reestablish themselves, like the brown pelicans that have been making a steady comeback as a breeding species on Galveston Bay?

I have to remind myself from time to time about the ospreys and pelicans and otters, because the opposing view is hard to shake off. Here is my worst fear: it may be that no matter how hard we work to publicize bay conservation issues, curb nonpoint-source pollution, oppose harmful development, and restore lost marshland habitats, things will nevertheless grow worse for Galveston Bay because of the pressures of increasing human population.

Between April 2000 and July 2001 Harris County's population grew by more than 60,000 people, to 3,460,589 (Lezon 2002). A continuing boom of this kind results in habitat losses and worsening nonpoint-source pollution—in compromises. Water-quality improvements and wildlife comebacks notwithstanding, on balance the history of every single estuary along the United States coast basically tells this story of gradual decline. Is there any reason to suppose we can make things go differently on Galveston Bay?

One prefers to end a book on a positive note. Ten years ago I might have done so with conviction, watching the buildup of research and restoration activities all around Galveston Bay after it became part of the National Estuary Program.

Today I am uncertain. I have participated in organizations working to exert public pressure on politicians and resource agencies, and I have cheered as some elected officials realized that the pressure was coming from the voters who elected them. But I have also watched politicians stand silent while government agencies propose or support projects that are clearly going to be damaging to the bay. Politicians are strongly aware of their sources of campaign contributions, and the corporate and industrial power brokers promoting some of those projects are often the largest political contributors.

I have seen resource agencies respond weakly in opposing poorly conceived development—until they see a groundswell of public opinion and recognize that their response is not just going to be filed away and disappear forever. It may actually wind up in the newspapers, find a supportive constituency, and make a difference, as it is intended to do. But like the matter of retaining office for elected officials, the outcome depends heavily on how loudly the stakeholders are shouting. Sometimes even when they find plenty of public support for their position, agencies back off under political pressure. Resource agency personnel like to bewail the sad circumstance of politics interfering with management of natural resources, as if this were avoidable. It is not avoidable. We are all in this for the same set of resources. All politics is ultimately about resources.

And I have seen that despite long effort and promising signs on the Chesapeake Bay, all is far from well there. Oysters were close to commercial extinction by 1993, with numbers around 1 percent of their historic levels. An adult oyster can filter up to sixty gallons of water a day, and there was a time when the oysters could filter all the water in the bay in three or four days. Today it would take the tiny remaining numbers of oysters in that bay a year to filter all its water.

"Wetlands Losses Continue," reads the front-page headline of a 1995 edition of the Chesapeake Bay Foundation's monthly newsletter *Save the Bay*. The article examines two widely held myths: that wetlands can no longer be destroyed—their destruction has been halted by state and federal permitting requirements; and that permit restrictions are so extreme as to cause many applicants to withdraw in frustration. A foundation study debunked both beliefs. The study revealed that far from progressing toward the goal of gaining two hundred thousand wetland acres by 2010, permit programs are not stopping wetlands losses and some mitigation projects fail to function properly. It showed instances of permit withdrawal due to exasperation with red tape to be extremely rare; projects died for reasons having nothing to do with the permitting process (Chesapeake Bay Foundation 1995).

Next I read that almost a third of the underwater grasses in the Chesapeake died during 2003, unable to survive as pollution blotted out their sunlight (Fahrenthold 2003). The immediate trigger was heavy rainfall that loaded rivers with nitrogen and phosphorus, which in turn provoked dense clouding of the bay with algal blooms. The underwater forest received too little light to grow. And then I learned that blue crab breeding stocks in the Chesapeake Bay have plunged 85 percent since 1990 (Parker 2003). The seafood industry, State of Maryland, and watermen are now sponsoring an experimental captive-breeding program to release young blue crabs into the bay.

Here is my second-worst fear: many resource management agency personnel and conservationists unwittingly perpetuate the myth or illusion that there is progress, restoration is being conducted, and everything is going to turn out okay—that we are following the formula laid out in the Galveston Bay Plan to fix things. We want to believe this, and we get some confirmation in positive results like the return of seabirds to reconstructed islands or marshes; indeed, I accept that without the efforts of these agencies and conservation groups, the birds and the fish would all be worse off than they are.

The formula for a healthy bay exists. It is the political will to insist on it that needs work. We do not want to read or think about things growing worse, let alone try to find the time and energy for remaking our political fabric in green and rearranging our lives to abandon pesticides and bulkheading. But to the extent that we allow ourselves to compromise about intrusions on bay resources and pat ourselves on the back for accomplishments rather than emphasize *and challenge* the continuing losses, we overlook the halving of the quart jar down to the shot glass. And we risk doing real environmental integrity a serious disservice.

My suggestion is to keep an eye peeled for ospreys and otters as reminders of the value of vigilance and activism. The tiny lives of vanishingly small plants and animals drifting in the bay's warm shallows are the key to all its riches, but they are not immediately absorbing. The satisfaction of progress in the right direction is much easier to sense in the passage of dolphins or the image of a brown pelican diving or an osprey winging over with a squirming fish—exclamation points that tell us why we should do no harm.

For years I have nursed the quiet hope of seeing sleek river otters gamboling in Pine Gully, the bayou where I live, halfway up the western shore of the bay. Early in 2004 local naturalists John and Gloria Tveten advised me that the chances of this were improving. Otters were being seen with some frequency much farther up the waterway at the Baytown Nature Center, practically in the shadow of the ship channel industries. I am not holding my breath, but I am hoping.

RESOURCES

The resources selected here are presented in alphabetical sequence by organization and topic, with contact details. All the hotlines are grouped together. Numerous additional conservation organizations are listed in a directory published by Citizens' Environmental Coalition (see listing). The two sources most useful for exploring on one's own were both developed by state agencies: the Great Texas Coastal Birding Trail and the *Beach and Bay Access Guide* (see listings).

All about Wetlands and Wildlife

Some excellent Web sites are devoted to the wildlife and natural history of southeast Texas. One of the best is http://texasnaturalist.net/, offering numerous links and including background articles spanning ten years. Emphasis is on birding, but there is also information on everything from amphibians and butterflies to wildlife rehabilitators.

A site devoted to wetlands along the upper coast, including parks and beaches, is http://www.texaswetlands.org/uppercoast.htm. Driving directions are given for each location, and links provide additional detail.

Bayou Preservation Association (BPA)

P.O. Box 131563
Houston, TX 77219-1563
713-529-6443
Fax: 713-529-6481
bpa@bayoupreservation.org
www.bayoupreservation.org

The BPA monitors local bayous and fights for them as needed. It has a stated mission: "To protect and restore the richness and diversity of our waterways through activism, advocacy, collaboration and education." Founded in 1966 as the Buffalo Bayou Preservation Association to prevent channelization of that waterway by the U.S. Army Corps of Engineers, the group later widened its scope and dropped the "Buffalo" from its name. Constituent bodies today are bayou associations for Armand, Brays, Buffalo, and Carpenter bayous; Clear Creek and Cypress Creek; and Dickinson, Greens, Halls, Sims, and White Oak bayous. BPA publishes a quarterly newsletter called *Bayou Forum* and conducts public outreach on bayou issues through seminars and workshops supported by the Jake and Terry Hershey Foundation.

The BPA recognized that wrangling with the Harris County Flood Control District and Corps of Engineers over channelization of bayous for flood "control" was largely a dead-end road: those agencies are merely responding to citizen pressure for flood control in the face of ever-greater floods deriving from increasing urban development. BPA directors realized they had to change their tack and go to the city planners, developers, and landowners (Shanley 1998). Hence a mid-1990s offshoot of the Bayou Preservation Association is the Bayou Lands Conservancy, dedicated to protecting riparian lands through conservation easements and preventing development of flood-prone property where green space and urban wildlife habitat are more appropriate. Landowners transfer various development rights to the BPA, establishing safeguards against uses that could damage the scenic, ecological, or natural resource values of the property.

BPA has been a major participant in the Buffalo Bayou Partnership, a multidisciplinary team developing a master plan for the bayou, including conservation areas and interpretive guidance along thirty miles of waterway from Barker's Reservoir in West Houston to the San Jacinto Battleground State Historical Park on the ship channel. BPA has had a hand in redeveloping Allen's Landing downtown, tree planting in selected locations, promoting of no-mow zones and use of native plants, and helping fight a proposal to channelize Clear Creek.

Beach and Bay Access Guide

Where to get to the shore, the beaches, and out onto the bay is the subject of the *Texas Beach and Bay Access Guide* published by the Texas GLO (2002). It can be ordered from the Texas Coastal Management Program, P.O. Box 12873, Austin, TX 78711-2873; 1-800-998-4GLO or 512-475-3401; www.glo.state .tx.us.

The book covers the whole Texas coast with maps showing boat ramps and other access points on the bays and adjacent lakes and rivers. Listings indicate facilities available and contact details. Similar listings are also included for national wildlife refuges, wildlife management areas, and chambers of commerce and visitor centers, again with contact information, including Web sites. For each county there is a general locational map, and then more detailed maps at a larger scale showing how to get to the various points.

There are eleven access points around Trinity Bay in Chambers County, eight of them with boat ramps. Some consist of little more than a boat ramp.

Others offer a bait camp, picnicking, camping, or birding opportunities. Galveston County has eighty-one such access points listed, about half on Galveston Island and the Bolivar Peninsula. Some are also sites on the Great Texas Coastal Birding Trail. Four are on the south side of Clear Creek and Clear Lake, and several more are dotted along the western shore of Galveston Bay and its tributary bayous. Harris County offers another twenty-six access points, twelve with boat ramps.

Beneficial Uses Group (BUG)

Galveston Bay has lost some 30,000 acres of marsh since 1950. As a result of citizen pressure to avoid endless additional damage to Texas bays through dumping of dredge spoil from ship channel maintenance, deepening, and widening, the BUG was born. A coalition of government agencies, including the Environmental Protection Agency and Texas Parks and Wildlife Department, the BUG determines how best to use the spoil for establishing and restoring marshes and bird islands to compensate for losses to subsidence, erosion, and coastal development. The BUG is creating a 6-acre bird island, more than 100 acres of oyster reefs, and some 4,250 acres of intertidal marsh, about a third of this at Atkinson Island, where the upper Houston Ship Channel enters the bay (TPWD 2000).

Restoration of productive fish and bird nursery areas is neither straightforward nor inexpensive. Habitat managers are still learning how to plant a marsh for maximum success in mimicking a natural marsh. Preliminary efforts have revealed that although the human-made marshes quickly develop plant biomass much like that of natural marshes, they do not approach the productivity levels of the original habitats. A study of ten created salt marshes found densities of shrimp and crabs only 25 to 40 percent as high as in natural marshes, and fish densities were also lower by up to 30 percent. One conclusion was that more edge is needed, and creation of channels to increase the amount of edge within constructed marshes is a strategy being pursued; channels may help animals move in and out with the tide (Minello 1997).

Boating and Sailing

Monthly publications for boaters include the newspaper *Mariner's Log* (distributed free at many restaurants in the Clear Lake area; 281-488-1108) and the subscription magazine *Telltales* published in Kemah (281-334-2202; waterfrontpublishing@earthlink.net).

Offering multiple links and a wealth of information is the Galveston Bay Information Site Project at http://members.aol.com/USWebNews/. Weather forecasts and warnings, wind speeds, and tidal predictions can be found here. For charts and other boating information, there are links to the sites of the ports of Houston and Galveston, the Houston pilots' Web page, and chart publishers. The site also features extensive listings of events and attractions on the bay.

Links to the sites of a series of marinas, sailing clubs, and boating stores can be found at http://www.kemah.net/areamarinas.html, maintained by the City of Kemah. Links are also given for several fishing charter organizations and for the U.S. Coast Guard and Galveston Bay Power Squadron, for boat safety courses. Some two dozen boating organizations are listed, with contact information, at www.kemah.net/Orgs.html. A third useful site is Sailing Gulf Waters (http://gulfwaters.com/HTML/links.html), which features links to numerous sailing clubs, magazines, and boat builders and chandleries.

The Galveston Bay Cruising Association based at Seabrook Shipyard (281-291-0360; gbca@gbca.org; http://gbca.org/) offers information about sailing in the Houston-Galveston area and the Gulf of Mexico, including race schedules, and it organizes ocean races each year.

Books

Books celebrating the bay and offering ways to get to know it are not numerous. A few stand out among those cited in the references. Journalist Gary Cartwright's *Galveston: A History of the Island* is a spirited account of Galveston's heyday, giving background about places visitors can easily see. Naturalist John C. Dyes's *Nesting Birds of the Coastal Islands: A Naturalist's Year on Galveston Bay* profiles the extravagant riches of bird islands few of us have seen.

Aerial photos of the Galveston Bay system in *Above and Beyond* by Rob Parrish and Chris Kuhlman help make sense of the landscape. The book can be ordered from Chris Kuhlman at Above and Beyond Publishing, CK Productions, 1002 Todville Rd., Seabrook, TX 77586; 281-474-2333; clk@ckpro.com; www.ckpro.com.

Photographer Richard Bricker's *Pearls on Galveston Bay* has a close focus on the oyster luggers of Smith Point—craft that are a Galveston Bay speciality but that may soon recede into history as working boats. Contact him at 1020 Shoreacres Blvd., La Porte, TX 77571, or call 281-471-2683 to order a copy. For broader focus, environmental lawyer Jim Blackburn's handsomely illustrated *Book of Texas Bays* reaches far beyond Galveston Bay to examine all the bays along the Texas coast, detailing the difficult politics surrounding conservation of each. The July 2003 special issue of *Texas Parks and Wildlife* magazine on the theme "The State of Bays" likewise covers all the estuaries along the coast.

A book devoted entirely to the natural treasures of Galveston Bay is Jim Stevenson's *Wildlife of Galveston*. To order it, contact him at Rt. 1, Box 1856, Galveston, TX 77554; 409-737-4081. Trained as a biologist, Stevenson is a birding guide, an environmental consultant, and the publisher of the quarterly newspaper *Galveston Bay Gull*. His book is strong on birding destinations and does an especially fine job of introducing readers to some underexposed occupants of the bay—sponges, jellyfish, urchins, starfish, and other small animals in the large world of marine invertebrates.

It is exciting to see something of a crescendo of publications on bay-related subjects: Stevenson's *Wildlife* came out in 1999; Bricker's *Pearls* and the *Texas Parks and Wildlife* special issue came out in 2003; Blackburn's book appeared in 2004. Following these in 2005 was *Water for Texas*, edited by Jim Norwine, John R. Giardino, and Sushma Krishnamurthy, tackling questions of future water supply, including freshwater inflows for estuaries.

Canoeing and Kayaking

Houston Canoe Club
P.O. Box 925516
Houston, TX 77292-5516
713-467-8857
www.houstoncanoeclub.org

Established in 1964, this club is the area's oldest and largest canoe and kayak club. General meetings are held the second Wednesday of each month at 7:00 P.M. at the Red Cross Building, 2700 Southwest Freeway (north side, between Kirby and Buffalo Speedway). Another body to contact is the Bay Area Paddlers (www.bayareapaddlers.com), and paddling stores are also good sources for finding out about locations and events.

Citizens' Environmental Coalition (CEC)

3015 Richmond, Ste. 720
Houston, TX 77098
713-524-4232
Hotline: 713-524-4ECO
issues@cechouston.org
www.cechouston.org

For more than thirty years, the CEC has served Houston as a regional initiative supporting dialogue, collaboration, and education on environmental issues. A coalition of close to a hundred nonprofit organizations in the Houston-Galveston area, it created and manages the Houston Environmental Center, established in 1998, where about a dozen local groups have office space, allowing them to work together more effectively. Other organizations benefit from use of meeting rooms and other resources at the center. CEC hosts Earth Day celebrations and presents the annual Synergy Awards for Environmental Excellence, honoring contributions to conservation.

CEC publishes the monthly newsletter *Environmental Exchange*, with news, perspectives, and a calendar of events; the CEC Web site and weekly e-mail news service *Environmental News Update* are also good resources. Possibly the most useful is CEC's annual *Environmental Resource Guide*, giving full listings of contact information and background on dozens of conservation groups, government agencies, and environmental hotlines in the area.

Coastal Conservation Association (CCA)

6919 Portwest, Ste. 100
Houston, TX 77024
713-626-4234
1-800-201-FISH
www.joincca.org

Founded in the late 1970s as the Gulf Coast Conservation Association but later renamed the Coastal Conservation Association, this is the group whose fish-shaped orange red sticker is seen on pickup trucks around the bay. Its original impetus was conservation and restoration of species of interest to sport fishermen, chiefly redfish and speckled trout. Fishermen realized that offshore fisheries do not begin and end offshore. The blue-water game fish depend on a healthy food supply from the bays (Murray 2002).

CCA has state chapters all along the Gulf and Atlantic coasts and publishes the bimonthly magazine *Tide*. Membership consists of some eighty thousand recreational saltwater anglers, who are proud of their role in supporting conservation measures.

Dolphins

Texas Marine Mammal Stranding Network
4700 Ave. U, Bldg. 303
Galveston, TX 77551
1-800-9-MAMMAL (1-800-962-6625)
www.gulfbase.org (click on institutes and organizations)

A 1990 study suggested an estimated population of about a thousand bottlenose dolphins occupying Galveston Bay and surrounding Gulf waters, with perhaps two hundred of them usually resident in the bay. Bottlenose dolphins are seldom found more than a hundred miles from shore or in water deeper than three thousand feet. They are attracted to shallow and food-rich inshore waters and are most often seen near the passes connecting the bay with the Gulf, such as the Bolivar Roads. They may, however, be seen almost anywhere in the bay, including off Seabrook, El Jardin, and Shoreacres well up the populated western shore. Mating behavior and newborn young have been observed in Galveston Bay year-round (GBF, "Bottlenose Dolphins," n.d.). Keep an eye peeled. The hotline for strandings is 1-800-9-MAMMAL.

Dunes

Dunes are hardly a notable feature of Galveston Bay today, but there was a time when they lined the Gulf shore of Galveston Island, and they deserve more re-

Pontoon dock and boat, 1957.

spect. I was impressed at what I saw in the low dunes from the boardwalk at one of Galveston's pocket beaches one midsummer afternoon. The boardwalk runs for perhaps two hundred or three hundred feet from the parking lot to the shore, through a strip of terrain consisting of humps that seem to call for quotation marks if one is going to call them dunes. The well-vegetated humps stretch a few hundred yards to either side of the boardwalk before running out at the fences of neighboring homes, where owners have scraped them flat and mown the grass.

By late July, every low green thing in Texas is struggling with the heat. The well-trimmed neighboring lawns were desiccated to khaki crispness and bare of flowers, all but dead. By contrast, the modest dunes of the pocket park were a riot of energetic life, even in the numbing summer heat. Birds darted among the scrubby bushes with sharp *chips* and a low *whirr* of wings. Butterflies bobbed by. In the dunes a dozen kinds of tough native plants bloomed despite their exposure to the salt breeze and the full fury of the sun in the apparently inhospitable environment of pure sand.

For property owners who want to create or protect dunes as a storm buffer rather than bulkhead beach frontage, the Texas GLO has a free brochure called *Dune Protection Guide* (request it from the Texas GLO, Coastal Division, 1700 N. Congress Ave., Austin, TX 78701-1495; 512-936-0683, 1-800-778-4GLO; http://www.glo.state.tx.us/).

Another resource is *Plants for Coastal Dunes of the Gulf and South Atlantic Coasts and Puerto Rico*, published by the U.S. Department of Agriculture (USDA), encouraging revegetation of dunes because vegetated dunes are far less subject to erosion than naked ones. According to this book, unlikely though it may sound, the plants in fact profit from the salt air: "Salt spray is a major source of plant nutrients in dune soils. It provides potassium, sodium, calcium, and magnesium" (USDA 1984, 4). The book describes how to trap sand and use boardwalks to prevent vegetation damage.

Ecotours

Skimmer Nature Tours
3406 Yupon Dr.
Dickinson, TX 77539
281-337-7420
skimmer@ev1.net
www.skimmernaturetours.com

Skimmer Nature Tours, operated by George Regmund and Mary Alice Trumble, has highly experienced guides to take out small groups. Specialists in birding, they offer one-day local excursions when not taking out groups to far-away places like the Amazon or Hawaii. They aim to give each client an unforgettable experience in the study of natural history, and they also give classes and workshops.

Regmund grew up in Corpus Christi and was on the staff at Armand Bayou Nature Center from 1976 until 2002. He has led natural history trips to Arizona, California, Maine, Costa Rica, Trinidad and Tobago, Canada, Mexico, and many areas of Texas. Trumble was director of education at Armand Bayou. Check their Web site for guided spring visits to the Houston Audubon Society's High Island sanctuaries to view numerous woodland birds as they reach the Texas coast after their migratory journey across the Gulf of Mexico, and for boat trips to North Deer Island Sanctuary in Galveston Bay to see thousands of nesting colonial waterbirds.

Thanks partly to the Master Naturalist training program coordinated by the Texas Agricultural Extension Service, a growing cadre of people is introducing others to the riches of the local environment. Terry and Becky Sheehy of Wetlands Adventures conduct custom birding tours for small groups, each arranged specifically to suit the season and participants (713-582-2231; www.saltgrass flats.com).

Ivory Jo Charters, based at the Nassau Bay Hilton Marina on Clear Lake (713-213-9663; www.ivoryjo.net), conducts tours focused on the local fauna, flora, and cultural heritage, besides its private charters for anniversaries and the like. The *Ivory Jo* is a rebuilt navy utility boat drawing only thirty inches of water and is thus able to maneuver in shallow inlets and tributaries. Skippers Capt. James Hunter and Capt. John Lynch are both knowledgeable about the area, and they add a naturalist guide for specialty groups.

Guided harbor tours and group trips to refuges, bird islands, and other points of natural interest and beauty are periodically offered by conservation groups and paddlers' organizations as well as by commercial guides. Bay and bayou tours are sometimes included as field trips during the State of the Bay symposium. For contact detail, see resources entries for Houston Audubon Society, Galveston Bay Estuary Program, Galveston Bay Foundation, and Canoeing and Kayaking; and see Galveston Island in chapter 7.

For much birding and other natural history information in the bay area, pick up a copy of the free newspaper called the *Galveston Bay Gull* (409-737-4081; natrix@airmail.net), found in some boating and convenience stores and restaurants. Published by Jim Stevenson and serving the Galveston Ornithological Society, this quarterly paper might be called the first ecotourism periodical in the area. Stevenson also guides numerous birding trips.

Fishing and Fishing Guides

The online *Texas Saltwater Fishing Magazine* (www.tsfm.com) covers saltwater fishing all along the coast from Boca Chica to Sabine Pass. Subscription costs fifteen dollars a year.

Fishing guides advertise in numerous local publications, notably *Tide* magazine (see Coastal Conservation Association) and *Telltales* and the *Mariner's Log* (see Boating and Sailing). Boat stores, marinas, and chambers of commerce also often have contact detail for fishing guides. A Web search for fishing charters produces plenty of possibilities. The following sites are among those that list guides with phone numbers and e-mail and Web contact details:

http://www.saltwaterfishingguides.com
http://texas.fishingcharter.net/
http://www.txsaltwaterfishingguides.com/
http://www.fishgalveston.com/

Galveston Bay Conservation and Preservation Association (GBCPA)

P.O. Box 323
Seabrook, TX 77586
281-326-3343
gbcpa@ev1.net
www.gbcpa.net

GBCPA was founded in 1974 in reaction to a stunning U.S. Army Corps of Engineers proposal to build a twenty-five-foot-high levee along the waterfront all the way from Morgan's Point to Kemah. Bayfront property owners and others organized to defeat the proposal (GBCPA 1994). Through the 1970s and 1980s GBCPA worked to keep out supertanker terminals at Bayport and Pelican Island and for inclusion of the bay in the National Estuary Program (see chapter 5 for more detail).

Galveston Bay Estuary Program (GBEP)

Bay Plaza One
711 Bay Area Blvd.
Webster, TX 77598
281-332-9937
http://gbep.tamug.edu/

As described in chapter 5, Galveston Bay is part of the National Estuary Program, creating an multiagency set of partnerships with the mandate of protecting health of the estuary while also supporting economic and recreational activity. GBEP is not an advocacy group but largely a coordinating body, designed to help everyone achieve a comprehensive approach via the Galveston Bay Plan. GBEP has published a wealth of scientific information about many aspects of the bay and conducts a State of the Bay symposium every other year; publications are listed on its Web site, many downloadable. The proceedings of the first symposium were a kind of inventory, titled *The State of the Bay: A Characterization of the Galveston Bay Ecosystem.* Later symposia have followed narrower themes—such as the focus in 2003 on the contribution of local communities to bay conservation work

Galveston Bay Foundation (GBF)

17324A Hwy. 3
Webster, TX 77598
281-332-3381
Fax: 281-332-3153
gbf@galvbay.org
www.galvbay.org

Founded in 1987, the Galveston Bay Foundation states as its mission "to preserve, protect and enhance the natural resources of the Galveston Bay estuarine system, and its tributaries, for present users and for posterity." It is a membership organization with a large board of directors representing almost every conceivable bay stakeholder group. GBF works through public workshops; the quarterly newsletter *Galveston Bay Soundings;* teacher and volunteer training; bay tours; and volunteer conservation activities, including routine water-quality monitoring and marsh restoration through planting of cordgrass. Volunteers also participate in mitigation planning for wetlands protection and in a variety of committees for oil spill response and management planning on the bay.

GBF has sponsored the Bay Day festivals at Sylvan Beach in La Porte and Discover Galveston Bay activities ranging from canoeing jaunts to bayou tours on the *Bay Ranger,* swamp and rookery expeditions, and walking visits to the Texas City Dike and ExxonMobil's Baytown refinery. *Soundings* began publication in March 1989. Paging through back issues gives excellent background about citizen involvement on behalf of the bay.

Bed-and-breakfast on the bay is an option in Seabook or Kemah, where older homes have been refurbished to this end.

Galveston Bay Information Center

Jack K. Williams Library
Texas A&M University–Galveston
200 Seawolf Pkwy.
P.O. Box 1675
Galveston, TX 77553
409-740-4703
Fax: 409-740-4702
gbic@tamug.tamu.edu
gbic.tamug.edu/gbb.htm

A starting point to learn more about almost any aspect of the bay is the Galveston Bay Bibliography maintained by this information center. The "Bay Bib" contains more than six thousand references to historical and contemporary works, from basics such as the Galveston Bay Estuary Program series to other research, published and unpublished reports, videos, photographs, charts and maps, computer files, journal articles, press releases, and manuscripts. Regularly updated, the "Bay Bib" is in a searchable database format. Other libraries have earlier printed versions. For help with finding material, contact staff at the information center offices in the TAMUG library in person, by phone, or by e-mail. Items can be borrowed direct or by interlibrary loan, and more than half of the items in the "Bay Bib" are to be found at the Jack Williams Library.

Galveston Historical Foundation (GHF)

502 20th St.
Galveston, TX 77550-2014
409-765-7834
Fax: 409-765-7851
foundation@galvestonhistory.org
www.galvestonhistory.org/

The GHF operates nine museums and historic properties, including the Texas Seaport Museum and the tall ship *Elissa*, and works in the community to preserve the historic architecture and the cultural heritage of the island. It has earned recognition for restoration of the historic commercial district on the Strand, and it sponsors the Dickens on the Strand festival and the Galveston Historic Homes Tour.

Great Texas Coastal Birding Trail (GTCBT)

Texas Parks and Wildlife Department
4200 Smith School Rd.
Austin, TX 78744
http://www.tpwd.state.tx.us/birdingtrails/

For hikes and getting acquainted with the kinds of habitat around the bay, a fine resource is the upper Texas coast map in the three-map series of the GTCBT. This map is centered on Galveston Bay and includes birding sites from the Louisiana border south to Freeport. Maps of the upper, central, and lower coast segments of the trail can be ordered at three dollars each from the Texas Cooperative Extension Bookstore at 1-888-900-2577 or online at http:// tcebookstore.org/ (click on TCE Bookstore).

The trail was jointly developed by the Texas Parks and Wildlife Department and the Texas Department of Transportation in a pioneering effort designed to promote less well known nooks of the state among bird-watching residents and visitors. Detailed directions are supplied for finding each site. Some are beaches or established parks, wildlife refuges, and nature centers; others are fairly obscure and would be difficult to find without the map and the brown-and-white sign identifying a stopping point on the GTCBT.

Sites are grouped into loops that can be visited in sequence, which allows planning for outings lasting just two or three hours, all day, or several days. And the sites are numerous. Galveston Island has more than a dozen. There are ten on the Bolivar Peninsula and many more around the bay. Not all are strictly coastal. Armed with this map, one need never again wonder where to go for a pleasant walk to enjoy natural places and the rich birdlife around the bay.

An unnerving aspect at some GTCBT sites that are on private industrial property is that entry points may have locked gates and signs discouraging unauthorized access. Often there is no one around at all—no concession stand, no ticket booth, no one to ask. I have stood around wondering whether possession of a GTCBT map means I am authorized to proceed despite the warnings, then noticed that beside a padlocked gate and a sign proclaiming "Private Property," there is in fact an opening in the fence and a well-trodden footpath: birders are invited.

Thanks to my GTCBT map, I have watched the amusing show of a reddish egret darting and dancing about after fish in the surf at Quintana Beach County Park near Freeport, apparently unperturbed by the presence of bathers. Some places call to be revisited at different seasons. The High Island bird sanctuaries, noted for concentrations of songbirds during the weeks of spring migration, have also supplied me with a fall retreat for a Thanksgiving Day turkey-sandwich picnic. On a winter walkabout on the Lake Anahuac levee, I found a pink host of roosting spoonbills and a crowd of dozens of sandpipers, fluffed up and crouching together for warmth on the shore. A Fourth of July return visit yielded a gorgeous purple gallinule preening in the early sun, with four fuzzy black youngsters bumbling in the reeds around her.

As is noted on the GTCBT Web site, Texas was the first state to create a birding trail, and the idea is being copied all across the country. Wildlife trails and trail maps provide exactly what nature tourists need for satisfying exploration. And the wildlife benefits, because this kind of tourism encourages landowners and communities to conserve habitats, providing visitors ever-greater opportunities to enjoy the natural riches of Texas. The following Web sites are among the numerous ones of relevance to birders:

www.texasbirding.net

www.birding.com/wheretobird/texas.asp

www.texasnaturalist.net

Gulf Coast Bird Observatory (GCBO)

103 W. Hwy. 332

Lake Jackson, TX 77566

979-480-0999

www.gcbo.org

The stated mission of the GCBO is the study and conservation of birds and their habitat in and around the Gulf of Mexico, to promote stewardship and be a catalyst for bird conservation. It is located on Buffalo Camp Bayou, off Highway 332 outside Lake Jackson. Its Web site includes directions to get there and a series of informative articles about the drama of bird migration on the Texas coast.

Gulf Restoration Network (GRN)

P.O. Box 2245
New Orleans, LA 70716
504-525-1528
www.gulfrestorationnetwork.org
 The GRN is a coalition of some three dozen local, regional, and national organizations dedicated to conserving the health of the Gulf of Mexico and restoring it to an ecologically sustainable condition. Priority issues are Corps of Engineers' dredge and fill activities, nutrient loading of Gulf waters, toxic discharges, prevention of coastal wetlands losses, and maintenance of sustainable fisheries. GRN has published a series of blistering critiques of the Corps of Engineers, including *The Costly Corps* (1996) and *Destruction by Design* (1999).

Hotlines

Be aware that the term *hotline* means different things to different people. You may get a recording rather than a human being; you may need to leave a message; the response may be less than instantaneous; and you may merely be given other numbers to call. That is the nature of hotlines.

Eco Hotline
713-524-4ECO
 The Citizens' Environmental Coalition provides answers to questions arising about environmental matters and referrals to other entities.

Environmental Violations
1-888-777-3186
 Calls to this line go to the Texas Commission on Environmental Quality and are routed to the relevant regional office.

Hazardous Waste
713-551-7355
 This City of Houston hotline provides information on safe disposal and storage of household hazardous waste and gives recommendations for less toxic alternative products.

Injured Wildlife
713-643-WILD
www.wrande.org

Calls to this hotline go to a licensed rehabilitator to help with injured or orphaned wildlife, a service of Wildlife Rehabilitation and Education (WR&E). Caring for wild animals and birds requires a special permit from the U.S. Fish and Wildlife Service. Licensed volunteers receive an average of about six thousand animals a year in the Houston-Galveston area, most of which are cared for at the volunteers' homes. Those that can be released into the wild are in due course released, and those that cannot often go into service in education programs. The Texas GLO has made a commitment to build a rehabilitation center for oiled wildlife on the Gulf Coast, and hopes are that when this is not in use for oil spills, it can be used for routine rehabilitation and wildlife education (Medlenka 2002).

Marine Debris
1-800-832-8224
Dumping from boats and ships is illegal. Report any marine dumping or persistent marine debris.

Marine Mammal Stranding
1-800-9-MAMMAL (1-800-962-6625)
Any dolphins or whales found on beaches, dead or alive, are under U.S. government protection—call the Texas Marine Mammal Stranding Network. Anyone discovering a dead animal should call to give its size, location, and general condition. For live animals, call for help. A live animal should not be returned to the sea because it will probably strand again. First aid is encouraged: move the animal to shallow water, being careful not to damage its flippers by putting too much strain on them. Ensure that its blowhole is above water, keep the animal wet, try to protect its skin from the sun, keep pets and crowds at a distance, and stay with the stranded animal until help arrives.

Oil Spills
1-800-424-8802 (National Spill Response Center)
1-800-832-8224 (Texas State Emergency Response Center)
The Texas GLO is the lead state agency for oil spills in Texas coastal waters. Report all spills immediately to GLO and/or the National Spill Response Center. For general information about the oil spill program, contact 512-475-1575 or visit the GLO Web site at www.glo.state.tx.us.
GLO also operates a Small Spill Prevention program, noting that used engine oil is the single-largest source of oil pollution in Texas waters: "It is estimated that 18 million gallons of used oil are improperly disposed off in Texas each year, more than the amount spilled by the *Exxon Valdez*" (Texas GLO 1998). For wildlife affected by any oil spill, call the WR&E hotline for injured wildlife (281-332-8319) or pager (713-604-0303).

Sea Turtles

409-771-2872

Call this number to report nesting or stranded turtles. To volunteer to help, call Carole Allen, Gulf Coast director for the Sea Turtle Restoration Project, at 281-444-6204. More about turtles can be found at www.ridleyturtles.org and www.seaturtle.org.

Most of the sea turtle nesting in the United States today occurs on Florida beaches. Texas has many fewer turtles, and the scientific community wants to know about them. Under a headstart program, eggs collected elsewhere were incubated safely so that they could hatch on South Padre Island. The tiny turtles entered the Gulf there, to become imprinted on the area. They were then captured and raised in safety for their first few vulnerable months before release. In 2002 thirty-seven females returned to nest on Texas beaches, most on Padre Island, one near Freeport, and two near San Luis Pass (Clark 2002).

Water Quality

To report any type of chemical spill or hazardous material spill, whether in water or on land, call the Texas State Emergency Response Center at 1-800-832-8224. Water pollution in Galveston County can also be reported to the Water Pollution Section of the Galveston County Health District at 409-938-2251 (24 hours). This body monitors and samples surface waters of Galveston County, maintains a water-quality database dating from 1972, and answers and investigates water pollution and hazardous materials complaints.

Houston Audubon Society (HAS)

440 Wilchester Blvd.
Houston, TX 77079
713-932-1639
houstonaudubon@houston.rr.com
www.houstonaudubon.org

The Houston chapter of a national birding and conservation organization, HAS has a proud record in providing conservation education, establishing wildlife sanctuaries on the Galveston Bay shore and islands, and encouraging pro-environment legislation. It publishes the monthly newsletter the *Naturalist*, conducts field trips and outreach programs, and conducts the Freeport Christmas Bird Count.

Maps and Charts

For underwater topography maps and charts of Galveston Bay made of waterproof, tearproof plastic, consult Fish-n-Map at 303-421-5994 or go to www.fishnmap.com. The maps have one-foot contours in the bays and five-foot contours in the Gulf. They also show locations of marinas, boat ramps, and other facilities. *Telltales* magazine (281-334-2202) has a laminated depth chart for Redfish Island.

Houston Wilderness

P.O. Box 66413

Houston, TX 77266-6413

713-524-7330

Fax: 713-525-9600

info@houstonwilderness.org

http://www.houstonwilderness.org

This new organization aims to raise broad public awareness about the varied ecosystems of the twenty-four county region surrounding Houston and to encourage people to explore the area. With the purpose of improving environmental stewardship, Houston Wilderness has conducted an extensive inventory of regional natural and recreational resources. The intent is to partner with chambers of commerce in ensuring that Houston is recognized as an ecologically rich, desirable place to live, work, and visit. The organization offers volunteering opportunities, and a useful calendar of events appears on its Web site.

Nonpoint-Source Pollution

Rain brings life, but it can also be dangerous to the bay. A growing body of evidence makes clear that even as municipal and industrial point sources of pollution have come under stricter controls in recent years, the nonpoint-source pollution affecting many water bodies through runoff is steadily worsening (see chapter 5). There are things we can do and avoid doing at home—regarding fertilizers, pesticides, the kinds of plants we grow, and how we dispose of waste— to keep from contributing to this load.

The Galveston Bay National Estuary Program has published a *Galveston Bay Area Residents Handbook* intended to help people avoid contributing inadvertently to nonpoint-source pollution. As that booklet points out, some 7 million Texans from Dallas to the coast—more than half of all Texans—live in communities in the Galveston Bay watershed. What goes down our drains and washes off our yards directly affects the bay. More than 60 percent of the permitted discharges of wastewater in the state also eventually reach Galveston Bay. Less spectacular than major spills but at least as damaging to the bay are the cumulative effects of everyday events such as rainfall runoff, sewage plant bypasses, and leaking barges.

All of this means that the actions of individuals make a difference, because there are millions of us. Dispose of household toxics safely. Do not pour solvents, pesticides, paint thinners, engine oil, or household cleaning products with hazardous ingredients down the drain or into storm sewers. Take them to a recycling center or hazardous waste collection site. Call 713-551-7355 for details about when Houston's collection center is open.

Home owners are quick to blame farmers for pesticide and fertilizer pollution in rainwater runoff into Galveston Bay, but today more of these kinds of pollutants come from urban areas than from the countryside.

Scenic Galveston

409-744-7431

This is the organization responsible for ensuring conservation of the marshes flanking the Gulf Freeway north of the causeway to Galveston Island. The John O'Quinn I-45 Estuarial Corridor was created when Scenic Galveston raised the funds to purchase close to a thousand acres of intertidal wetlands. The group has coordinated remediation of degraded sections and replacement of wetlands and bird islands, and the property is open to public use as a site on the Great Texas Coastal Birding Trail.

Texas Commission on Environmental Quality

Houston Regional Office
5425 Polk Ave., Ste. H

Houston, TX 77023-1486

713-767-3500

Fax: 713-767-3520

www.tceq.state.tx.us

Texas Parks and Wildlife Department

4200 Smith School Rd.

Austin, TX 78744

1-800-792-1112 (general information line)

512-389-4828 (boat registration)

512-389-4505 (fishing)

1-800-792-1112 (state parks)

512-389-4505 (wildlife)

1-800-937-9393 (magazine subscriptions)

1-800-792-4263 (report violations to Operation Game Thief)

512-389-8900 (park reservations)

512-389-4310 (Texas Conservation Passport)

U.S. Army Corps of Engineers

Galveston District

P.O. Box 1229

Galveston, TX 77553-1229

409-766-3004

Fax: 409-766-3049

www.swg.usace.army.mil

The wide-ranging role of the Corps of Engineers, covering channel maintenance and the issuing of permits for projects affecting the shoreline and waterways, gives it immense power over Galveston Bay.

U.S. Coast Guard

Group Galveston

Commanding Officer

P.O. Box 1912

Galveston, TX 77551

409-776-5633

Fax: 409-776-4728

http://www.uscg.mil/d8/groups/grugalv

Functions include port and marine safety and security, aids to navigation,
and monitoring and enforcement on the waterways for illegal discharge of pollutants. The Coast Guard's Group Galveston Web site features numerous links,
including links for charts and boating safety.

BIBLIOGRAPHY

Akkerman, Dora F. (Sam). 1998. *From Buffalo Bayou to Galveston Bay: The Centennial History of the Houston Yacht Club, 1897–1997.* Houston: Houston Yacht Club.

Antrobus, Sally. 1999. "Think Regional on the Megaport." *Bay Runner,* September, 3.

———. 2000. "Some People Get Their Exercise by Jumping to Conclusions: A Few Clues about Jim Blackburn." *Bay Runner,* October, 3–4.

Banks, Suzy. 2003. "Watch the Birdie!" *Texas Journey,* March–April, 27–32.

Barrington, Carol. 1999. "Galveston Bay Foundation." *Texas Highways,* June.

Bayou Preservation Association. 2003. "Eyes on the Bayou." www.bayoup reservation.org (accessed November 16, 2003).

Bay Runner. 1997. "Another Man's Treasure." November, 27.

Bayshore Sun. 2002. "Zoning Discussed." June 15.

———. 2003. "Council Tables Port Plea." June 11.

Bill Cherry's Galveston Memories: A Collection of Stories First Published in the Galveston County Daily News. 2000. Galveston: VanJus Press.

Bixel, Patricia Bellis, and Elizabeth Hayes Turner. 2000. *Galveston and the 1900 Storm.* Austin: University of Texas Press.

Blackburn, James B. 1998. *Report on the Blackburn-Formosa Agreement.* Houston: Privately published.

———. 2004. *The Book of Texas Bays.* College Station: Texas A&M University Press.

Bomar, George W. 1983. *Texas Weather.* Austin: University of Texas Press.

Bricker, Richard W. 2003. *Pearls on Galveston Bay: The Oyster Luggers of Smith Point, Texas.* Shoreacres, Tex.: Published by the author.

Cabeza de Vaca, Álvar Nuñez. 1997. *Cabeza de Vaca's Adventures in the Unknown Interior of America.* Translated by Cyclone Covey. Epilogue by William T. Pilkington. Albuquerque: University of New Mexico Press.

Cartwright, Gary. 1991. *Galveston: A History of the Island.* New York: Atheneum-Macmillan.

Casteel, Pamela. 2000. "Dolphin Watching in Galveston Bay." *Houston Chronicle, Texas* magazine, March 5, 12–14.

Chambers County (brochure). N.d. Anahuac, Tex: Wallisville Heritage Park.

Chesapeake Bay Foundation. 1995. "Wetlands Losses Continue." *Save the Bay,* February, 1.

Christensen, Roberta Marie. 1992. *Pioneers of West Galveston Island.* Austin: Nortex Press.

Clark, Gary. 2001. "Birding Team Sets Big Day Record in Texas." *Houston Chronicle,* May 18.

———. 2002. "A Woman with a Big HEART." *Houston Chronicle,* September 6.

CNN Online News. 1996. "Oil Spill off Texas Stretches for Miles." Posted March 19, 1996. http://www.cnn.com/US/9603/oil_spill/ (accessed April 17, 2003).

Costanza, Robert, R. D'-Arge, R. de Groot, et al. 1997. "The Value of the World's Ecosystem Services and Natural Capital." *Nature* 387 (May 15): 253–60.

"Curly's Corner: A Piece of the Past." 2002. *Lake and Bay Log,* February.

Daniels, A. Pat. 1985. *Bolivar! Gulf Coast Peninsula.* Crystal Beach: Peninsula Press of Texas.

———. 1992. *A Fascinating Voyage on the Bolivar Ferry.* Crystal Beach: Peninsula Press of Texas.

Dawson, Bill. 1991. "The Challenge of Christmas Bay." *Houston Chronicle, Texas* magazine, September 15.

Dean, Cornelia. 1999. *Against the Tide: The Battle for America's Beaches.* New York: Columbia University Press.

Dunn, Gail. 1993. "Throwaway Reefs." *Texas Parks and Wildlife,* December, 23–25.

Dyes, John C. 1993. *Nesting Birds of the Coastal Islands: A Naturalist's Year on Galveston Bay.* Austin: University of Texas Press.

Edwards, Janet R. 1993. "Gateways to the Gulf." *Texas Parks and Wildlife,* August, 29–35.

Environmental Protection Agency (EPA). 2002. *National Estuary Program: Bringing Our Estuaries New Life* (poster). Washington, D.C.: EPA Office of Wetlands, Oceans, and Watersheds.

Epperson, Jean L. 1995. *Historical Vignettes of Galveston Bay.* Woodville, Tex.: Dogwood Press.

Evans, Mark. 2000a. "At the Water's Edge: Chambers County." *Texas Shores,* Fall, 22–26.

———. 2000b. "Water-Borne Cruises Put Marine Life Up Close and Personal." *Texas Shores,* Fall, 27.

Fahrenthold, David A. 2003. "Chesapeake Bay Grasses Dying Off." *Houston Chronicle,* May 30.

Farley, Barney. 2002. *Fishing Yesterday's Gulf Coast.* College Station: Texas A&M University Press.

Fertl, Dagmar, Mike Jackson, and Suzanne Yin. 1994. "Otters in Galveston Bay Waters?" *Bay Soundings* 6, no. 3 (Fall): 1–3.

"Financial Reports and Trade Data, Port of Houston Authority." 2003. PHA Cargo Mix by Volume, Exports by U.S. Customs Districts and Ports. Galveston Bay Conservation and Preservation Association, Publications. www .gbcpa.net/financial_reports_and_trade_data.htm (accessed September 24, 2003).

Flood of a Lifetime, June 2001, Houston. 2001. Video, 90 minutes. ABC Eyewitness News. Houston: KTRK Television.

Fox, Anne A., D. William Day, and Lynn Highly. 1980. *Archaeological and Historical Investigations at Wallisville Lake, Chambers and Liberty Counties, Texas.* Archaeological Survey Report no. 90. San Antonio: Center for Archaeological Research, University of Texas at San Antonio.

Foxworth, Erna B. 1986. *The Romance of Old Sylvan Beach.* Austin: Waterway Press.

Freedenberg, Henry, and Robert B. Rica, eds. 1990. *Environmental Geology and Genetic Sequence Analysis of the Trinity River Valley—Delta Region, Chambers and Liberty Counties, Texas.* Field trip guidebook, November 17. Houston: Environmental/Engineering Committee of the Houston Geological Society.

Fulghum, Clay. 1988. "What to Do with Those Old Oil Rigs." *EPA Journal* 14, no. 5 (June): 35–36.

Fuller, Becky. 1998. "Texas City Unveils Port Plan." *Bay Area Sun,* July 22, 1.

Galveston Bay Conservation and Preservation Association (GBCPA). 1981a. *Newsletter,* Spring.

———. 1981b. *Newsletter,* Fall.

———. 1983. *Newsletter,* Winter.

———. 1994. *Newsletter,* March.

———. 2000a. "Ports Break Promises: The Long Beach Experience." Press release, September.

———. 2000b. "What about the Texas City Alternative?" Press release, November.

———. 2002a. "Bayport EIS Risks Violating Due Process." Press release, September.

———. 2002b. "National Security Issues at Bayport." Press release, September.

———. 2003a. "Bayport Lawsuit Filed: We Need the Truth." Press release, June.

———. 2003b. "Fonteno Bayshore Park Proposed for Bayport." Press release, January.

———. 2003c. "A Park at Bayport: How Likely Is It?" Press Release, July.

———. 2003d. "Port Is Draining Harris County Taxpayers." Press release, August, based on full report at http://www.gbcpa.net/financial_reports _and_trade_data.htm.

Galveston Bay Estuary Program (GBEP). 1997. *Proceedings: State of the Bay Symposium, III* (January 10–11). Austin: Texas Natural Resource Conservation Commission.

Galveston Bay Foundation (GBF). 1990. *1990 Annual Report.* Houston: GBF.

———. 1998. *1999 Calendar: Who Uses Galveston Bay?* Houston: GBF and Exxon.

———. N.d. "Bottlenose Dolphins of Galveston Bay." Fact sheet. Houston: GBF.

———. N.d. "Galveston Bay Sediments." Fact sheet. Houston: GBF.

———. N.d. "Galveston Bay: What's It Worth to You?" Fact sheet. Houston: GBF.

Galveston Bay National Estuary Program (GBNEP). 1995. *The Galveston Bay Plan.* Publication GBNEP-49. Houston: GBNEP.

———. N.d. *Galveston Bay Area Residents Handbook.* Houston: GBNEP.

Glass-Godwin, Nela. 1991. "Piping Plover." *Texas Parks and Wildlife,* February, 46–48.

Gulf Restoration Network (GRN). 1996. *The Costly Corps: How the U.S. Army Corps of Engineers Spends Your Tax Dollars to Destroy America's Natural Resources.* New Orleans: GRN.

———. 1999. *Destruction by Design: Army Corps of Engineers' Continuing Assault on America's Environment.* Edited by Heidi Lovett. Compiled by Mark Beorkrem and Cynthia Sarthou. New Orleans: GRN.

"Gulf Shrimpers Must Reduce Bycatch." 1997. *Marine Conservation News* 9, no. 3 (Autumn): 1.

Handbook of Texas Online. "Lynch's Ferry." http://www.tsha.utexas.edu/handbook/online/articles/view/LL/rtl1.html (accessed October 2002).

Harral, Sue. 1992. "In Search of Seabrook Sydnor." In *A Day at the Bay* (Seabrook Celebration program, October 1–3), 6–7. Seabrook, Tex.: Seabrook Association.

Hastings, Karen. 1993. "When Salt Was King." *Houston Chronicle, Texas* magazine, July 4.

Henson, Margaret, and Kevin Ladd. 1988. *Chambers County: A Pictorial History.* Norfolk, Va.: Donning.

Hoese, H. Dickson, and Richard H. Moore. 1998. *Fishes of the Gulf of Mexico: Texas, Louisiana, and Adjacent Waters.* 2d ed. College Station: Texas A&M University Press.

Hofstetter, Robert P. 1967. *The Texas Oyster Fishery.* Rev. ed. Coastal Fishery Series 6, Bulletin no. 40. Austin: Texas Parks and Wildlife Department.

Holley, Mary Austin. 1990. *Texas.* Austin: Texas State Historical Association.

Holmes, Ned S. 1999. Address to Houston Property Rights Association luncheon, June 25. Tape in possession of the author.

Horton, Tom, and William M. Eichbaum. 1991. *Turning the Tide: Saving the Chesapeake Bay.* Washington, D.C.: Covelo, California Island Press.

Houston Audubon Society. 2001. "Smith Point Hawk Watch." *Naturalist,* September.

Houston Chronicle. 1997. "The Explosion." Special section, April 13.

———. 2000. "Advertising Supplement." Special section, June 25, 1.

Houston Post. 1981. "Group Aims Lawsuit Threat at Facility in Texas City." March 16.

Kietnz, Renée. 2002. "Archaeologists in Aggieland: Nautical Explorers from A&M Hunt History in the Sea and the Lab." *Houston Chronicle, Texas* magazine, July 7, 8–13.

Klopp, Lucile B. 2002. *A History of El Jardin del Mar.* Privately published. (Available from El Jardin Community Association, P.O. Box 1115, Seabrook, TX 77586.)

Koeppel, Dan. 2003. "5 Days, 5 Nights, 3,000 Miles, and 10 Hours of Sleep (but Who's Counting?)." *Audubon,* March, 94–101, 131.

Larson, Erik. 1999. *Isaac's Storm: A Man, a Time, and the Deadliest Hurricane in History.* New York: Crown Publishers.

Leary, Sarah Pounds. 1967. *The Crabs of Texas.* Rev. ed. Coastal Fisheries Series 7, Bulletin no. 43. Austin: Texas Parks and Wildlife Department.

Lezon, Dale. 2002. "Houston-Area Population Booming." *Houston Chronicle,* April 30.

Lieth, H., and R. H. Whittaker, eds. 1975. *Primary Productivity of the Biosphere.* Ecological Studies 14. New York: Springer-Verlag.

Living in the Bay Area. 2001. Supplement to the *Citizen* (Clear Lake), September.

"Loss at Seabrook." 1990. In *A Day at the Bay* (Seabrook Celebration program, October 6), 55–56. Seabrook, Tex.: Seabrook Association. Originally published in *Times-Picayune,* September 10, 1900.

McComb, David G. 1986. *Galveston: A History.* Austin: University of Texas Press.

———.1999. *The Historic Seacoast of Texas.* Paintings by J. U. Salvant. Austin: University of Texas Press.

———. 2000. *Galveston: A History and a Guide.* Austin: Texas State Historical Association.

McEachron, L. W. 1987. "Crabs" (pamphlet). Rockport: Texas Parks and Wildlife Department.

"Major Oil Spills Jolt Gulf of Mexico, Houston Ship Channel." 1990. *NewWaves* 3, no. 3, September. http://twri.tamu.edu/newsletters/New Wave/nw-v3n3.pdf (accessed April 22, 2003).

Maril, Robert Lee. 1986. *Cannibals and Condos: Texans and Texas along the Gulf Coast.* College Station: Texas A&M University Press.

"Marine Commerce 101." 1999. Special issue, *Texas Shores* 32, no. 3 (Fall).

Marshall, Thom. 1988. "Gilbert: No Normal Hurricane." *Houston Chronicle,* September 25, 32A.

Maupin, Melissa. 1998. "The Shell Game." *Texas Parks and Wildlife,* December, 19–25.

Meason, George, and Greg Cubbison. 1988. *Pocket Guide for Speckled Trout and Redfish: Galveston Bay System Edition.* Houston: Pocket Guide.

Medlenka, Carla. 2002. "A Wild Life Offers Much Wisdom." *Small Change* 12, September–October, 10.

"*Mega Borg* Oil Spill." 1990. http://www-gerg.tamu.edu/menu_aboutus/borg .html (accessed April 23, 2003).

Minello, Thomas J. 1997. "Created Salt Marshes as Habitats for Fishery Species." In GBEP, *Proceedings: State of the Bay Symposium, III* (January 10–11), 45–48. Austin: Texas Natural Resource Conservation Commission.

Moore, Kathleen Dean. 2001. "A Weakened World Cannot Forgive Us." Interview by Derrick Jensen. *Sun*, March.

Morrison, Donita. 1988. "Seabrook-Kemah Bridge." In *A Day at the Bay* (Seabrook Celebration program, October 1), 16–18. Seabrook, Tex.: Seabrook Association.

Moulton, Daniel W. 2003. "Some Impacts of the Galveston Bay Estuary on the Regional Economy" (abstract). In *Sixth Biennial State of the Bay Symposium* (January 14–16), 171. Houston: GBEP and Texas Commission on Environmental Quality.

Moulton, Daniel W., and John S. Jacob. 2000. *Texas Coastal Wetlands Guidebook.* Texas Sea Grant Publication TAMU-SG-00-605. Bryan: Sea Grant.

Murray, Pat. 2002. "Looking beyond the Bays." *Saltwater Texas*, September–October, 12.

Nailon, Robert W. 1990–91. "Everything You Ever Wanted to Know about Oysters, but . . . " *Bay Soundings* 2, no. 4 (Winter): 1–4.

National Wildlife Federation. 1992. *The TED Experience: Claims and Reality.* Washington, D.C.: Center for Marine Conservation, Environmental Defense Fund, and National Wildlife Federation.

———. 1998. *Higher Ground: A Report on Voluntary Property Buyouts in the Nation's Floodplains.* Washington, D.C.: National Wildlife Federation.

Norwine, Jim, John R. Giardino, and Sushma Krishnamurthy. 2005. *Water for Texas.* College Station: Texas A&M University Press.

Office of Earth Science. 1998. *Astronaut's Guide to the Houston–Galveston Bay System: Human Interactions with Its Geology, Geography, Hydrology, Meteorology, and Biology.* Compiled by David Amsbury, Cynthia Evans, Joseph Caruana, Patricia Dickerson, Amy Liu, Marco Lozano, Kamlesh Lulla, Julie Robinson, Brad Rundquist, Sue Runco, Leslie Upchurch, Kimberly Willis, and Justin Wilkinson. Houston: NASA, Johnson Space Center.

Olmsted, Frederick Law. 1962. *A Journey through Texas.* 1857. Reprint, Austin: Von Boeckmann-Jones Press.

Oswalt, Lori. 1992. "Toxic Discharges: A Continuing Concern." *Bay Soundings* 3, no. 5 (Spring): 6–7.

Parker, Gretchen. 2003. "Lab-Bred Crabs Claw Way to Success." *Houston Chronicle*, August 3.

Parrish, Rob, and Chris Kuhlman. 1993. *Above and Beyond: The Original Aer-*

ial-Pictorial Guidebook to the Galveston Bay System. Bellaire, Tex.: Above and Beyond Publishing.

Pomeroy, David C., Jr. 1988. "Seabrook, Texas: Historical Chronology 1919–1986." In *A Day at the Bay* (Seabrook Celebration program, October 1), 11–15. Seabrook, Tex.: Seabrook Association.

"Port of Houston History." 1991–94. Serialized in 13 parts. *Bay Soundings* (Galveston Bay Foundation), Spring 1990–Summer 1994.

Progress. 1981. "GBCPA Strives for Environmental Preservation." Supplement. Houston: Exchange News/Daily Citizen.

Quammen, David. 1998. "Backwater Boondoggle." *Audubon*, January–February.

Racine, Marty. 1999. "Working and Living on the Half-Shell." *Houston Chronicle, Texas* magazine, February 14, 8–14.

Rappole, John H., and Gene W. Blacklock. 1994. *Birds of Texas: A Field Guide*. College Station: Texas A&M University Press.

Richardson, Don. 2000. "Beginning Birding: Migration and How It Works." *Spoonbill* 49, no. 4 (April): 2–4.

Roach, Will, and Steve Spencer. 1992. "Produced Water: What Is It and Who Cares?" *Bay Soundings* (Galveston Bay Foundation) 4, no. 3 (Fall): 4–5.

Robison, B. C. 1989. "Galveston Bay under Siege." *Houston Metropolitan*, April, 50–53, 75, 77.

Roy, Arundhati. 2001. *Power Politics*. 2d ed. Cambridge, Mass.: South End Press.

Sanders, Deborah. 1991. "Deepdene to Casa Mare." *Bay Area Resident*, September.

Seabrook Police Department. 2002. Dispatch recording, December 19–20. CD in possession of the author.

Shanley, E. B. 1998. "White Oak Bayou" (Watershed Representative Report). *Bayou Forum*, Fall, 4.

Shanley, Kevin. 1998. "It's the Watershed, Stupid!" (letter from the BPA President). *Bayou Forum*, Fall, 1.

Shanley, Kevin, and Ernie Sears. 1997. "The Little Thicket." *Bayou Forum*, Summer, 5.

Singer, Grace L. 1979. People and Petrochemicals: Changing Perceptions in New Jersey and Texas. Address at annual meeting of Galveston Bay Conservation and Preservation Association, Houston Yacht Club, January 11.

Sipocz, Andrew. 1993. "Seabrook's Pelicans." In *A Day at the Bay* (Seabrook Celebration program, October 1–3), 30–31. Seabrook, Tex.: Seabrook Association.

Smith, Elizabeth. 2002. "Redheads and Other Wintering Waterfowl." In *The Laguna Madre of Texas and Tamaulipas*, ed. J. W. Tunnell, Jr., and Frank W. Judd, 169–81. College Station: Texas A&M University Press.

[Smith, Frank]. 1984. "Chairman's Message." *Bayou Forum*, April.

Sonoma Technology. 1999. *Assessment of the Health Benefits of Improving Air Quality in Houston, Texas.* Final Report STI-998460-1875-FR by Frederick W. Lurman et al., prepared for the City of Houston. Petaluma, Calif.: Sonoma Technology, California State University Institute for Economic and Environmental Studies, and University of California-Irvine Department of Community and Environmental Medicine.

The State of the Bay. 2002. 2d ed. Publication GBEP T-7, AS-186/02. Edited by Jim Lester and Lisa Gonzalez. Houston: GBEP and Environmental Institute of Houston, University of Houston–Clear Lake.

The State of the Bay: A Characterization of the Galveston Bay Ecosystem. 1994. Edited by Frank S. Shipley and Russell W. Kiesling. Publication GB-NEP-44. Houston: GBNEP.

Stevens, Hugh. 1997. *The Texas City Disaster, 1947.* Austin: University of Texas Press.

Stevenson, Jim. 1999. *Wildlife of Galveston.* Galveston: VanJus Press.

Stoeltje, Melissa Fletcher. 1999. "A Tale of Two Waterfronts." *Houston Chronicle, Texas* magazine, July 4, 6–14.

Storm Signals. 2001. Special issue on Tropical Storm Allison. Quarterly newsletter of the Houston/Galveston National Weather Service Office, Dickinson, vol. 58 (Summer), 16 pp.

Swinton, John. 2003. "Compromise and Deceit" (letter). *Outdoors Unlimited*, April, 21.

Texas Coastal Management Program. 1996. *Coastal Wetlands in Texas* (brochure). Austin: Texas GLO.

Texas Department of Health. 2001. "TDH Study Shows Fish, Crabs from Most of Galveston Bay Safe to Eat." Press release. http://gbic.tamug.edu/ss/pr.html (accessed April 14, 2002).

Texas General Land Office (GLO). 1994. *Great Texas Beach Trash-Off* (brochure). Austin: Texas GLO.

———. 1998. *Small Spill Prevention* (brochure). Austin: Texas GLO.

———. 2002. *Beach and Bay Access Guide.* Austin: Texas GLO.

———. 2003. "Oil Spills," GLO data. bayinfo.tamug.tamu.edu/gbeppubs/s&t2002/Part8OilSpills.pdf (accessed April 17, 2003). Analysis at http://trendstat.harc.edu/projects/oilspills/OilSpills1.html (accessed December 6, 2004).

Texas Natural Resource Conservation Commission (TNRCC). 2000. *A Green Guide to Yard Care.* Austin: TNRCC.

Texas Parks and Wildlife. 1999. Special issue: "World's Best Birding," April.

———. 2003. Special issue: "The State of Bays." July.

Texas Parks and Wildlife Department (TPWD). 1986. *Shrimp* (brochure). Austin: TPWD.

———. 1999. *Sea Center Texas* (brochure). Austin: TPWD.

———. 2000. "Pardon Our Dredging: Galveston Bay Marsh Creation Continues." Press release, February 21. http://www.tpwd.state.tx.us/news/news/
000221a.htm (accessed November 2, 2003).

Thomas, D. J. 2003. "Buffalo Bayou's Development Project Recognized." *Houston Chronicle*, Perspectives, February 23, 23.

Tunnell, John W., Jr., and Frank W. Judd. 2002. *The Laguna Madre of Texas and
Tamaulipas*. Gulf Coast Studies no. 2. College Station: Texas A&M University Press.

Tveten, John L. 1979. *Exploring the Bayous*. New York: David McKay.

———. 1993. *The Birds of Texas*. Fredericksburg, Tex.: Shearer.

Urban, Jerry. 1989 (spill compilation). "'Dumb Luck' Keeps Spill Contained,"
Houston Chronicle, June 26; "Oil Cleanup Goes on Despite Rain, Winds,"
June 27; "Skipper Cites Lack of Map in Wreck," June 28; "Witness De-
scribes Crash of Ship into Oil Barge," June 29; "Spill Unlikely Source of
Oyster Bed Oil Find," June 30; "Port, Corps Blame Each Other as Silt
Chokes Bayport Channel," July 1; "Dredging Bids Sought for Bayport Chan-
nel," August 16. http://infoweb5.newsbank.com/bin/gate (accessed Octo-
ber 23, 1998).

U.S. Army Corps of Engineers, Galveston District. n.d. *Galveston Seawall* (brochure). Galveston: U.S. Army Corps of Engineers.

U.S. Department of Agriculture. 1984. *Plants for Coastal Dunes of the Gulf
and South Atlantic Coasts and Puerto Rico*. Soil Conservation Service,
Agriculture Information Bulletin 460. Washington, D.C.: Government
Printing Office.

U.S. Department of Transportation, Maritime Administration. 2003. *Port Statistics, Waterborne Traffic Statistics*. www.MARAD.dot.gov/ (accessed September 24, 2003).

U.S. Fish and Wildlife Service (USFWS). 2000a. *Brazoria National Wildlife Refuge Complex*. Angleton, Tex.: USFWS.

———. 2000b. *Texas Midcoast National Wildlife Refuge Complex: Birds* (brochure). Angleton, Tex.: USFWS.

———. 2000c. *Birds of Anahuac National Wildlife Refuge*. Anahuac, Tex.:
USFWS.

———. 2002. Letter, Frederick T. Werner, Assistant Project Leader, Clear Lake
E. S. Field Office, to Col. L. Waterworthy, U.S. Army Corps of Engineers,
Galveston District, re: Permit 21520. April 25.

Voyage of Rediscovery: Replica Ships Retrace Columbus' Historic Voyage.
1992. Commemorative ed. Corpus Christi, Tex.: Bay Area Press.

Wallstin, Brian. 2001. "Damage Control." *Houston Press*, December 13–19,
23–31.

Ward, G. H., and N. E. Armstrong. 1992. *Ambient Water and Sediment Quality of Galveston Bay: Present Status and Historical Trends*. Publication
GBNEP-33. Webster, Tex.: GBNEP.

Warner, William W. 1976. *Beautiful Swimmers: Watermen, Crabs and the Chesapeake Bay.* Boston: Little, Brown.

Weems, John Edward. 1999. *A Weekend in September.* College Station: Texas A&M University Press.

Werner, Frederick T. 1993. "The Galveston Bay Shore Environment: Where Wetlands Meet Waves!" *Bay Soundings* 5, no. 2 (Summer): 1–3.

Wheaton, Elizabeth Lee. 1948. *Texas City Remembers.* San Antonio: Naylor.

White, Christopher P. 1989. *Chesapeake Bay: A Field Guide.* Centerville, Md.: Tidewater Publishers.

White, W. A., T. A. Tremblay, E. G. Wermund, Jr., and L. R. Handley. 1993. *Trends and Status of Wetland and Aquatic Habitats in the Galveston Bay System, Texas.* Publication GBNEP-31. Webster, Tex.: Galveston Bay National Estuary Program.

Wiggins, Melanie. 1990. *They Made Their Own Law: Stories of Bolivar Peninsula.* Houston: Rice University Press.

Williams, John M., and Ivor W. Deudall. 2002. *Florida Hurricanes and Tropical Storms, 1871–2001.* Exp. ed. Gainesville: University Press of Florida.

Wilson, Marsha. 1999a. "Texas Leading Nation with Innovative BUG Project." *Texas Parks and Wildlife,* March, 8.

———. 1999b. "New Island in Galveston Bay." *Texas Parks and Wildlife,* September, 12.

Winningham, Geoff. 2003a. *Along Forgotten River.* Austin: Texas State Historical Association.

———. 2003b. "Buffalo Bayou from Every Angle." *Houston Chronicle,* Texas magazine, February 9, 6–10.

Withers, Kim. 2002. "Seagrass Meadows." In *The Laguna Madre of Texas and Tamaulipas,* ed. J. W. Tunnell, Jr., and Frank W. Judd, 85–101. College Station: Texas A&M University Press.

Withers, Kim, and Suzanne J. Dilworth. 2002. "Fish and Invertebrate Fisheries Organisms." In *The Laguna Madre of Texas and Tamaulipas,* ed. J. W. Tunnell, Jr., and Frank W. Judd, 223–52. College Station: Texas A&M University Press.

INDEX

Page numbers in **bold** indicate items appearing in captions for color photos.

Galveston Bay Cruising Association, 59,
190
Galveston Bay Estuary Program, 46, 104,
168, 196, 197, 203
Galveston Bay Foundation, x, xi, 16, 105–
107, 159, 168, 196
Galveston Bay Information Center, 197
Galveston Bay Plan, 46–48, 104, 185, 196
Galveston Bay Power Squadron, 190
Galveston causeway, 54, following 112
Galveston County Fair and Rodeo, 164
Galveston County Health District, 202
Galveston harbor: port development, 8–
10, 14; Houston takeover rejected, 10,
109–110, 111
Galveston Historical Foundation, 108–
111, 145, 172, 198
Galveston Historic Homes Tour, 165, 198
Galveston Island, 9, 133, 145–46
Galveston Island State Park, 146
Galveston Ornithological Society, 195
Galveston waterfront, 108–111
Galveston Wharf Board, 110
game fish, 56
garfish, xii, 182
Gatorfest, 156, 167
Gayolynn Ann Griffin (tug), 91–92, 96
geese, 64, 151, 157, 158
General Land Office, Texas: bay access,
56, 150, 188; and oil spills 95, 201; and
restoration, xi, 162, 193
Gibb Gilchrist (ferry), 147
Glyptoxanthus erosus, 33
gnatcatcher, 169
Goose Creek oil field, 15
Grand 1894 Opera House, 109
Grandcamp (ship), 144–45
Greater Houston Partnership, 15, 131
Great Storm of 1900: death toll and dam-
age, 17–18, 52, 58, 75, 147; and port
development, 9, 15; storm surge 72–76
Great Texas Birding Classic, 63, 162–63
Great Texas Coastal Birding Trail, 3, 61–
62, 70, 137, 146, 148–49, 156–57, 187,
204
grebe, 65
Grimes, John, 93, 128
groundwater withdrawal, 102
guided hikes, 137. *See also* tours
Gulf Coast Bird Observatory, 169, 199–200
Gulf Coast Waste Disposal Authority, 98

"Gulf Ghost" (art car), following 112
Gulf Intracoastal Waterway, 68, **following
112,** 151
Gulf Restoration Network, 48, 200
Gulf Stream, 8

harbor tours, 145, 194–95
Harris brothers, David and William, 131
Harris County commissioners, 131–32
Harris County Flood Control Distict, 84,
106, 188
Harris Ranch, 117, 131, 181
hawks, 157
Hawkwatch, 19, 168–70
hazardous waste, 200, 204
Hendley Row, 109
herons, 3, 63, 64, 137, 141
Heterocrypta granulata, 35
High Flyer (ship), 144–45
High Island, 17, 19, 68, 149, 194, 199
Holmes, Ned, 116, 118
horned lizard, 139
hotlines, 200–202
Houston, Sam, 8, 11, 20, 140, 203
Houston Audubon Society, 18–19, 65, 111,
148–49, 173, 194, 202
Houston Canoe Club, 191
Houston-Galveston Area Council, 122
Houston Lighting and Power Company,
105
Houston Pilots Association, 93, 106
Houston population, 38, 184
Houston Property Rights Association, 116
Houston Ship Channel: early dredging,
10–16; pollution and spills, 39–41, 94,
96–97; proposed deepening to fifty
feet, xi, 100, 104–108, 112, 124–25,
180; and seafood, 176, 177; tours and
trails, 19–22, 140–43
Houston Wilderness, 203
Houston Yacht Club, 57–60, 123
hummingbird, 157, 169
hundred-year floodplain, 84
Hunter, Capt. James, 194
hurricanes: Alicia, 72, 80; Carla, 72, 78–
79, 108; effects on bays, 73, 86–88;
statistics and predictions, 72–73, 80–
81; storm of 1915, 15, 18, 76; storms
making Texas landfall, 73–74, 77–80,
87. *See also* Great Storm of 1900;
storm surge

ISBN 1-58544-460-X